GNYSS THE MAGNIFICENT

GNYSS THE MAGNIFICENT
Three Verse Plays

Glyn Maxwell

born 1962

Chatto & Windus
LONDON

Published in 1993 by
Chatto & Windus Ltd
20 Vauxhall Bridge Road
London SW1V 2SA

A CIP catalogue record for this book is available
from the British Library

ISBN 0 7011 5723 2

Photoset by
Pure Tech Corporation, Pondicherry, India

Printed in Great Britain
by Mackays of Chatham, PLC
Chatham, Kent.

Contents

GNYSS THE MAGNIFICENT

GNYSS THE MAGNIFICENT

Dramatis Personae:

VICTOR EMMANUEL GNYSS, the Lord of the New Republic

In the year '83:

MAXIMILIAN, his bodyguard

DAMSEL, his daughter

COLONEL COSKER, formerly Captain of the Guard

DANE, an historian

ZARA, his wife

COLONEL IVAN, son of Grand Duke Petran

A SOLDIER

In the year '62:

DUKE LOPEZ
GRAND DUKE PETRAN
DUKE SUAREZ
DUKE ALEXIN } the Heroes of the '48 Revolution
GRAND DUKE TESSEL
DUKE ULRICH

MARTIN POLDER, Gnyss's speechwriter

DAMSEL as a child

LADY LYDIA, Gnyss's wife

CAPTAIN JACOB CRACK, a soldier of fortune

ROSANNA,
THORN
"SHADOW" } his girl Crack's Team
ZACARELLI

COSKER, Captain of the Palace Guard

GRANCHEV
KALT
HAIN } Palace Guardsmen
FODEN

NATALIA VALDEZ, a prostitute

HEIDI FISHER, a student
"LAZARUS", a poet
MANNI, a schoolboy
BAUER, a photographer
A PORTRAIT PAINTER
WOMEN GUESTS at the Banquet

The play takes place in and around the Palace of the New Republic and on an uninhabitable wilderness known as "the Given-up Land", in the year '83 and the year '62.

ACT I

The Palace, in the year '83.

GNYSS *is in his armchair, reading the whitebound edition of a book called "Gnyss the Magnificent". There comes a knock on the door. A pause, then enter* MAX

MAX
  The Duchess is here now.
  I told her, and it's the truth, she should not assume
  Either that you were up or you were in here,
  Lord Victor Emmanuel, but that I'd look
  And see with my own eyes.
GNYSS   And what did you find?
  What can we tell the intemperate little Duchess?
  And will she believe, or even listen, Max?
  All her life her father has told her where
  To search for specific stars, or when to expect
  Rain, or how to distinguish right from rubbish,
  But still, at a creeping-up age she will get drenched,
  Talk rot and point her telescope at a cloud.
  I'd watch her very closely as she comes,
  Max, she may forget why she is coming,
  Bursting into my day.
MAX   It seemed important.
GNYSS
  Ah, then she has her urgent mood and will stamp
  And stamp until she's done.
MAX   She seemed impatient.
GNYSS
  And so she is, impatient to succeed,
  Me, that is: all through the summer days
  She turned her pouting look upon the sun
  Until it hid. Then it was my turn.
  Sun and father, equally uneasy
  For sitting on our thrones. Tell her, Max,
  Start at the bottom stair,
  And do not stop until the last, but then
  Do stop, for if she has a mind to ascend
  To heaven this morning I won't forbid it. I may
  Go myself. So fetch the sulking angel.

"The Lord Gnyss, pictured in '51,
With Damsel Caroline Gnyss, his only daughter,
Nine months old." Somebody's black-and-tan
Prank on the Lord Gnyss. I was never this man.

Enter DAMSEL. GNYSS *hastily hides the book*

DAMSEL
What are you hiding, daddy? There are three things
To tell this morning, I'll tell them in any order,
Except that the one, there's one I can't remember
Yet, will have to be last, or at least second.
I don't know what it is but it dangles there
With a feeling of could-be-good but probably-bad.
That happens to me. What do you want to hear,
The bad I can or the bad I can't remember?
Except you look quite happy.

GNYSS   I am, why not?
Ageing in the Age of Me, Damsel.
Tell me the bad bad news.

DAMSEL   It's not that bad.
What are you hiding? Well, it's the docks again.
Swollen mobs of ordinary people
And Colonel Manolo threatening them and asking
For infantrymen, hoses, ammunition.
They knocked a warehouse down but it was empty.
That made them awfully cross. Your agent reckoned
They would have set the sea alight if you could.
Instead they hang about.

GNYSS   Colonel Manolo
Can have his matériel. This can't go on.
What other news.

DAMSEL   I haven't remembered the third
Thing but this is the second: the grape harvest,
Meaning wine, daddy, meaning the people
Happy, you understand? meaning exports
Out to the Islands, the grape harvest? is terrible.

GNYSS
That's sun and rain, that's Nature, Damsel, cruel
And beautiful. But I think our cellar is full.

DAMSEL
Max says it's more than full.

GNYSS   – So who's the Lord,

[6]

Max? This week it's fishermen. Next week
We'll have the damned illiterate farmers out
Rioting from shire to shire. Am I
Responsible for the stubbornness of the sun,
Or the vandal frost? Let the winegrowers press
Fishermen underfoot and bottle that!
There's a buyer in this chair.
DAMSEL   Daddy, hush.
There is no news of rioting elsewhere.
Even the docks are quiet this morning. Look,
It's a white book you're hiding.
GNYSS   I'm not hiding.
Can I not read as I rot?
DAMSEL   I know what it is,
You fantastically vain daddy!

She finds the book

GNYSS   "Magnificently",
Damsel, look, it says: "Gnyss the Magnificent",
In print, you have to believe.
And let me show you a picture . . .
DAMSEL   Oh I've remembered.
GNYSS
Who'd recognise these people?
DAMSEL   What a curious
Coincidence. Or maybe it's not one.
Maybe you read the book about yourself
Every morning! How do I know you don't do?
GNYSS
Look at this beauty.
DAMSEL   You you mean, not this ugly
Newborn shape.
GNYSS   Nine months.
DAMSEL   Nine months of what,
Screaming out, being cold, being stared at.
GNYSS
I doubt if you remember a thing.
DAMSEL   I'm glad.
But I did just now. Remember the third thing.
The book reminded me. That's where I know the name.
GNYSS
Whose damnable name?
DAMSEL   Dane, daddy.

Professor E. V. Dane, a historian
At your own Institute of Studies.
GNYSS   Dane?
Never heard of him.
DAMSEL   Look who wrote your book.
GNYSS
    . . . E. V. Dane. Well yes. He did. This print
Is difficult enough, but when it's tiny . . .
E. V. Dane, well yes. Did we ever meet him?
DAMSEL
No, the work was done at the Institute
And sent here, then you read it and agreed
Or disagreed and off it went for printing.
GNYSS
So a ghost-writer. He's dead?
Is that the news? Then "ghost-writer" 's a joke,
Isn't it? I can tell it to the colonels.
DAMSEL
I'm sure they'll laugh. The news about E. V. Dane
Is not he's dead but that he's disappeared,
Gone from the Institute of Studies.
GNYSS   Scholars.
Pointlessly coming and going and never welcome.
Why is this any news?
DAMSEL   It may not be news,
Daddy, but in my career
As Lady-in-Everlasting-Waiting for you,
Magnificently aged as you are,
To abdicate at last in favour of youth
While it's still youth, one of my many chores
Is to tell you what has happened that appears
To make no sense. This appears to make no sense.
GNYSS
On about abdication again. So, let's
Have him write a big book about you, why not,
And call it "Damsel the Damned Impatient", yes?
When he turns up again.
DAMSEL   It's all gone.
Papers, furniture, pictures, photographs,
Traces, clothes. The Special Unit has been,
And done its work. Professor Dane has vanished
Or been abducted.
GNYSS   Maybe *he* abducted.

Maybe his daughter's poised to move in,
Pantherlike, to start on a new volume.
DAMSEL
They found a colleague of his.
A Dr Pryce, and something came to light.
GNYSS
Babbling scholars all. Why don't they help
With hauling in the rotten grapes?
DAMSEL   Daddy,
Listen or don't. I have a whole day
To stretch and waste, waiting to turn to something
Other than daughter.
GNYSS   I'll listen and take your time.
DAMSEL
Dane wrote this book.
You commissioned the Institute, the Institute
Commissioned him, because he wrote the best,
But his field was ancient-ancient, not modern.
Tribes were what he studied, tribes and stones.
Then he tells this Dr Pryce of another plan.
GNYSS
So what? These are historians not colonels.
DAMSEL
He tells this Dr Pryce of a second book.
GNYSS
A Guide To Stones: Grey, Brown and Black Ones.
DAMSEL
He tells this Dr Pryce:
There is another history to be written.
GNYSS
So? What else does a shovelling old bookworm
Do with himself?
DAMSEL   Daddy, it's not a commission.
Books on history, politics or ideas
Can only be commissioned, under the wing
Of the Institute.
GNYSS   Well it's an excellent Institute.
That's why.
DAMSEL   So why has he run away?
GNYSS
Some pebble's caught his eye. You think I care
What happened or not in his field? In any case,
The law covers only books on the modern age.

[9]

DAMSEL
  This is a book on the modern age, daddy.
  He told this Pryce, who told the Special Unit –
  He's rewriting "Gnyss the Magnificent".
GNYSS   It's written.
  It's in my hands.
DAMSEL   Apparently yes, and no.
GNYSS
  Nonsensical. Good day, Damsel.
DAMSEL   Good day. . . . Oh,
  Neither of us has gone. Can I continue?
  He's not rewriting it all, only some.
  Chapters Six and Seven he had to alter.
  Pryce says he saw a pile of photographs,
  But Dane came in. And when he last saw Dane,
  Dane was in a fever, claiming his work
  Was twenty-one years late, but even now
  Would shake the State apart.
GNYSS   They're all insane,
  Historians, aren't they? Envious of those
  Who make their history. Twenty-one years late?
  That means his work relates to . . . '62.
  – So if he's mad, have the Unit pick him up.
DAMSEL
  What do you think the Unit's trying to do?
  Daddy, he's disappeared!
GNYSS (*leafing through*)   Let me see . . .
  Chapters Six and Seven . . . yes, of course:
  These action-filled accounts.
  Chapter Six: "The Men of Word and Deed".
  Chapter Seven: "Death in the Gallery".
DAMSEL
  About the assassinations?
GNYSS   Yes, maybe
  The mad professor believes I was killed that day.
  That's called, I think, revisionist history.
DAMSEL
  April the 7th, '62. I remember
  Being asleep that day and remembering nothing.
GNYSS
  This academic may have been wide awake
  But he wasn't there so how can he write a book?
DAMSEL
  He wrote this one.

[10]

GNYSS   At the Institute he wrote it.
　That's where all the material is, and plenty.
　Plus several survivors, still surviving.
　No abdications yet. Enough of this.
　I think your prof has fallen prey to his last
　Lunacy: he worked too hard in the dark.
　The only danger is to impressionable minds
　He cannons into. Have the Unit redouble
　Their search. We'll catch this Dane in a sealed net.
　We've read his magnificent tome. Have done with it.
　Until tomorrow, daughter.
DAMSEL
　Troops in the docks, no wine for anyone,
　State historians feverish, on the run,
　Twenty-seven years on the same throne . . .
　Those all rhyme, don't they, daddy? So long.

Exit DAMSEL. GNYSS *picks up the book, and reads*

VOICE OF DANE
　"By the year '62, Victor Emmanuel Gnyss, now one of
the seven surviving Heroes of the '48 Revolution, had
been undisputed Lord for six years, two years longer than
the period allowed for by the Revolutionary Constitution
of '48. Though his hardline policies had brought
prosperity to the provinces and stability to the State
institutions, there existed certain jealous souls who felt
that his reluctance to hand power back to the Seven as a
group represented at best a dangerous precedent, at worst
a betrayal of the '48 Constitution itself . . ."

SCENE II
An Antechamber in the Palace, twenty-one years earlier,
in '62.

Enter GRAND DUKE PETRAN *and* DUKE LOPEZ

LOPEZ
　Four years of Barberis, four years of you,
　Four years of Lord Victor Emmanuel Gnyss,
　And then another. Then another. This
　Trouble you, Petran?

[11]

PETRAN   You know it does.

LOPEZ

Or are my mathematics in revolt?
Six is more than four, I still believe.
Now some are thinking one is more than six.

PETRAN

Ear to the mob, again, Lopez, my friend?
The mob believes that one is the only number
Needed if the mob is of one mind.
Would you invite them up?

LOPEZ   In the extreme.

PETRAN

The State is quiet, the countryside is calm,
The mob dispersed, at lunch in twos and threes.
By all means hammer on every door in the land
To make your earnest constitutional point,
But you'll disturb them at the meals they have.
They know they do not starve, and Gnyss is Lord.

LOPEZ

So nail the old dictators up again,
You mildest of all men! Why are we meeting
At all if all is well? Let's hurl ourselves
Into some old-time adoration and pray
There never comes a day the insulted Heroes,
Yourself, Suarez, Alexin, timid old Tessel,
Nudge within an inch of power again!

PETRAN

We're meeting to discuss the news I have.
Suarez and Alexin and we two
Can make good news of it, you know.

LOPEZ   Know?

I don't. Trust? There's some of that left. Hope?
Stale as my baptismal sweetmeats. Pray?
You settle for that.

PETRAN   I shall. Here come the others.

Enter DUKE SUAREZ *and* DUKE ALEXIN

SUAREZ

Chaps, damn Palace is like my favourite chocolate,
Softly-centred with guess what? These women.
From the ripe to the young to the very young to, chaps,
Look at the eyes of young Alexin: dancing.

LOPEZ

He never saw a woman?

[12]

SUAREZ   Leave him, bully,
  You didn't see: they might have stopped your noise.
LOPEZ
  What have women to do with this?
SUAREZ   Oh nothing.
  Nothing to do with anything, women.
  That's why I'm a lover of snails, and Alexin,
  He likes to watch the desert as it advances.
  Petran gazes in ponds. One day, Lopez,
  Perhaps we'll know what women were for. Or never.
ALEXIN
  You want to hear my wish?
LOPEZ   No, and that's mine.
PETRAN
  All right, be calm and listen.
  You three, we four, here meet as a group opposed
  To Victor's – after six years – remaining
  Lord of the Republic. We acknowledge,
  I think we all acknowledge his expert handling
  Of the Grain Riots in '59, and last year
  His economic policy, which,
  Not one of us can gainsay, has left us
  Richer and stronger. No force has been used
  Against us, no attempt made to rewrite
  The Constitution to make his tenancy legal,
  No sudden switches of power. He is popular –
LOPEZ
  So are we, Petran.
SUAREZ   Yes, '48,
  Remember '48 – who hung our banner
  Over the Palace roof while the army split
  And all the miserable oligarchs turned tail?
PETRAN
  You, Suarez.
SUAREZ   Who stood his ground all night,
  Barely a man but belting out our anthem?
PETRAN
  The history I know. The boy was Alexin.
ALEXIN
  To no avail without the help of you all!
LOPEZ
  While Tessel drew up charts and charters, hoping
  The guns would stop and the pageantry get going.

[13]

SUAREZ
And Ulrich rubbed his palms together and said:
"This bears out my basic prognosis." I'll
Bear his out.
LOPEZ   I'll be there then.
PETRAN   Victor
Emmanuel was with us, he fought,
Was scarred like you and stood his ground like you.
SUAREZ
But now he tells us: "Heroes are one thing,
You need economists too."
LOPEZ   Planners. Charters.
SUAREZ
Prognosticators.
LOPEZ   Ministrators.
ALEXIN   Experts.
LOPEZ
So where were all those chatterers when the ramparts
Burned and the corrupted Coalition
Burned beside or fled like rats forever?
SUAREZ
Where was Mr Polder?
Not there in '48, not of the Eleven,
Not one of us, and now he hangs from Gnyss
Like a brass medal and pens his soothing speeches.
LOPEZ
The ultimate in scribblers, smart and yellow.
ALEXIN
I loathed him from the minute before the minute
I saw him.
PETRAN   Victor has heard all this, he knows it.
On nine occasions in the Chamber Council
We've asked that an Election be called,
That calmly and with dignity we take
Our case outside the Citadel. Out there
The flags of '48 still fly from churches
And cottages: they cheer when we pass by.
LOPEZ
When Ulrich passes by, if he ever did,
They say "I thought he'd died."
SUAREZ   If they saw Polder,
They'd think the Coalition had been trawled
From Hell, apologising.
PETRAN   I have asked

[14]

Victor a tenth time and he has replied –
Yes. Plans are underway this morning
To present the People a true democratic choice:
To carry on indefinitely with Gnyss
As Lord, or to transfer the reins to us.

ALEXIN
Us – us four?

LOPEZ   Better than seven.

SUAREZ   That's fair.
Us, not Ulrich. Polder we can exile,
Put Tessel out to grass, and Victor Emmanuel?

LOPEZ
A long, circling holiday.

PETRAN   Exactly ·
His suggestion, Lopez, and made
This morning without malice.

ALEXIN   When's the poll?

PETRAN
On Monday of next week, in four days.

SUAREZ
Four days? It's far too soon!

LOPEZ
Afraid we'll lose, Suarez? Sooner the better.

SUAREZ
But we have to organise!

ALEXIN   Present our case.

LOPEZ
Our case is unanswerable. A better idea
Is to plan the Festival of our victory:
The arts and anthems, memories and glories
Of '48!

SUAREZ You go ahead. I'd rather
Go and make some friends in the bigger castles.

ALEXIN
I'll circle all the names of my acquaintance.
I'm well-liked in the East.

PETRAN   We are well-known
And liked where there are decent citizens,
Honourable revolutionaries. No one's
Forgotten '48.

SUAREZ   They won't forget
'62 in a hurry. Come on, Alexin,
Let's move among the populace. I hear
They have some of those women things out there.

Exit SUAREZ *and* ALEXIN

LOPEZ
So how come Gnyss gets out of bed this morning
Answerable to the Constitution?
PETRAN   He feels
His work is done, the country quiet, stable.
In his words, the Republic has returned
To what it was meant to be beyond the fighting:
"A land for arts of peace."
LOPEZ   Another of Polder's?
One of his usable phrases?
PETRAN   Well, Lopez,
Look what you've ignited with your sparks.
Say nothing of the election.

Enter GRAND DUKE TESSEL, DUKE ULRICH *and* MARTIN
POLDER

ULRICH   Was that Suarez
And the boy Alexin on their way in a hurry?
What happy errand is that, I wonder . . . but,
I'll elect to hold my peace.
TESSEL   Grand Duke Petran,
I'm glad I find you. Good day, Duke Lopez.
Grand Duke Petran, if I might have a word . . .

TESSEL *and* PETRAN *go aside*

ULRICH
Lopez, voting to stay at home today?
You may be in the minority.
LOPEZ   I may.
I am wholly outnumbered by the races
Of weasel, snake, flea, fly and germ.
ULRICH
Hmm, you nominate us among them? Martin,
Duke Lopez is a candidate for a sulk.
LOPEZ
And you elected unopposed for a blade
One dusk in the dark. You, Ulrich,
Press your hands so close together they fuse.
Close your eyes and pray you do not lose.
ULRICH
I'm not standing, sir.

[16]

LOPEZ   You won't be. Sir.

Exit LOPEZ

TESSEL
  Bad blood again, and unaccountably
  Flowing between Heroes.
PETRAN   Lopez's temper
  Is short, and Ulrich's sense of decency
  Short on sense and decency.
TESSEL   True, true
  Maybe, but you've convinced me this idea
  Of voting has some merit, so long as all sides
  Know me willing to serve, whatever the outcome.
PETRAN
  A cool breath on a hot morning, Tessel.
  My words were a calm flame, but my friends: petrol.
TESSEL
  Hmm, though the Lord is pleased with the idea.
  Confident, of course. I only hope
  The good you mean to come of it does come.
ULRICH
  Grand Duke, of course it will!
  We're all good friends, all revolutionaries
  Together, eh, Grand Duke?
PETRAN   There'll be no evil.
  There'll be the people's will, and our reaction.
  And then the world rolls on.
ULRICH   Faster and faster,
  With six dukes a-clinging as it spins.
  Let's hope whoever wins honestly wins.
PETRAN
  Indeed. You talk as if
  You shared the morals of the Coalition.
  Duplicity is extinct. Good day to you.

Exit PETRAN

POLDER
  "Duplicity is extinct." But it distinctly
  Passed between his lips and pattered my eardrums.
  Ba-da-da-da da dum-dum. Ah now it's gone.
TESSEL
  Well. I too must be gone, Duke Ulrich,
  Mr Polder. The Banquet is tomorrow,

[17]

And the Lord, who knows it may be his last Banquet
As Lord of the Republic, hopes to make it
An unforgettable night. Important guests,
If you understand me . . .

Exit TESSEL

ULRICH   Do we understand him?

POLDER
  "Important guests" – ba-da-dum da. I hazard
  His import is . . . guests who are important.

ULRICH
  Now I understand your meteoric
  Rise to influence, Martin. So to the future.
  Are we ready?

POLDER   Our desperadoes are,
  Crawling to glory over the wilderness.

ULRICH
  The rider you sent?

POLDER   Returned,
  Apparently none the worse for seven hours
  Out on the Given-up Land. The mask he wore
  Seems to have sheltered him from the rotten air.
  The horse is another matter. But: the group
  Are making steady progress, they are armed
  As you instructed and morale is high.

ULRICH
  Why not when they know nothing? In the mean time,
  Let's be seen less together, Martin. The Palace
  Fills with strangers, girls, some whim of the Lord's,
  I take it. Singers, dancers, easy women.

POLDER
  Blurs on the edge. No help for the clear thinker.

ULRICH
  Quickly, Martin. That's the voice of the Lord
  Plus wild offshoot: the permanently
  Appended daughter.

Exit POLDER *one way; enter* GNYSS *and* DAMSEL *the other*

DAMSEL (*to* ULRICH)   Look, do you like poets?
  You, Ulrich, do you like them? My father,
  He's the Lord, he doesn't, but as I do
  We need it to be settled whether they're good.

ULRICH
  Good as their poems, perhaps.
DAMSEL   You mean their works?
ULRICH
  You think of them as "works"?
DAMSEL   I found this.

She shows ULRICH *a piece of paper*

ULRICH (*to* GNYSS)   How did she come by this?
GNYSS   You'd like to know?
  I'd like to know myself.
DAMSEL   Isn't it fine?
  Fine, I think it is. Look, it starts
  There, and ends there, with breaks there,
  There, there and there.
ULRICH   Most everywhere.
GNYSS
  You like the shape, don't you, Damsel?
DAMSEL   Yes,
  That is one thing I like. And what he says.
ULRICH
  But what he says is wrong, Miss Damsel.
DAMSEL   You know
  His name? It's Lazarus.
GNYSS
  Not a real name but yes, he's well-known
  In – circles, different circles from our own.
DAMSEL
  I've had a dream about a circle, daddy.
GNYSS
  Ulrich, I need Polder.
  Tell him I need his help with a short speech
  To the apple-growers.
ULRICH   You mean you're pitching for votes?
  But surely –
GNYSS   No, I'm not pitching for votes,
  Ulrich, I'm doing my best to run the Republic,
  In spite of these irrelevancies of asking
  Peasants to roll dice for the Heads of State.
  So get me Polder. Is everything prepared?
ULRICH
  I don't –
DAMSEL Look Ulrich, is everything prepared?

GNYSS
  For Saturday, the group portrait?
ULRICH   Oh yes,
  Of course, I saw the painter arrive this morning.
  The – seven of us to meet in the Gallery.
GNYSS
  Yes, exactly, good. And our visitors?
ULRICH
  Are on . . . their way.
GNYSS   Behold a surpassing servant,
  Daughter. When I'm duetting on the harp
  With another Lord, you'll need a man like this
  To be and do and say what's necessary.
  And go when meant to go.
ULRICH
  Of course, of course. Good day, Miss Damsel, Lord.

Exit ULRICH

DAMSEL
  But actually he's horrid, isn't he, daddy?
GNYSS
  Yes, but what he is is right. Your "Lazarus"
  May seem a peach of a soul but he tells lies.
DAMSEL
  I also like the smell of this paper.
GNYSS   That's
  A smell I like myself, daughter. Clean.
DAMSEL
  Clean, but inky, look. I like this poem.
  I did, but then I saw my wicked stepmother
  Stepping in our direction.

Enter LADY LYDIA

LYDIA   Victor, explain,
  Please, why strange women infest the Palace,
  Some in states of virtual undress,
  Most of dubious walks of life, and all
  Asking the way to different quarters. Well?
GNYSS
  I thought you liked the company of ladies.
LYDIA
  There are no ladies here.

[20]

GNYSS   Then let me show you
  Written proofs of the innumerable times
  You've told me too few women wield any power.
LYDIA
  None do, not one of the Seven.
GNYSS   But not one woman
  Wielded a thing that night in '48.
  Our power has been the upshot of our daring.
LYDIA
  Disgraceful words. Hundreds of women fought.
GNYSS
  Finally, yes, they did, but not that night.
LYDIA
  So why are they here? You want them to fight each other?
GNYSS
  I felt perhaps you could all meet up together,
  Form a group of something. Don't you see how
  Democratic I'm being?
LYDIA   How democratic
  All your Dukes are suddenly being! And how
  Stupid you suddenly think I am, your wife.
  Send them away at once. I insist.
GNYSS
  I absolutely won't. They are my guests.
  And yours. Some are going to attend the Banquet
  Tomorrow night.
LYDIA   All smiles for the Election.
  The cynicism of the man, of men.
GNYSS
  Whatever my motives, good will come of it:
  A say for our neglected womenfolk.
LYDIA
  Folk? Among your folk there are at least
  Three whores and a clothes-model, and then her –
  Your daughter running around among them all!
  What will Damsel learn?
GNYSS   What Damsels become
  If they don't watch it. Lydia, enough.
  Banquet tomorrow, portrait Saturday,
  Election Monday, then the Victory Dinner!
LYDIA
  Yes but whose?
GNYSS   The true Victor. Enough!
  Be on your way. My love.

[21]

DAMSEL (*reading*)
    "The lava thickens in the crust.
    The blood is pounding under the hide.
    No one man can hold it. All must
    Move fast, or be blown aside."
 Then there's a break, and then –

GNYSS *snatches the poem away*

GNYSS
 A very long break, daughter. No more of this stuff.
 One man can hold it. And he's had enough.

Exit GNYSS *and* DAMSEL

SCENE III
The Given-up Land, '62.

A marshy, eerie green. Enter, creeping, in protective masks,
CAPTAIN JACOB CRACK *and his band of mercenaries:* SER-
GEANT THORN, ROSANNA BARON, "THE SHADOW" *and,*
last, LIEUTENANT ZACARELLI, *who is walking backwards.*
CRACK *takes off his mask*

CRACK
 Team, don't be alarmed. I am now informed
 By Contact that exposure to this air
 Is possible for a spell. You may experience
 Giddiness or nausea, or a slight
 Echo to everything, but no chronic damage.
 Apparently tests were done. We'll trust in science.
 An hour is the maximum. Any more than an hour
 Is hazardous in the extreme. Therefore
 We limit ourselves to minimum conversation.
 Now this is Sergeant Thorn. Rosanna, sweetheart,
 Sergeant Thorn. Sergeant, Rosanna Baron.
 We know this woman only as "the Shadow".
 She was assigned to us as the best there is,
 Sergeant, as you yourself were, that is,

Equal best. She'd die for the Republic.
Obviously she hasn't said that as such,
But it goes with the job, Sergeant, as you know.
The rear man is – excuse me, Zacarelli,
Would you mind paying attention?
ZACARELLI (*taking off his mask*)
   Just seeing the way we came here, Captain Crack.
CRACK
   No need to know the way we came. We never
   Retreat, do we?
ZACARELLI   We don't. We certainly don't.
CRACK
   I was saying prior to this it is possible
   To breathe the air for sixty minutes without
   Chronic internal damage.
ZACARELLI   Who would, though?
   It's revolting, as air goes.
CRACK   Then I was saying
   Talk must be kept to an absolute minimum.
   Then I was introducing Sergeant Thorn.
   Sergeant Thorn, Lieutenant Zacarelli.
   Known in the trouble-spots of this wicked world
   As "Captain Crack's Best Man".
   This is of course not to say he's any better
   Than you or the Shadow, as you're the best there are,
   – Not forgetting Rosanna, who's just – the best.
   In fact you're all shit-hot but I'm in charge.
ZACARELLI
   Good morning, evening, night or whatever the hell,
   Sergeant. Of course, being "Captain Crack's Best Man"
   Has nothing to do with bravery or skill,
   Fitness or a good head in a crisis:
   It means I'm the unlucky git who dies
   Early on in the action, so the Captain
   Can show he's human, master a little tear
   While saying "Zacarelli, my best man . . ."
   It's true, I read the books. There's always one.
   Never the Captain's honeybunch, or the thug
   (No offence) or the one who never speaks,
   Always the one who lightens the atmosphere
   Who gets it. Right in the stars. The tear-jerk.
   Do the job with a scowl, oh you'll be fine.
   Can't see you shedding a tear.
   Can't see you at all, as it happens.

[23]

THORN (*taking off his mask*)
  With your permission, Captain, may I submit:
  I already find this man not a little irksome,
  And wish it to be generally known
  I'd prefer his conversations with himself
  Were as of now conducted with himself,
  Sir!
ZACARELLI (*to* CRACK)
  Did you get all that?
CRACK   Zacarelli,
  Keep your idiot thoughts to yourself. Sergeant,
  Trust me: he's the man you want on your team.
ZACARELLI
  At it again, you see?
  Why not hang a placard round my neck
  Saying "Shoot at this"? Yeuch, this air . . .
CRACK
  Save your breath for breathing it, soldier.
  Now listen up, all of you.
  A rider came last night with information
  I have, naturally, eaten but memorised.
  At dawn on Saturday morning, thirty-six
  Hours from now, we reach the Republican Palace.
  The North Gate was sealed many years ago,
  Giving out as it does on this infected
  Wilderness. There's a sheer drop beneath it.
  Contact will have opened the Gate and lowered
  A rope into the marshes. Once in the Palace,
  We will be hidden for the remaining hours.
  Where, we will be told. The rider gave me
  This photograph of those we have to hit,
  Circled here, here, here and here.
  These are the sworn enemies of the People,
  Apparently. Our Contact is this man.
  Details of our payment will be forthcoming.
  Concentrate for now on these faces.
ZACARELLI
  How do we know which one's the East Gate?
CRACK
  It faces us as we approach.
ROSANNA   Jacob,
  You said North Gate.
ZACARELLI   Really? Was it North?

CRACK
  Yes, wasn't it? East, North. Yes, North.
  But hang on, where's the sun?
ROSANNA   Somewhere about.
  I'm sure that's West.
ZACARELLI   How long ago did you eat it?
  Perhaps we could still –
CRACK   I memorised it, okay?
THORN
  I heard North. He said North.
  Finito. Let's get going.
CRACK   Good idea.
  Let's move on out!
ROSANNA   You pinhead, Zacarelli.

Exit THORN, CRACK, SHADOW *and* ROSANNA

ZACARELLI
  Check, check, and double-check. It's the only way.
  This best man wishes the worst was yesterday.

Exit ZACARELLI

ACT II

The Palace, '62.

An Antechamber. There is a large armchair, five smaller chairs, and a table set with glasses of sweet-looking wine. Who comes comes dressed for a Banquet. Enter LOPEZ, SUAREZ *and* ALEXIN

LOPEZ
What is this meant to make us think? We all
Drink the same and trust each other? I half
Expect my name on one that's an off colour.
SUAREZ
As you are always. You know how many times
Alexin and I fielded the same question
From widows otherwise ripe to vote our way?
LOPEZ
I'll guess: "How I like your smiles, Honourable Suarez,
And how I love your snaps of the boy Alexin,
But are you in cahoots with that death's-head
Lopez?"
SUAREZ   Along those lines.
ALEXIN   But then we answer:
"Yes, but he's on oath at the very least
To grin if elected." That goes over well.
LOPEZ
If Lords would observe the Constitutions, all
Might snort eternally, safe in their own beds.
SUAREZ
Imperilled in ours!
ALEXIN   Whole villages!
LOPEZ   So,
What were your widows' answers, out in the counties?
SUAREZ
Good, Lopez, good. Good, in fact,
Once you forget the constitutional details
And go full throttle into a history lesson –
Banners, flames, Alexin, Lopez, Petran
And furious lionly me, that summer night –
The eyes mist and the cross is in your hands.

LOPEZ
  We have no need of stories. We've the Law.
ALEXIN
  Law's a bore to husbands cutting hedges,
  Duke Lopez, but to see a chap with his shears
  Clutched to his breast, imagining he was there
  In '48, single-handedly pruning
  The necks of the plutocrats like overgrowths:
  It brings a sob to the throat.
SUAREZ   A vote to the slip.
ALEXIN
  And the Heroes' Party to power.
SUAREZ   We have not heard
  A single citizen at odds with us.
  It's ours. So I want another of these, old chap,
  Whatever the poison.
ALEXIN   Drink and be elected!
LOPEZ
  To '48.
SUAREZ/ALEXIN   '48!
LOPEZ   To '62.

They drink. Enter TESSEL

TESSEL
  Ah, have I missed the toast? Typical me.
  Unless it was I on the toasting side, Duke Lopez,
  Duke Suarez, Duke Alexin. In good spirits?
SUAREZ
  Never better. A-betting on ourselves.
TESSEL
  The fever of these days is, after all,
  A favourable contagion! I had had fears
  Of rivalry and discord at the election.
SUAREZ
  That happens when the rivals are close rivals,
  Tessel. We've been arranging strategies
  Economic, military, artistic . . .
  And a first-class ticket for Victor Emmanuel
  Across the world on a liner.
TESSEL   Ah, he is most
  Confident. Support in the Western regions
  Is quite assured.
SUAREZ   Far from it, we were there.

ALEXIN
  And we're home free in Arrowvale, Whitedale
  And all the East and South-east.
SUAREZ   I grant you,
  Victor might hold the Islands – that's 'cause his face
  Is on the bottles of wine and we can't be bothered
  To sail there and compete with that. And true,
  They might just swing to him on the Given-up Lands:
  Population negligible, green
  And plural-headed.
ALEXIN   But they don't get two votes!
TESSEL
  Well, as long as you know me willing to serve
  In any capacity after, whatever the outcome.
LOPEZ
  Though then he should declare for whom he voted.
SUAREZ
  Hell's teeth, Lopez. I am increasingly glad
  You didn't come on the stump with us.
LOPEZ   This circus.
TESSEL
  There is one thing I'd like a chat about.
SUAREZ
  Me too but not the same, I imagine.
TESSEL   Oh?
  Well it's the Palace Guard: Captain Cosker
  And all his men, there always seem to be more.
  The Lord has been evasive over the form:
  Do they remain his Guardsmen if he loses?
LOPEZ
  Not in hell. They guard the Lord, whoever.
  Gnyss reverts to private citizenship.
SUAREZ
  But if we feel a changing of the Guard
  Is healthy: well, we hold the right to ditch
  This spook Cosker and bring in our own people.
LOPEZ
  And we shall use it.
ALEXIN   Speak of the Devil's butler.

Enter the Palace Guard: CAPTAIN COSKER; GRANCHEV,
KALT, HAIN *and* FODEN. *Evidently they are Gnyss's men.*
Then: GNYSS, DAMSEL *and* PETRAN. *Then, to one side,*
ULRICH *and* POLDER

GNYSS
   The Dukes have drinks? Then Guardsmen, you have drinks!
   Friday night is the cancellation of cares,
   Suspension of the stuffy workaday laws
   Governing us free-breathing, fair
   Republicans! I declare
   All talk of our forthcoming peaceful bout,
   Our democratic joust, our happy fight,
   Illegal, punishable by grand forfeit!
   Tonight we are mandated to be gluttons,
   My friends, for there is much to celebrate
   Here on this famous night at the pulsing heart
   Of our red-blooded state! A toast!
   To the Republic! The night of '48!
ALL
   To the Republic! The night of '48!
GNYSS
   My friends, another toast, to a great man,
   Soon to be my rival at the polls,
   Ever to be my friend, whatever befalls!
   To the Grand Duke Petran!
ALL   To Petran! A speech!
PETRAN
   Friends, it is not my night, it is Victor's night,
   Who, as he knows and accepts the People's right
   Gently to move him aside in the gusts of change,
   And pass the documents of State to those
   Who served him loyally, holds no grudge or ill-will –
   He holds instead the approaching grand Banquet!
   So showing his love and trust for the six men
   Whom History has blindly elected to term
   "Heroes" – the Dukes Tessel, Lopez and Suarez,
   Ulrich, Alexin, my unmeriting self . . .
   A toast to the other five! To the five Heroes!

They toast and break into groups

LOPEZ
   Some Heroes, others just this side of helpful.
ULRICH
   Running guns is one thing, running a State
   Takes decidedly more.
LOPEZ   Of the People's taxes.
POLDER
   A common misconception.

[29]

ALEXIN   Aimed at the common.

SUAREZ
  Alexin, is there a nasty odour in here?
  Could it perchance be the Men of Derring-Don't?
  I thought I smelt some lingering comment.

ULRICH
  I thought I saw a pair of Dukes lingering
  Far from the gentlemen's chambers only today.

SUAREZ
  Is that what you do for love as you calculate?
  Me, I don't mind who watches with their fingers.

ULRICH
  Filth in person.

SUAREZ   Effigy
  With an abacus.

ULRICH   Cess of the whole Palace!

SUAREZ *and* ULRICH *square up, and are restrained by*
ALEXIN *and* POLDER. GNYSS *comes over*

GNYSS
  Same as it always is.
  One hero is another's hatred. Friends,
  Look at each other, all of you. Who planned
  The glorious path of brightness into the core
  Of the dull, teeming oligarchy? He did.   (ULRICH)
  Who climbed the roof of the Palace so that for miles
  In all directions citizens were stirred
  By our one, fluttering flag? That was this man. (SUAREZ)
  Others plotted, others perished,
  Some bled, some only staunched the bleeding –
  All were Heroes. All were Heroes.
  Then as now, as all the People know you:
  The Men of Word, who see what can be done.
  The Men of Deed, who do what can be seen.
  The Men of Word and Deed. The Lord between.
  Now all shake hands. Strangers are coming in.

They shake hands limply and split back into their factions.
GUARDS *escort in* LADY LYDIA, *reluctantly leading in* NA-
TALIA VALDEZ, HEIDI FISHER *and the* WOMEN GUESTS

GNYSS
  All passions spent, bring on the beautiful ladies

To brim our hearts again! Lydia, my love,
You have so many dazzling companions.

LYDIA
Grand Dukes, Dukes, Gentlemen. I was asked
To bring these women to eat at the Banquet.

GNYSS   Lydia,
Do better, let's try.

LYDIA   These are the delegates
To the first Republican Conference on Women:
"Women of all Walks of Life".

GNYSS   These two,
What are the walks these ladies represent?

LYDIA
This woman is called Natalia. She . . . walks
With men for her living.

GNYSS   Doubtless she'll walk with us
While the night grows, won't you, Madame Natalia?

NATALIA
Won't I, will I, say what you mean or say
Nothing, Lord. Don't waste your smirk on me.

GNYSS
I'm sure in time we'll all say what we mean,
Won't we, friends? Who is this young lady?

LYDIA
She's just –

HEIDI   You can see who I am, I'm just a student.

GNYSS
Indeed we can. So whom do you represent,
The League of Just Students?

HEIDI   I don't understand.

LYDIA
The girl is bewildered, Victor.

GNYSS   In that case,
We'll unbewilder her with a fine wine.
Daughter, look, she's about your age.

DAMSEL   Not really.
But she is about my size, but what does that mean?

GNYSS
I can see you two getting on quite well together.

DAMSEL
Why? She's much too shy, and so am I.

TESSEL
You are both most welcome here, as official
Representatives of, er, what you represent.

GNYSS

And down to business in the morning, ladies?

NATALIA

Maybe. That's our business, isn't it, ladies?

LYDIA

I beg your pardon? – Yes, that's our business.

GNYSS

Now let me introduce our proud walkers
To the Republic's finest.

GNYSS *and the* GUARDS *lead* NATALIA *and the* WOMEN
away, followed by LYDIA *and* TESSEL. DAMSEL *stops*
HEIDI *by the elbow*

DAMSEL

You, do you know a poem? Listen to this . . .
          "A cloud has eaten up the sun.
          A man has eaten up the both.
          His name is known to everyone.
          One day it will be oath, oath."
I like that "oath, oath", that saying it twice.
"Oath, oath" – it really annoys my daddy,
Me saying it twice, in fact me saying it at all.
He threw it on the fire but by that time
I had it off by heart.
              "The homes are broken into huts.
              The huts are broken into by
              The Men they call the Brave. The ruts
              Lead to a City, and lead high."

HEIDI

          " . . . The lava thickens in the crust,
          The blood is pounding under the hide.
          No one man can hold it. All must
          Move fast, or be blown aside."
"Song of the Written Cross", by Lazarus.

DAMSEL

Hmm, being a poetry-lover like I am,
You maybe can solve the problem. My father,
He's the Lord at the moment, he says Lazarus
Is a liar and bad, but his poem's good.

HEIDI   And true.

DAMSEL

I don't know that. It's just some little pictures,
Isn't it? I don't know what it's up to.

HEIDI
Stop if it annoys him, Miss Damsel.
It ought to. He would call it propaganda.
DAMSEL
He would? What's that? Not really poetry?
HEIDI
It can be that.
DAMSEL   Well look, it is it here.

GNYSS *comes over*

GNYSS
Making a scholarly friendship, are you, dear?
DAMSEL
It's a private talk, daddy, about the Arts.
GNYSS
I'm glad it's about the Arts. I have a surprise . . .
(*to* ALL) Grand Dukes, Dukes, my Ladies and Gentlemen,
Another guest, a most distinguished guest,
Not one whom my opponents would expect
To meet in the passages of our Great Palace,
But let it be evidence:
In our Republic no one is unwelcome,
Whatever the walk of life, whatever the view.
I commend to you an interesting young fellow,
A special Banquet surprise for my daughter
Giddy with poetry . . . Bring on Master Lazarus!

LAZARUS *is escorted in by* COSKER *and* KALT

DAMSEL
Fantastic! I can ask him the one thing.
HEIDI
But this is impossible.
LOPEZ   Suarez, what does this mean?
SUAREZ
What do you think? Advanced electioneering.
ALEXIN
I don't see a cameraman.
SUAREZ   Don't sweat, there'll be one.

GNYSS *brings* LAZARUS *to* DAMSEL *and* HEIDI

GNYSS
Young man, this is my curious daughter Damsel.
Tread lightly, she believes you're a genius.

[33]

LAZARUS
I'm happy to meet you, Damsel.
DAMSEL   You're a poet.
If I said a line of yours, would you know the next?
LAZARUS
I better had.
GNYSS   But would you say it aloud?
LAZARUS
I better had.
GNYSS   Wherever, whenever?
LAZARUS   Whoever.
HEIDI
I'm an admirer of you – your work – sir.
GNYSS   .   See?
You've got the Academy too, young man. I believe
You ought to consider politics!
LAZARUS   I do . . .
Consider it, all the time.
GNYSS   And so you should.
We need more people like you, you create a balance.
DAMSEL
Look at this talk! Is he going to read a poem?
GNYSS
At dinner, yes, aren't you, Master Lazarus?
LAZARUS
If I'm invited to read, I shall.
GNYSS   And eat!
I hope you don't believe you're exempt from that,
The way you are from morals, and so on.
LAZARUS
What do you mean by that, sir?
GNYSS   Be at ease!
Time to encounter Men of Words and Deeds.
An unartistic bunch for the most part,
But full of fervour. Lopez acts like a poet.

GNYSS *and* LAZARUS *go to meet the* DUKES *and* WOMEN.
NATALIA *joins* DAMSEL *and* HEIDI

NATALIA
So where did he first meet you?
HEIDI   He never met me.
NATALIA
Fine. Why are you here?

HEIDI   I'm from the College.
  He, the Lord, invited me here for a forum,
  "Women In All Walks –" like the Lady said.
NATALIA
  You're doing well. Learnt your lines like a walk-on.
HEIDI
  What do you mean? This is his daughter, Damsel.
NATALIA
  I know who she is. Look about you, honey:
  What kind of a forum is this? Dancers, strippers,
  Gypsies, whores: you see us around a table?
  What is our business here?
HEIDI   There is an election,
  Isn't there? Look there for the man's reasons.
NATALIA
  I have six senses. Each is telling me
  A different word that's adding to a warning,
  But why and what and how and who? A blank.
  But I don't believe his story and nor do you.
DAMSEL
  He never believes. He didn't believe that poem.

DAMSEL *wanders off*

NATALIA
  Listen, what's your name –
HEIDI   Heidi.
NATALIA   Listen.
  I was fed this line about a forum
  And told, as you were told, to tell this story,
  But don't you see –

GUARDS *come too close for her to go on*

GNYSS
  Grand Dukes, Dukes, Ladies,
  Gentlemen, and Poet! Your attention please!
  One final guest remains. Tessel reminds me –
  I'm starting to turn forgetful in my age! –
  There is one final guest, in many ways
  The most important of all . . . But he's only a boy.
  Only a boy, I hear you muttering, why
  Is a boy important in such company?

Only that for the year of '62,
This is the Star Pupil of All Schools,
And only that he was born in '48,
To parents who in that year fell as heroes,
For freedom! I myself am 48,
A chance inspiring me to nominate
This orphan born in a year of pain and glory
As the Star Child of the Revolution! Young Manni!

MANNI *is brought in by* FODEN *(who always remains near him as his guide), with the photographer* BAUER. GNYSS *sits in his chair and signals* MANNI *to take the next one.* DAMSEL, LYDIA *and* LAZARUS *take the others.* BAUER *prepares his camera*

SUAREZ
  The publicity stunt to stunt all publicity stunts.
  His brat, an ark of beauties, a dissident poet,
  And some prodigious swot from the humble life.
  Final ingredients: sepia and soft-focus.
  Let's stuff the election and kill him.
PETRAN   Easy, Suarez,
  Look upon it as desperation.
LOPEZ   Damn him,
  Squeezing our shared glory into his cup.
ALEXIN
  We might avoid tomorrow's portrait.
PETRAN   No,
  Then we show the fear Victor is showing.
SUAREZ
  I wish his fear had half the look of fear,
  Petran. And to think we put him in there
  As a stabilising influence, a cipher.
PETRAN
  Trouble with a cipher, Suarez,
  It's not just nothing. It's also everything
  To everyone.
LOPEZ   But you can't remove a cipher.
PETRAN
  You can't remove a friend.
LOPEZ   If you're a friend.
ALEXIN
  There's still two days to go.
SUAREZ   And a trio of nights.

Let's meet the ladies from all walks of life:
The Men of Talk are talking them to death.

SUAREZ *and* ALEXIN *move in on* NATALIA *and the* WOMEN

GNYSS
In all of History,
Has more in the way of irritation to kings,
Emperors, sultans, potentates and tsars,
Down to your humble lords, been down to war,
Famine, plague or ideology – which,
Young Manni, which?
MANNI   Er . . . ideology.
GNYSS
The answer is none at all! The crowning glory
In Irritation's Annals is the man
Getting his camera ready. What's his name?
MANNI
He's Mr Bauer from the Republican Times.
GNYSS
Is he indeed. You're going to be famous, Manni,
With all that that entails.
MANNI   What does it entail?
GNYSS
Patience with your Mr Bauer, Manni.
So what is "Manni" short for – "Manikin"?
Manikin, a little Man. That's it,
The greatest little Man in the Republic.
Damsel, I'm going to arrange for you to marry
This Manikin!
DAMSEL   Oh no you're not, daddy.
GNYSS
– That's bloody impolite, isn't it. Isn't it?
Poet, what do you think? Poem coming on?
Ha! You can read at the wedding party, can't you?
Do wedding poems at all? or just fictions?
LAZARUS
I'll try my hand –
GNYSS   He'll try his hand. There, Damsel,
You have a poet laid on, what more do you want?
Imagine how famous Manni will be by then!
Manni, what do you think of her?
LYDIA   Victor!
These are very young people.

GNYSS   So they don't think?

MANNI

  I'm very pleased to meet your daughter, sir.

DAMSEL *runs out*

GNYSS

  Good answer, she's a treasure. Lazarus,
  A poem please.

LAZARUS   What kind of poem?

GNYSS   A poem!

  You ask a gardener garden and he gardens.
  You ask a fisherman fish and he damn well fishes.
  What trade is this with a stare and a silence, uh?
  Later, Lazarus, give you time to think.
  I'd like to ask about your influences.

LAZARUS

  Influences?

GNYSS   I have my tastes, you know.

LAZARUS

  Of course –

GNYSS   We're not all bonehead lawgivers.

BAUER

  The camera's ready, sir.

GNYSS   Don't interrupt.

  Mindless, really mindless. Lazarus,
  By all means be a prophet in my own home.
  Am I going to win this vote or not?

LAZARUS   I believe

  You'll win on Monday, sir.

GNYSS   And Manikin.

MANNI   Sir?

GNYSS

  Does he have a vote?

LYDIA   He doesn't have a vote.

GNYSS

  How would you vote, Manni?

MANNI   For democracy.

GNYSS

  Good, he should have a vote, it's a mark for me!
  Give this boy the vote! Votes for Children!
  Take all the votes of cameramen and give them
  To boys and girls! Disenfranchise all
  Technicians! All except Mr Bauer, eh Manni?
  Where's Damsel gone?

LYDIA   She'll be in the cloisters.
GNYSS   Oh,
  We'll have the student in the empty chair.
  Hey, sweetheart, come and join us! Sit down there.

HEIDI *sits, so the group is* GNYSS, MANNI, LAZARUS,
LYDIA, HEIDI

  Manni, hold my hand. Let's take the picture.
BAUER
  Everyone smile, please.
GNYSS   Mr Bauer
  Of the Republican Times says "Everyone smile"
  Or he'll do what. I say "Everyone smile"
  Or I'll ban children, photography, the lot.
  And poetry. Can't say fairer than that.
  Take it, take it.

*A one-second silver flash, accompanied by the whirr of the
exposure, and everyone on stage freezing, denotes the taking
of a photograph here and at several subsequent points. It is
denoted thus:* FLASH/FREEZE

  Fame at last, poet. Your books will sell
  And you can dress like us. Lydia, please
  Try and coax your stepdaughter up
  Out of her well of woes. This Manikin's
  Going to propose, aren't you, Manni? Now,
  Food, food! Manni, you'll sit with me
  And talk matters of State. Poet, you take
  The just student and make her just like you.
  Now everybody follow me two by two!

GNYSS *leads* MANNI *off, followed by* COSKER *and* FODEN
as their guards. Then PETRAN *with* LYDIA, *who has found*
DAMSEL; LAZARUS *and* HEIDI; SUAREZ *and* NATALIA;
LOPEZ, ALEXIN *and* TESSEL *each with one of the* WOMEN
GUESTS; *then* GRANCHEV, KALT, HAIN *and* BAUER. *Left
behind are* ULRICH *and* POLDER

ULRICH
  Tomorrow can't come soon enough, Martin.
  He's agitated. Something's going to blow.
POLDER
  Not tonight. Tonight is mere heat,

Men at the purest posture. Our Great Lord
Is, I assure you, certifiably mad,
But the Men of Deed will drink and do nothing.
ULRICH
While our own men of a different deed are out
Crawling over the radiated land
Armed to the green teeth. Did you check the crypt?
POLDER
Perfect. Awaiting them.
ULRICH   You have the painter?
POLDER
Under the floor of the barracks.
ULRICH   Why hide him?
Who's afraid of a portrait painter?
POLDER   Duke.
Secrecy is complete or its opposite.
ULRICH
Of course. I must – steady myself on edge.
Let's pick the meat, and swill the wine, and watch.

Exit ULRICH *and* POLDER

SCENE II
The Given-up Land.

The same green marshlight. Enter CRACK, SHADOW,
THORN, ROSANNA *and* ZACARELLI. *They take off their
masks*

CRACK
This is it: the wall of the Citadel.
The Gate is forty feet from where the ground
Fell away when whatever happened – happened.
ROSANNA
Where's our rope, Jacob?
CRACK   Probably there.
It's probably of a camouflaging colour.
THORN
We stopping here, Captain? If so, let's stop.
CRACK
Check: we'll bed down here. Zacarelli,
Thorn and Shadow, you better get some sleep.

Rosanna and I will take first watch. At one,
Shadow and you, Zacarelli.
ZACARELLI   I like a good chat.
CRACK
Thorn and I at three. Helmets back on.
Who knows what havoc the air plays with your dreams?
Remember, team: it's our last night in the open.
It's all a breeze from here: we do the hit,
We're paid and we make our low profile exit,
Identities provided by Contact.

THORN, SHADOW *bed down.* ZACARELLI *is facing the
wrong way again*

Zacarelli, what are you doing again?
ZACARELLI
It's as well to know the way you came, Captain.
CRACK
For the last time, it isn't. Not only that,
It's negative and it's bad for team morale.
We're going forward, soldier, to the wire.
ZACARELLI
It's also a fascination with the terrain.
Why did it all go green?
ROSANNA
We didn't come here to be fascinated, you moron.
We came to erase the enemies of the Republic.
Didn't we, Jacob?
ZACARELLI   But why not pink? Why green?
CRACK
Believe it and go to sleep, Zacarelli.
ZACARELLI   I will,
But what if I never see this place again?
CRACK
For God's sake, man, be positive. We're killers,
Not balladeers.
ROSANNA   To never see it again
Would be too soon for me.
ZACARELLI   That Sergeant Thorn –
What do we know about him?
ROSANNA   That he's the best.
ZACARELLI
Seems we know that about just about everyone.
He bothers me.
ROSANNA   Compared with you, Zacarelli,

He bothers me about as much as the death
Of a fly by natural causes.
ZACARELLI   All very well,
If that doesn't bother you much.
CRACK   Listen to him:
Pieties from the best shot in the business.
ZACARELLI
Here we go on the epitaph trail again.
You all know very well, when I'm blown to bits
There'll be no time to honour my last wishes
To have a fun-packed funeral, with tunes
In 3–4 time. You'll still be shooting people.
Can't see old Sergeant Thorn arranging the flowers.
Sorry I'll miss the Shadow's moving oration.
ROSANNA
You'll make it, Zacarelli, you always do.
ZACARELLI
You won't be telling me that when I don't, will you?
I've read all the books: the joker never makes it,
He dies still doing a gag. But that wouldn't happen.
CRACK
Number One in a fight, and stories scare him.
ZACARELLI
For the millionth time, I'm over the hill with this!
I'm terrified.
ROSANNA   I love him, he cracks me up.
CRACK
This time tomorrow, lieutenant, you'll still be at it,
Bothering someone under a different name.
Now go to sleep. You're on with the Shadow at one.
ZACARELLI
Can't wait. Gossip, banter, cut and thrust.
Hell. Hell! I've a family, you know.
I left the house a thousand years ago.

ZACARELLI *beds down*

ROSANNA
He has a family?
CRACK   Something went wrong.
She slung him out for something. They lived
Way up North, cold as you like, where the air
Is said to be clear again.
ROSANNA   What happened here?

[42]

I know I'm not supposed to care, but sometimes . . .
You know, Jacob, this was once a place.

CRACK
Honey, I know, and there were once people,
Villages and games on the holidays.
Wind, rain, snow, sunshine – ha,
We sound like Zacarelli.

ROSANNA   What's with him?
He's never been like this before.

CRACK   Don't worry.
The best can be a little unorthodox
In our line, love.

ROSANNA   It's just that we always do
And say all the same things, I mean, for luck.
And Zacarelli's changing the pattern, you know?

CRACK
I know, but that's irrational thinking, sugar.

ROSANNA
Like how we never kiss on the night before.

CRACK
Well. It's worked so far. We lead the lives
We want to lead, with liberty and money,
And keep the Republic strong. It's a small price,
To kiss whenever we wish to kiss, but never –

ROSANNA
Kiss on the night before. That makes you just
As irrational as me, Jacob. Fine.

CRACK
It wouldn't worry me to break that pattern.
We are professionals. We have a plan.
According to this Contact, it's foolproof.

ROSANNA
But is it kissing-proof?

CRACK   Don't tempt me, Rosanna.
Please, don't tempt me, Rosanna.

ROSANNA   I won't try.
I'll think my thoughts beside you, but you won't
Know I'm here, nor what they're all about.
And we'll shake hands goodnight.

They shake hands and sit staring forwards

The Antechamber, outside the Banquet.

LYDIA, NATALIA *and* HEIDI *are in the chairs*

NATALIA
So this is how it's done where the air is pure.
The women expelled to the cold corridor
To stare each other out, while the drunken dukes
Ping-pong abuse or gossip like – women.
LYDIA
My husband sports his Friday worst tonight.
HEIDI
He did let Lazarus read. I never thought –
Lazarus in the Great Republican Hall.
Was that an honour to hear? Reading for them?
NATALIA
I've no idea what it was.
LYDIA   A nature poem.
Nothing to do with what he's notorious for.
HEIDI
Admired for.
NATALIA   Aren't you just the radical.
You and your student forum. Why not start
The speeches now?
HEIDI   I don't know what you mean.
I never met him before.
NATALIA   Did I ask you that?
LYDIA
Leave her alone.
HEIDI   I can look after myself.
LYDIA
So can we all in a classroom. This is a Palace,
And madam, if I had my way you'd be out
Doing the thing you do, not staining the halls
With your profession.
NATALIA   Staining, lady wife?
What do you think we saw in here tonight?
A saintly fraternity? This is a sty.
It's not a sty. The dukes I was stuck between
Would find a sty too prim.
Doing the thing I do. What do I do?
Satisfy citizens, so. Infantrymen?

Battalions. Harbourmasters, Governors?
Two at a time. Priests. You need to ask?

LYDIA
Nauseating rollcall.

NATALIA   What about Dukes?

LYDIA
I daresay.

NATALIA   Dare. What about Grand Dukes?

LYDIA
There are only two.

NATALIA   I counted only one
One foggy morning. What about the Lord?

LYDIA
I shouldn't be at all surprised.

NATALIA   So don't be.

LYDIA
I haven't seen his chamber for a year.

NATALIA
Nor I, but at the age of this bluestocking,
All the time. So what do I want to know?
What have we three honestly got in common?
What have all the women here in common?

LYDIA
There is no mystery, madam. Why shouldn't Victor
Ask the women he knows?

NATALIA   But how does he know them?

HEIDI
My name is Heidi. I never met the man.

LYDIA
Kaboom goes your theory, madam.

NATALIA   Don't you
Feel something? Women in safe quarters,
A dissident who whispers nature poems
At smug aristocrats? And all those Guardsmen?
Natalia's getting out of here tonight.
And so should you be. This ain't no forum.

HEIDI
But if it's all a lie –

Enter COSKER, GRANCHEV, KALT *and* HAIN

NATALIA   What do you want.

COSKER
We've been assigned.

[45]

We've been assigned, and we're the Palace Guard,
To ensure there's nothing not to your liking,
And to escort you if you so desire
Convivially to bed.

NATALIA   We don't desire.

COSKER

You don't? Is that the case?
Then you must know the writer of the poems,
Who won't recite for us, however gently
We urge him to delight us.

LYDIA   Where's my husband?

COSKER

Husband, husband . . . your husband
Is still at his spirits, a dark one and a clear one.

LYDIA

Who else is there?

COSKER   The small boy and his guardsman,
The Lord's daughter, a sottish cameraman.
Pictures are being taken, and a fine time
Is being had by all.

LYDIA   Where are the Dukes?

COSKER

There's Dukes in the Gallery, Dukes in the library,
Dukes in the cloisters, Dukes in the scullery . . .

NATALIA

Oh God get me out of here. I'm leaving now.

COSKER

Granchev shall escort you.

NATALIA   Over my corpse.

COSKER

Hain and Granchev shall together escort you
Discreetly, far behind, Miss Natalia Valdez.
We might as well all go together. Ladies?

LYDIA

Cosker, take us all to my own quarters.

COSKER

Lady, lady, both these guests have special
Private quarters.

LYDIA   I'm quite aware of that.
I'm telling you now to take us all to mine.

COSKER

It shall be done. It's simpler to escort
Three to the one, than three distinct locations,
Isn't it? Let's all proceed together.

[46]

The GUARDS *escort the* LADIES *out. Enter* GNYSS, *as if he had been waiting for the coast to clear, stealthily, like a boy*

GNYSS
He-he, I think they've gone! Come on, children,
New chairs to sit in, all change again!

Enter MANNI *and* BAUER, *who are a bit drunk, and* DAMSEL *and* FODEN, *who aren't. They sit in the chairs*

DAMSEL
We're all sleepy, aren't we. Are you, Manni?
MANNI
Not at all at the precise moment Damsel.
GNYSS
Geniuses don't sleep, you ignorant daughter.
It's cameramen who sleep.
Go to sleep, Mr Bauer.
BAUER   I am asleep.
GNYSS
Good, you're a bit of a bore when you're awake.
Shouldn't he take some pictures?
BAUER   I'm asleep.
GNYSS
Not if I want some pictures you're bloody not.
But I don't. I'm going to sleep.
MANNI   Good night, sir.
GNYSS
I think you should call me Victor Emmanuel.
MANNI
I'll do that, Victor Emmanuel.
GNYSS   So tell me:
What do you make of it all, the powerful life?
MANNI
Very exciting and at the same time simple.
GNYSS
Simple it isn't. Simple?
MANNI
You say what to do, and they do what you say.
GNYSS
Ha! A genius: listen, Damsel, listen,
You have to marry him now.
DAMSEL   I don't see why.
He doesn't look like much.

GNYSS   Why should he
Look like much. He's pure, pulsing brain!
What makes the grass grow green?
MANNI   The chlorophyll.
GNYSS
From where does the zephyr blow?
MANNI   It blows from the west.
GNYSS
Square root of one hundred and sixty-nine?
MANNI/DAMSEL   Thirteen.
GNYSS
Who was the Lord in '50?
MANNI   Barberis.
DAMSEL
I knew that too. He was a friend of mine.
Look, I'm going to bed. Finally, Manni,
I was quite pleased to meet you, but I don't know
If I'll ever meet you again.
GNYSS   Not in the morning.
He's off, up, out, away, early.
In fact we're all of us off to bed. Mr Bauer,
Wake up so you can go to sleep. Damsel,
My much-too-advancing daughter,
Take Manni and Mr Bauer to the Silver Wing
And set their clocks to six. Ha! Goodnight!
See you in the newspapers, ol' Manni.
MANNI
Good night, Victor Emmanuel. Good luck
With your election.
GNYSS   What? Oh, hmm.

Exit DAMSEL, MANNI and BAUER

                         Guard.
Foden, is it? I want them out by nine.
Get them breakfast in their quarters, then,
Out. Not five past nine, not one past nine.
If I see or hear of either of those two
After nine o'clock, you're gone. Got it?
FODEN
I'll have 'em a million miles from the Gate by nine.
GNYSS
That's far enough. Stay with them.

Exit FODEN

You say what to do, and they – ?
They do what you say. Hmm . . . Do they.

ACT III

The Palace, twenty-one years later, in '83.

GNYSS, *the 69-year-old of Act I, is in his armchair. There is
a knock on the door. After a pause, enter* MAX

MAX
  Colonel Cosker is here.
GNYSS   Give me a minute,
  Max, I need some time. He can wait below.
MAX
  He could have, but he didn't, Lord Victor.
  He followed me up the staircase. When I said
  "Colonel Cosker is here", I did mean here.

Enter COSKER, *exit* MAX

GNYSS
  Can the Lord not have a minute nowadays,
  Cosker?
COSKER I feel the minute may grow in value
  After our short discussion, Lord, as opposed
  To before.
GNYSS   And why is that?
COSKER   One needs, does one not,
  To act always in full possession of all
  Vital data, and by that, Lord, I mean
  There is some news.
GNYSS   About the dock strike?
COSKER   That
  Situation is under the tight control
  Of Colonel Manolo, but this is not the news.
GNYSS
  And the wine-growers?
COSKER   Are signing a roll of paper
  So infinitely long one is led to wonder
  Why they are not paper-millers instead.
  But this is not the news either. The news
  Originates from the Office of Information
  Attached to the Victor Emmanuel Institute
  Of Studies.

GNYSS   So. They've run this Dane to ground.

COSKER

  Of him there is no trace. What has been found

  Are papers, lodged in the waste ducts of the building.

GNYSS

  Papers? So, what papers? Who was looking

  In the waste ducts, for God's sake? Revolting.

COSKER

  In answer to the second question: I was.

  In answer to the first:

  Photocopies of photographs of you.

GNYSS

  Of me?

COSKER   Quite recognisably.

GNYSS   Of when?

COSKER

  The year '62, Lord Gnyss. Then.

  Approximately April 7th,

  A Saturday, mid-afternoon. That time.

GNYSS

  That time.

COSKER   Let's not be round-about with this.

  If this – bolted professor has had access

  To such materials, by whatever means

  They came into the light – we were not aware

  Of anything existing – he could do

  A degree of damage, Lord. This might explain

  The abruptness of his flight.

GNYSS   . Photographs?

  There were no photographs.

COSKER   What if there were?

  And one showed them to two showed them to four . . .

GNYSS

  This isn't sedition, Colonel. It's High Treason!

COSKER

  Of course it is.

GNYSS   So find him and arrest him!

COSKER

  I have so many soldiers in the throes

  Of this endeavour, the anarchists could rise

  And go home bored, finding no one to fight.

  There is no trace.

GNYSS   His family.

[51]

COSKER As I say,
There is no trace.
GNYSS Fingerprints somewhere!
. . . Something was unexplained, Cosker, something
Didn't happen that day, a door unshut,
A space unsealed, a window hanging open . . .
Something we forgot. I was seeking it
All last night – what was it?
Something's wagging its tail. I need some time
To think, – my God, am I never to be left
Alone again? The Lord? Can you not find
A single man with the whole of the fucking army?
COSKER
There was a man named Fodén.
A Palace Guardsman, Lord, when I was Captain.
He came from the southern hills, his papers stamped
Setmoor County. He was employed for a month,
And then he disappeared. It was on that day.
So, we assumed he perished in the assault,
Or had had prior warning. In any case
He was never seen again. The matter was closed.
GNYSS
Why was it closed? It doesn't look closed now.
It smells wide bloody open. Photographs.
There were no photographs.
COSKER
It was a time of danger and of treason,
Remember? There were some significant matters,
Issues of great importance –
GNYSS Great importance?
What's of greater importance than the fact
That somebody may be alive who saw it happen,
Who didn't want it to happen?
COSKER History knows
Precisely what happened: it's there in your white book.
A fine historian wrote it.
GNYSS A wretched traitor
Wrote it! How can you stand there and say that?
COSKER
Do, please, not think me cold to the implications.
My face was on the photocopies too.
While I stand here and am harangued by you,
I am your army. The rest is a search patrol.

All right, all right. So back to the work. Foden.
– Close the bookshops, Colonel, every one.
Indefinitely. Encircle, strip and search
Every publishing firm in the Citadel
And all employees. Shut the Institute
Of Studies until further notice. Send me
The editor of the Republican Times. Scan
Personal columns. Go to every home
Tenanted by a Dane or Dean or Daniel or
Every damnable D in the land. Secure them.
Clear the jails if necessary. Treason
Erases theft, fraud, rape, murder.
Tell Max to triple the Palace Guard. The entire
Military is at work until this traitor
Scribbles the day on a stone wall with his nails.
Begin, Colonel.

COSKER   Consider it all performed.

Exit COSKER. GNYSS, *against his own will, picks up the whitebound edition of "Gnyss the Magnificent" and finds a page*

VOICE OF DANE
"It is thought that at approximately dawn on Saturday 7th, the band of mercenary killers gained access to the Republican Palace, either through disused ventilation ducts leading out to the irradiated desert known as the 'Given-up Land', or via the old North Gate, which was believed to have been sealed over with concrete. Only treachery within the Palace could have been responsible for opening either of these fatal apertures. As the assassins crept into the hallowed Temple of Freedom, its Lord and his fellow-revolutionaries – may their names ever be praised – slumbered peacefully in their quarters. The sun rose, bathing the eerie wilderness in bottle-green light, and the snake was in the garden . . ."

The book falls out of GNYSS's *hands and he stares ahead*

The North Gate at dawn, 7th April, '62.

Enter FODEN, MANNI *and* BAUER, *hushed.* MANNI *and*
BAUER *stare out in wonder at the green glow of the Given-up*
Land

BAUER
   It's hillier than I imagined.
FODEN   Sshh.
   Just take your pictures, right? You asked to see it,
   And here it is. Not many has seen that sight,
   And it's more than my job's worth to show it you.
   If you're not out by nine they'll string me up,
   And I like my little number here.
MANNI   Look . . .
   Look what it does to the sunrise: beautiful.
FODEN
   Beautiful, he says, and a breath can kill yer.
   Poison, that is, pure and simple: poison.
   Hundred-and-ten percent. No additives.
MANNI
   There's a rope here. The air can't be that bad
   If people can climb down.
FODEN   Why there's a rope
   Is someone else's bundle, not mine.
   The air is bad. How bad it is is not
   Strictly my kettle neither. It's very bad.
   Now take your snaps and make a Guardsman happy.
   It's less than an hour to nine, and nine's the hour.
BAUER
   We're much obliged, mate. The blokes at the Times
   Would kill to get a shot like this.
FODEN   I'm sure.
BAUER
   Manni, take one of me: I'll stand at the edge.
FODEN
   Famous last words, if you don't mind me saying.

BAUER *gives* MANNI *the camera*

BAUER
   You know how to work the – oh, you obviously do.

MANNI
It's only a camera, Mr Bauer. Smile.

FLASH/FREEZE. *There is a thud, and* BAUER *falls out of sight*

No! Oh no!
FODEN   Stand back, sonny, he's gone.
Must've slipped.
MANNI   No, no, there was a sound, a –
FODEN
I'm getting you out of here, I told him, I said,
I told him, didn't I say –

Another thud and FODEN *drops dead.* MANNI *is petrified for a second, then runs off, back into the Palace. One by one,* CRACK'S TEAM *climb into view*

CRACK
No one mentioned a welcoming party.
Nice shooting, Shadow.
ZACARELLI (*to* SHADOW)   You could at least say, well,
"Don't mention it" or something.
THORN (*of* FODEN)   What about this?
CRACK
Push it over, drop it in the marsh.
He won't care what he breathes from now on.

THORN *and* ZACARELLI *carry* FODEN's *body off*

ZACARELLI
So when did your Contact tell you there'd be guards?
You said this gate was never used. It doesn't
Exactly cheer me up one notch from utter
Desolation to your basic terror.
I smell a rat and his gang.
ROSANNA (*finding a note*)   We were expected.
It's coded: C for Crack.
ZACARELLI   C for Crack?
C for Call the whole thing off right now.
CRACK
Nice work, petal. Yep, this is from Contact.
1500 hours . . . the Bluebell Gallery . . .
How to get there from our hideaway . . .
ZACARELLI
Hideaway? Now you're speaking my language.

[55]

CRACK
It seems to be some kind of crypt.
ZACARELLI   Fine,
It's a cryptic message.
THORN   I swore to myself: if that
Idiot makes a pun on "crypt", I'll kill him.
ZACARELLI
Kill me, just don't swear in front of the ladies.
Shadow here's been shocked into silence.

ZACARELLI *goes to the edge*

Goodbye, Given-up Land. Don't give up on us.
CRACK
How many times, Zacarelli? Stop looking backwards.
ZACARELLI
You have to in life, it's full of colours and girls.
Forwards is blank as blank can be, but I'm sure
We'll fill it up with bulletholes.
THORN   You bet.
I'd die for this Republic.
ZACARELLI (*to* ROSANNA)   Why does he keep
Pretending we're all this bunch of raving zealots?
We know it's only the money.
ROSANNA   Not only.
I'm doing it for Jacob.
ZACARELLI   Lucky Jacob.
CRACK
It all makes sense. This afternoon at three,
The Seven Heroes of the Revolution
Are posing for a portrait in this place
The Bluebell Gallery. Three will sit at the front.
Four will stand at the back. These are our men,
The enemy, and this man here. The painter
Is one of Contact's agents, not a painter.
ZACARELLI
What if they see he's rubbish? They're bound to look.
Even dukes can tell a talented painter
From a goon who can't draw ears.
THORN   We've got the gen,
Captain, shouldn't we get to the hideaway?
ROSANNA
He's right. What if these guards were on a shift,
And going to be relieved?

ZACARELLI   They're relieved now.
"Phew", I bet they're saying to each other.
CRACK
  Nice thinking, Sergeant Thorn and sugar. Yep,
  Let's hit that hideaway. We'll get this thing
  Memorised.
ZACARELLI   Oh good, I haven't eaten.
CRACK
  This stays with me, Zacarelli. It's our insurance
  Against a double-cross. It proves we're here
  Under the auspices of Contact.
ZACARELLI   What
  Double-cross? Oh, now I'm liking this
  About as much as that. To tell the truth,
  I'm homesick for the radiation.
CRACK   Team,
  Let's move on out. Long Live the Republic.
THORN/ROSANNA
  The Republic!
ZACARELLI
  Long live flies like us, who live in it.

Exit CRACK'S TEAM

SCENE III
Lady Lydia's bedroom.

LYDIA, NATALIA *and* HEIDI

HEIDI
  See, it's light outside.
NATALIA   It could be black
  As pitch forever for all I care, sweetheart,
  So long as we were outside in it.
HEIDI   Surely
  Something will happen soon, or someone tell us
  Why we're here.
NATALIA   We know why we're here.
  We got too close, we know too much. This lady's
  Loving husband scraped the streets for all
  The girls he ever had or ever told
  His secrets to. Now they are ours to share,
  Because the lady, you and me ain't

[57]

Going nowhere. Oh yes, but you're the exception,
Aren't you, Comrade Heidi, you turned up
To represent your walk of life at a forum.

HEIDI

I'll take you on for sarcasm, Natalia,
Any day. But I won't hide anymore.
Victor Gnyss – he came to the school one day.
He had his suspicions: drink, debauchery,
Men smuggled in. But none of it was true.
So he brought a barrel of wine and made it true.
And when the dancing stopped and the lights were out –

NATALIA

The Lord of the Republic and little you.

HEIDI

After, he said one day I'd be the mistress
Of the College of the Citadel – then nothing.
Then this – this invitation. He said it was time
He came good on his promise. "Come to the Palace,
Heidi, and we will talk. You understand me –"

NATALIA

"Come to the Palace, Natalia, you will have
Whatever you desire. For you understand me.
The other women there are nothing." Howdy,
Nothing.

HEIDI   Howdy yourself. I had that too.
I won't worry. Remember there's an election.
He doesn't want us compromising him. After,
I think we'll be free to go.

NATALIA   Free to go?
Why, where, how, with what we know?

LYDIA

Guard! This is intolerable. Guard!

Enter GRANCHEV

I say again, and I won't say it again:
Take me to my husband. Now, at once.

GRANCHEV

Gladly, but I can't, Lady Lydia.
I have to follow an order, and the order
Is: that the three of you remain in here
For your own safety.

LYDIA   Our own safety from what?

GRANCHEV
  From danger, at this very dangerous time.
NATALIA
  It's dangerous 'cause men with hollow skulls
  Stare ahead and follow orders. Nothing
  In our own lives is dangerous but men.
GRANCHEV
  I cannot enter into any discussion
  While undertaking –
NATALIA   Shut up and sod off then.

Exit GRANCHEV

  Men protecting us from other men.
HEIDI
  What about your stepdaughter,
  Lady Lydia, maybe she can see him.
LYDIA
  She's full of bad words against her father,
  But won't believe or hear them from another.
  Besides, she makes no sense.
NATALIA   I'm surprised
  She's not shut in with us and shares our dark
  Criterion.
LYDIA   That's an atrocious comment.
NATALIA
  And that's an ironic one, if you look at us.
  What do you think this man is doing – joking?
  He's bolting himself in place to rule this State
  Forever, the whole world can hike to hell,
  Or wait for his slaves to cart it here.
HEIDI   They're coming.

Enter COSKER *and* KALT, *with* LAZARUS

COSKER
  Lady Lydia, I do hope it's not
  Inconveniencing, but we'd be grateful
  If you and your fellow ladies would entertain
  This poet for a while. He's very weary.
  He read to us all night.
LYDIA   He can stay here.
COSKER
  Can he? We're glad you say that.
HEIDI   He can sit here.

COSKER
  We did purchase his books, but that's because
  We're all a little ill, our noses outrunning
  The Palace supply of paper.
LAZARUS   There are more books
  Than running noses, sir.
COSKER   There are other holes
  To wipe, poet.
LAZARUS   A line of poetry
  Known across the world absorbs the waste
  Of every thug on the planet. The memory
  Keeps it warm while all of us become
  The stuff we block our noses at. You
  Will die with poems crackling at your ears.
COSKER
  Really. See, ladies, a gentle sort,
  Keen on flowers and birds, as you'd expect.
HEIDI
  You must be a brave soldier, to insult
  A hungry poet while gripping a big gun
  So tight it turns your knuckles yellow.
COSKER   I am,
  I am a brave soldier, aren't I, Kalt?
KALT
  Quite a hit with the female sort as well.
NATALIA
  What females? Sows, bitches, ewes, mares?
COSKER
  I seldom have to pay, like those you know.
NATALIA
  Pillaging a town, you wouldn't have to.
  Call yourselves men-o'-war? Jellyfish.
KALT
  That don't apply to him.
NATALIA   Who wants to know?
  Get out, get out, get out of the Lady's bedroom!

KALT *and* COSKER *wilt and retreat*

LYDIA
  Thank you, Miss Natalia.

NATALIA   That's nothing.
That or fingernails in the weasel faces.
HEIDI
How are you, friend?
LAZARUS   I'm tired.
They talked to me all night. They never touched me.
And they'll be just as tired.
HEIDI   Close these eyes.
Stop these ears, let all obnoxious sound
Die away in the walls.

LAZARUS *goes to sleep, with his head on* HEIDI's *shoulder*

LYDIA
I think I know him well enough to know –
He knows he couldn't – get away with this.
NATALIA
Maybe he doesn't know he can't, love.
Maybe he knows he can.
Maybe that's what this is. Maybe he's that man.

SCENE IV
The Crypt.

Very dark. ZACARELLI *is sitting apart from the rest of the
team*

CRACK
Let's run through it all again. Thorn, Rosanna.
THORN
There are three chairs, three men sitting in them.
ROSANNA
Four men stand behind. It's for a portrait.
THORN
Contact walks away from the group to the door.
CRACK
And what does he say?
ROSANNA   "We need some extra bodies."
CRACK
"We need some extra bodies." Then what happens?
THORN
Baron, Shadow and I walk into the room
And stand behind the upright men.

[61]

ROSANNA   Zacarelli
   Covers us at the door. The painter says:
THORN
   "Hold it, gentlemen."
CRACK   "Hold it, gentlemen."
ROSANNA
   Then Jacob blows away the man in the chair.
THORN
   Baron, Shadow and I do the hits with these.
   After the execution, we form a line
   And give the Battle Salute of the Republic.
CRACK
   A-okay. One other vital detail:
   Before I hit the man in the chair, I'll say:
   "Long Live the Republic!" You got that?
   Zacarelli, you get all that? Where is he?
ROSANNA
   Over there by the urns.
CRACK   Oh not again.
   Zacarelli, say something, dammit!
ROSANNA   Jacob,
   He's been like this before, remember. The night
   We hit the diamond smugglers in the mountains?
   He came through then. It's pure concentration.
CRACK
   Okay, okay, at ease, Zacarelli.
   Nod your head if you understand the m.o.
ROSANNA
   Did he nod?
CRACK   It's dark in here, how do I know?
   No sense in arguing with the best there is.
THORN
   Captain, I have a point to raise.
CRACK   Sergeant.
THORN
   We're acting on the principle that if
   The Contact says do this, we do it, and if
   The Contact makes no mention, we don't do it.
CRACK
   Check. So what's your point?
THORN
   My point is, with respect, Captain Crack,
   The Contact makes no mention of you saying
   "Long Live the Republic!" at the point

You said you'd say it in the m.o. So,
My point is: it's a straying off of the plan,
And therefore makes our strategy a fraction
Jeopardisable, sir!

CRACK   "Long Live the Republic."
What's wrong with saying that?
We're doing this to save the damn Republic
From traitors, so what fitter thing to say?

THORN
Sir, I yield to no man in my love
Of this Republic, nor no woman either,
But the Contact don't say say it so don't say it.

CRACK
Sugar, what do you think?

ROSANNA   I'm not sure.
It's a shame not to say anything, but the Sergeant's
Point is valid. Ask the others.

CRACK   The others.
Zacarelli in cuckooland, and this
Wordless killing machine.

THORN   You're the Captain.
You don't go asking the panel.

CRACK   Fine, fine,
I'll say just what I like then, Sergeant Thorn,
If it's all the same to you.

THORN   It seemed worthwhile
To raise the point.

CRACK   You did and now let's drop it.
I want the two of you, Shadow and Thorn,
To follow the lieutenant into deep
Meditation. This is how we work,
Sergeant. Mental strength as well as precision.

THORN
I'll have a think. But you won't hear what I think.

CRACK
Sugarplum, this is it.
Two hundred and twenty minutes to go. I've got
That icy feeling that never fails. Tonight
We'll be rich and different people.

ROSANNA   Who will you be?

CRACK
A navy man, I thought, with a beard and a past.

[63]

ROSANNA
  I won't have a past, only a glittering future.
  My name will be . . . Blanche, and I'll be a blonde,
  A platinum blonde, and one day in the harbour
  I'll see a navy man with a beard and a past,
  Looking out to sea there.
CRACK   I won't turn,
  Then I'll turn and be dazzled. I'm dazzled now,
  But it's so dark.
ROSANNA   They'll never know we were heroes.
CRACK
  They'll know that heroes came. They'll never know
  Who they were.
ROSANNA   Or why they never kissed
  Before a mission.
CRACK   Why did they never kiss
  Before a mission?
ROSANNA   Because they had never died.
CRACK
  Why did they never die?
ROSANNA   Because, after,
  There was nothing to do but kiss.
CRACK   Don't move, Rosanna.
ROSANNA
  Don't move, Jacob, Captain.
  Blink, and let the hands go round till the hour
  Blanche and the mariner meet by the sea. There.

SCENE V
The Bluebell Gallery.

Three chairs in a row. Enter POLDER, *who rearranges them
slightly then stands back. Enter* ULRICH

ULRICH
  Behold the resurrection of the dead!
POLDER
  What do you mean by that? A ghost story
  Is of no use to us.
ULRICH   I mean, Martin,
  I just came up from the crypt. I saw your team,

[64]

Sitting around like a set of china humans,
Absolutely still. They didn't see me.

POLDER

There was no need for you to see them, Duke.

ULRICH

But yes, I make a hobby of humans! What
In hell have you gathered together? Are you sure
They're up to it?

POLDER   They meet our needs exactly.
Various pathological misfits
Asleep on a precipice they cannot see.
The Captain is a veteran of several
Violent escapades at the rim of war.
Desertion, vagrancy and alcohol
Account for his four followers. They are all
Touchingly courageous, hand-in-hand
With eminently gullible. Heroes.
That particular column of the doomed.

ULRICH

And will they do what they're supposed to do?
Predictability is all, Martin.

POLDER

Give them a bell, they ring it. Give them a boat
They get in it and sail it. Give them a plan
They execute it to the nth degree.
They'd slaughter their own selves if it were ordered,
Not without an innocent puzzlement
As the last blood ran out. They make the world
Go round in a red lagoon, the valiant kind.
What we've planned, they'll do.

ULRICH

They'd better do, or it's some tricky questions
For the Duke and Mr Polder. Your instinct
For human reflex – that's what the entire
New Republic hangs upon this hour.
By nightfall there will be a change of power
One way, or a sudden drastic other.
This has to work, Martin – will it?

POLDER   Duke.
Get nine sacks. That's how I'll answer that.
By nightfall our great leader
Will be alone with his two saviours,
One a Duke, and one a Duke tomorrow.
Ba-dum, ba-dum, I recognise the footfall.

[65]

ULRICH *and* POLDER *sit in the two outer chairs. Enter* GNYSS, *who sits between them and puts his arms around their shoulders*

GNYSS
And how's the world of dukedom?
ULRICH   Full of life.
GNYSS
And how's the crypt this morning?
POLDER   A shade deathly.
GNYSS
And how's the world of painting?
ULRICH   Black and white.
GNYSS
And how are our foreign visitors?
POLDER   All ready.

FLASH/FREEZE. *Pause.* FLASH/FREEZE. *Pause.* GNYSS *rises*

GNYSS
Right, let's get some lunch. Can't be painted
On an empty stomach. I also feel the need
To while away some time with the Grand Dukes
And rub my shoulders with some Men of Deed.
You never know when you'll get the chance again.
Come on, you Men of Word.
Into the world of men.

ULRICH *and* POLDER *rise and begin to follow* GNYSS.
FLASH/FREEZE. FLASH/FREEZE. FLASH/FREEZE. *They exit*

ACT IV

The Crypt. Very dark.

CRACK
  Fourteen hundred and thirty hours, team.
  That's thirty minutes to go, and falling. Thorn?
THORN
  Check, Captain.
CRACK   Rosanna?
ROSANNA   Check, Jacob.
CRACK
  Shadow?
ROSANNA She moved her head a bit to the right.
CRACK
  That's good enough for me. Check, Zacarelli?
  Snap out of it, Zacarelli.
ZACARELLI   – I have snapped out.
  I have snapped out, and it isn't "check" at all.
CRACK
  What the hell do you mean?
ZACARELLI   It isn't "check".
  It isn't check-check-check but it is chess
  And guess what pieces we are. I'm not coming.
THORN
  He's broken up, I knew it.
CRACK   Hold it, Thorn.
  He's my best man, remember: temperamental.
ZACARELLI
  Holy moly I'm not your best man, Jacob!
  I'm your worst fear, my nerves are shred to powder.
  Temperamental? Pluck any rotten husband
  Or failed father out of the frozen North
  And give him a little gun, and hide him away
  In a tomb in a lousy palace, having had him
  Lug his lungs in the shittiest air in the business
  Of being air you can breathe, sling him in here,
  Set him against entire armies, but never
  Forgetting to tell him, and prod him and then remind him
  That he's the best there is, when he knows damn well
  It's all about to be over, minus children,
  Minus cat called Wilson, minus wife,

[67]

You'd be temperamental, Jacob. Life
To me was life, not a modus operandi.
And I do not want to die being
Captain Crack's Best Man, I want to be worthless,
And gossip, and eat my morning meals in bed,
And then still not get up.
ROSANNA   We're losing him, Jacob.
  Do something.
CRACK   Zacarelli, listen to me:
  This plan has been checked and double-checked. We know
  All we need to know: that a plot's been laid
  By certain men to murder their own Lord,
  And bring the Republic down. We don't know why,
  But we know faces. This is the kind of work
  We always do: no questions, bang. And then,
  Rich and with new identities we go,
  To our new homes and names. By all means
  Laze in bed forever then, or get up
  Only to overspend, but –
ZACARELLI   Overspend?
  We're not the lucky prizewinners, Jacob,
  We're the money itself, we're being spent!
  Can't you feel it? Something is pulling us in,
  I felt it in the wilderness, I kept
  Looking back to be sure and it tugged me on
  Like I was a dog who left his life behind!
  We're starting to belong to someone, Jacob,
  We never have before!
THORN   We should consider, Captain,
  Terminating with extreme prejudice.
ZACARELLI
  Well go ahead, I'll tell you what it's like,
  And catch you a little later on a cloud
  And giving me the finger. Better consider,
  Sergeant Thorn, if we go out together,
  You may be allocated a neighbourly nimbus,
  Then I can tell you gags eternally
  And you can terminate to your heart's content
  But I won't stop till Judgement Day if then.
THORN
  Captain, he's a danger to us all.
CRACK
  Sergeant, we can look after ourselves.

ROSANNA
  Better make a decision quickly, angel.
  I think he's gone this time, he's talking nonsense.
ZACARELLI
  Something about our words: like in a dream
  You talk and the words are wrong, alien, new,
  And you never remember awake, when it's the morning,
  What they even were, and the plot and the reason
  All gone, all gone. You've only the emotion,
  Floating away.
CRACK   My God.
THORN
  He's out of control, Captain, may I submit:
  A liability. If I was in charge –
ROSANNA
  Well you're not, Jacob's in charge, and Jacob knows
  Zacarelli's the best he ever had.
THORN
  I'd like to meet the worst he ever had,
  But I guess he's eating bacon and eggs in bed.
CRACK
  This is a hard blow to absorb, Zacarelli.
  We've been on a hundred hits like this –
ZACARELLI   No we haven't.
  Those were the been and gone. This is the present.
  We lived through them and this is one we haven't.
  That makes it terribly different to me, Jacob.
  And I do not want another name. And the money
  Has turned to nothing but money.
CRACK
  Hell! Logic, military training, all
  Out of the window, dammit! You do your job.
  You do your job, that's all it comes down to!
  Your job is this, you do it 'cause you're paid
  To do it, you do it, you're paid, and there's an end.
  Otherwise, what? Nothing! Nobody doing
  Anything. Everything stopping. The world
  Waiting for just one job to get itself done,
  And this is the job, and the world is waiting. If not
  For the money, the heart and soul of the Republic,
  Freedom, honour, or the mere pride of a soldier,
  Do this job for Captain Crack. – Zacarelli?
THORN
  Sounds like he died of his own conversation.

[69]

CRACK
Hell, where are you?
ROSANNA   He's not where he was sitting.
THORN
He crawled away. We should have heard the clucking.
CRACK
Dammit, dammit, he was my best man.
ROSANNA
Hold hard, Jacob, he isn't now: forget him.
CRACK
Hell, okay – we won't have covering fire.
THORN
Covering fire, who needs it. I'm burning now.
CRACK
Okay, let's do it. What does Contact say?
THORN
"We need some extra bodies", sir!
CRACK   And sugar,
What does the painter say?
ROSANNA   "Hold it, gentlemen."
CRACK
"Long Live the Republic!"
THORN   And goodnight, treason.
CRACK
Arm up, team, and head on out.
THORN   Let's go!
(*to* SHADOW) You 'n' me, man, let's bring the shadows down!

Exit THORN *and* SHADOW

CRACK
Beautiful lady, see you over the bridge.
ROSANNA
Over the bridge and by the sea, my man.
CRACK
Don't even blow me a kiss.
ROSANNA   I wouldn't dream.
Just remember, Jacob, when you lost
Your best man and the time had come, of all
The best men in the world, the best was a girl.
Now take me into battle.

Exit CRACK *and* ROSANNA

[70]

The Bluebell Gallery.

*The Seven Heroes of the Revolution are in position for their
portrait. Standing, left to right from our perspective:*
ALEXIN, SUAREZ, LOPEZ, ULRICH. *Seated;* PETRAN,
GNYSS, TESSEL. *There is an easel with a blank canvas. Enter*
POLDER

POLDER
　Your Graces, I sincerely apologise
　For this delay but I do assure·you the artist
　Is on his way.
GNYSS　　　　　So what's delaying the man?
　Has he found seven other heroes of some other
　Revolution? Well well, these men of dreaming . . .
SUAREZ
　I reckon he's gone to stock up on his grey
　Oils, the greyer and oilier the better
　With Ulrich as a subject.
ULRICH　　　　　　　　More likely
　He's brushing up on his heraldic symbols:
　For instance, lions rampant for the cloak
　Of the Lord Gnyss, or, poised over the head
　Of the Duke Suarez a sword, pointing downwards.
LOPEZ
　He'll have to be a master of dissembling,
　Exploiting an arsenal of golden smiles.
　Them he will have to forge.
TESSEL　　　　　　　　Not in the front row,
　Happily, Duke Lopez. We three
　Will serve to remind the populace of how
　Harmoniously and undiscordantly
　We do behave, election or no election.
ALEXIN
　So is the election in doubt, all of a sudden?
　That could disappoint some seven hundred
　In the hills of my home shire.
PETRAN　　　　　　　　　It is in no doubt.
　Our people will conduct themselves in the manner
　Of our exemplary nobility.

GNYSS
We're all quite sure of that, Good Sir Petran.
I trust you've written your speeches.
PETRAN   I have done.
GNYSS
And I mine.
LOPEZ   What need of more than the one?
We know how Victory's spelt: so there's a speech.
ULRICH
By no means, Duke Lopez. You omitted a dozen
Exclamation marks and a wild salsa
Filched from the peasantry.
PETRAN   I have two speeches.
That is the essence of a democracy.
SUAREZ
Well Ulrich has two faces,
That is the practice of a democracy,
And will sorely tax the painter, if he's finished
Crayoning in the sky and his four windows.
TESSEL
I assure you he's a painter of great renown:
His reputation goes before him.
SUAREZ   Seems
It has to, so does everything else.
ALEXIN   I hear him,
Or someone – more than one.

Enter COSKER *and* GRANCHEV

COSKER
Your Graces, may we sue to witness this
Most auspicious occasion?
GNYSS   If you've truly
Nothing better to do than watch us has-beens
Immortalised for the electorate.
LOPEZ
Assuming anyone else appears on the canvas.
ALEXIN
Probably do us Men of Deed in pencil.
SUAREZ
Or lemon, so they can make us out as we burn.
TESSEL
Is this the painter now?

Enter KALT *and* HAIN

GNYSS
  Cosker, are you sure it's the Seven Heroes
  The painter means to paint, or the Palace Guard?
  I hope no one is neglecting other duties
  For this frivolity.
LOPEZ   Frivolity.
  So much for harmony, immortality.
COSKER
  All our duties are being performed, Lord.
GNYSS
  I hate to see the Guard enjoying themselves.
  Wipe those smiles off, we're the powerful ones.
PETRAN
  Now I can hear the painter.
  That's not the step of a soldier, is it, Victor?

Enter the PAINTER

PAINTER
  Graces, Graces, everywhere there are Graces!
  Seven Graces, a holy number of Graces!
ALEXIN
  Another poet. Is this a Lazarist?
PAINTER
  Exquisite, ah . . . the Heroes of the hour.
SUAREZ
  What's left of it. Get on with it.
PAINTER   Graces,
  Gentle Graces, I need you such a short time.
  Have such a short little time to spend with you,
  I hope to make best light of it.
PETRAN   Why
  Do you have a short time with us?
PAINTER   Noble Graces,
  I need you only the bite of an hour! I draw
  Your spirits on to my page, I breathe you in,
  And sketch your excellent souls on the tablet, white
  In anticipation of its ecstasy!
  Then I need you no more,
  And the meanest men can serve me for my models.
  Your time is precious, Graces.
  In minutes you will be free.

[73]

TESSEL   I understand.
  He doesn't need us for long. Then he requires
  Volunteers to form the shapes of men
  And be ourselves for the time it takes to paint.
  Are there any?
GNYSS   We can't spare Palace Guards
  All day and night.
POLDER   Lord, it is taken care of.
  Acting on the approximate measurements
  Of yourself and the Grand Dukes and Dukes, I have
  Enlisted servants of both height and build
  Not dissimilar. These await the call
  Even now, outside the door.
PETRAN   Painter,
  We were not inconvenienced by the sitting.
LOPEZ
  Speak for yourself: I want to get out of here.
SUAREZ
  Why not paint the impostors, anyway?
  Then they can have the election, and we can all
  Walk new walks of life.
PAINTER   I have begun!
  Work has begun on you!
  And will not end until we see you truly!
  . . . I am beginning to have you now, your breath
  Is floating through my fingers, see? to the canvas
  And forming into a Grace, another Grace,
  Another: you are there and you are here –
  Ach, the chill of my genius, from where
  Are you emanating? Another Grace has appeared!
  Oh, balance, pattern, swing! Ah,
  Four are captured, four are immortalised!
ULRICH   Four?
  Let's let some people go then. I'll open the door.

PETRAN *stands up suddenly.* ULRICH *opens the door*

  We need some extra bodies.
GNYSS   What's the matter,
  Grand Duke?
PETRAN   Stiffness suddenly, stiffness, Lord.

Enter CRACK, *who walks towards* PETRAN, *then* ROSANNA, SHADOW *and* THORN, *who move behind the Seven, directly behind* ALEXIN, SUAREZ *and* LOPEZ. ULRICH *remains at the door;* PETRAN *remains standing*

Is this man going to be me? Am I that tall?
CRACK
Oh – am I?
PAINTER   Hold it, gentlemen.

CRACK *hesitates*

ROSANNA
Say it, Jacob, say your damned line!
CRACK
Er – Long Live the –

FLASH/FREEZE. *The following sequence unravels in silence, punctuated by the* FLASH/FREEZE *of the pictures that are being taken, so the structure is that of a slow flickering film. The characters are either frozen or moving normally. This is what happens:* PETRAN *suddenly sees what's coming, draws a gun and shoots* CRACK *dead on the spot.* GNYSS *throws himself and* TESSEL *to the floor;* ULRICH *stands clear. Meanwhile,* ROSANNA, SHADOW *and* THORN *attack, respectively,* ALEXIN, SUAREZ *and* LOPEZ *from behind, with cord – none is successful, and the three become hand-to-hand struggles.* PETRAN *is the first to realise that* COSKER, GRANCHEV, KALT *and* HAIN *are levelling guns at all of them. Gradually, the six who are fighting realise it too.* PETRAN *raises his hands in a gesture of helplessness and disappointment, then all seven are gunned down.* GNYSS *and* TESSEL *stir on the floor. The* PAINTER *is long gone*

GNYSS
Loyal Tessel, you live! Am I alive?
TESSEL
Oh Victor, the devastation! Calamity!
Outrage! Catastrophe! Barbarity!
GNYSS
And Ulrich, you live too!
ULRICH   By some mercy
Mysterious and terrifying, I do!

GNYSS *and* ULRICH *embrace.* FLASH/FREEZE

TESSEL
Half the heroic generation felled
In a fell manner!
GNYSS   Dreadfully fell, Tessel!
Petran, my brother! Alexin, almost a son!
TESSEL
Suarez and Lopez, Lopez and Suarez, gone!
ULRICH
Now how I regret our enmity!
TESSEL   Too late!
GNYSS
Vicious assassination! Vile assault!
Guards, cover these horrors.

THE GUARDS *start to cover the bodies.* FLASH/FREEZE

Tessel, rage and action wait their turn
Behind despair and grief. After we mourn
The loss of Heroes, then we avenge the loss,
Find out who sent these slaves into our midst.
But one thing above all . . .
One favour dragged, dark green from the depths . . .
TESSEL
Anything out of this wild disaster, Lord.
GNYSS
Find and shield my daughter. Maybe danger
Lurks everywhere: if all my joys are over
And in the past with these great Martyrs of Deed,
Harm to Damsel –
TESSEL   I'll reach out through my sobs,
And pull her out of danger, find her, shield her –
Oh Victor, the devastation! Atrocity!

Exit TESSEL. *Pause*

GNYSS
I'm sure he's said that twice.

ULRICH *and the* GUARDS *burst out laughing.* FLASH/
FREEZE. GNYSS *takes a look at the "painting"*

Couldn't we find a man who can draw?
HAIN   I can draw,
Lord, but apparently don't look like a painter.

[76]

GNYSS
You don't, nor very much like a Guardsman either.
You look to me like a cook.
HAIN   I'm a good cook.
ULRICH
Victor Emmanuel, am I a Duke or a Duke?
GNYSS
You're a Grand Duke, Duke Ulrich, and where's
                                   Martin?
You're going to be one too.
POLDER   There are only eight.
GNYSS
What?
POLDER There are nine sacks;
And only eight inhabitants for them.
ULRICH   He means
Our intelligence told us there were five
Visitors coming, not four –
GNYSS   Well now there aren't any.
Who'd have expected the Grand Duke to be armed?
Now there's a cynic.

COSKER *comes over with more guns.* FLASH/FREEZE

COSKER   He wasn't the only one.
They were all armed but you and the old fool.
GNYSS
Amazing, in this day and age, in this
Democracy. Where's that cook?
COSKER
You're wanted, Hain.

HAIN *comes over.* FLASH/FREEZE

GNYSS   Dig out the chief assassin,
The one who came in first. Better just check
His pockets for the usual thrilling clue.
ULRICH
We know what he's going to find.
GNYSS   Oh – do you?
Learn what you know and what you think you know,
Ulrich. Here they come.

GNYSS *takes from* HAIN *the documents found on Crack*
                    Remarkable.

[77]

POLDER
  Ba-da-da-dum. This is the drum for us.
ULRICH
  Where's there a secret –
GNYSS   Guards, seize these men:
  Their faces are both ringed upon the papers
  Found here on this savage –
ULRICH   Oh for God's sake,
  Victor, you know they are, we brought them here,
  We set them up, you told us to work it out!
COSKER
  Interesting.
POLDER Death, this is watertight.
GNYSS
  You know as well as I do what happened:
  Miraculously I have survived an attempt
  To kill me on the eve of the Election,
  Though, tragically, four of the Heroes died
  Trying to shield their Lord. Now it transpires
  One single envious Duke and his protégé
  Were architects of this conspiracy.
ULRICH
  But everyone in the room knows this a lie!
GNYSS
  But everyone in the room is loyal to me,
  With two glaring exceptions. Take them away
  And keep them under lock.
POLDER   Say nothing, Duke.
  My mind is trying to work but it's slow work.

ULRICH *and* POLDER *are taken away by* HAIN *and*
GRANCHEV

GNYSS
  That's where scrabblers end. Now, Mr Kalt,
  Go after Grand Duke Tessel, and remember,
  My daughter's safety is the only point.

Exit KALT

  So what have I forgotten?
COSKER   Nothing, Lord.
GNYSS
  Rubbish, there's always something.

COSKER

The Special Unit are coming to take the victims.
The Editor of the Times arrives tonight
For the essential story. Obviously
We are going to have to cancel our Election.
Nobody but yourself seems to be standing.

GNYSS

I am the Lord, Cosker. You do not have
Elections to be Lord, you are the Lord.
They wanted to bring me down, my own brothers.

COSKER

They did indeed, and came within a whisker.

GNYSS

The chosen has no choice. Sorrow is his,
The loss of fellows. Loneliness is his.

COSKER

The mountaineer's loneliness, Lord.

GNYSS

I see my enemies at the cliff's foot,
Cosker. You have loyally served in this.
My daughter!

COSKER   Kalt has gone to protect her, Lord.

GNYSS

And all of the Devil's women?

COSKER   Will know him better.
And that reminds me, Lord.

GNYSS   I have an ache,
Here where I trusted a lady, here a Duke,
Here another, here where I loved . . . the Lord
Endures the pain of them all, locks it away.
Locks it away in the box of treasure.

COSKER   Lord.
You have not closed that box.
Three females and a male, all white persons,
Remain in a secure haven. If
You wish and you should know I do advise
Against it, they be let loose from the Palace,
And trusted ever after, we of the Guard
Will do your bidding instantly. Likewise,
The other option. As you shall command.
We might lock up the story to the general
Satisfaction of the public, i.e.,
Widening this late monstrosity
Of assassination to absorb the poet,

Your Lady – which equips the tragedy
With barbs to make each wedded citizen weep –
And two unlucky bystanders no one
Will greatly miss. And that's
How we lock it up. The other option
Obviously is to take the chance the poet
Switches mid-career, and the white females
Let it slip their minds.
As I say, it's as you shall command.

GNYSS

Why d'you find it so debatable,
You road of slime, you sub-contemptible
Wedge of deeds? Free them at the Gate.

COSKER

Free them at the Gate.

GNYSS   The North Gate.

COSKER

The old North Gate.

GNYSS   Free them,
Let them out of my Palace, your white persons,
Let them out of my Palace, Cosker.

COSKER   Yes,
I shall, but a last confirmation, please,
At such a critical time: the four persons
Remaining at your Grace's pleasure, comprising
A woman, a young girl, a creature of no
Moral worth and the publisher of lies,
To be freed forthwith at the North Gate of the Palace?

GNYSS

Mmm.

COSKER   Consider it done. Immediately?

GNYSS

Mmm.

COSKER   Consider it done.

Exit COSKER

GNYSS

Murderers all, murderers and thieves.
Whores and liars and slobberers and slaves.
We'll lock the door on all of them. We have
Locked it. I can hear it. It's enough.

SCENE III
A cottage, twenty-one years later, in '83.

A little desk and chair. Enter PROFESSOR DANE, *who sits and reads from a blackbound book*

DANE
"Lazarus. Song.

Into the desolate heart I travelled,
        Into the blown heart.
Beside the tracks of the dead I waited,
        The just dead.
Across, when I had to cross, the impassable bridge,
        I did cross, my ladies,
And Now is Ever, my people,
        And now you know.

Beside the adders and cats I sang,
        To the sick cats,
Over the arc of the sky they had me,
        Our old sky.
Down, when I had to move, the distorting tunnel,
        I did move, my ladies,
And Now is Ever, my people,
        And still you know.

So, from the mock and murder I fly
        My own murder.
Towards new desolate hearts I travel
        To your hearts.
Up, when I have to rise, the eternal well,
        I will rise, my ladies,
For Now is Ever, my people,
        And ever you know."

Enter ZARA DANE, *with a letter*

ZARA
Manni, a letter's come. You read so well.
DANE
I know who this is from. This is from Pryce.
ZARA
I waited for you to finish the poem, in case

I might disturb you in the rhythm, but no,
I bet I wouldn't have done.
DANE   I'm sure you wouldn't.
Let me just read what he says . . .
ZARA   What does he say?
DANE
    . . . My God, yes it's out, it's out, it's everywhere!
ZARA
The book? Oh heavens! Where?
DANE   The Institute,
The paper, the press, the university towns!
" 'Gnyss the Magnificent II' " he says, "is the talk
Of every man on the street!" But the other side –
Shots, arrests in the Citadel, new Laws –
But no, it's found its way to the barracks! Zara,
These books are in the hands of the State Army!
"The Third Battalion, under Ivan Petran,
Looks set to mutiny now, in loyalty
To the Grand Duke's memory. Regions to the East
And South are reporting massive public unrest,
And statues of the Lord are burning!" Zara,
It's happening, it's happening! "One bookshop
Is closed, another opens, Emmanuel:
You can't see anyone's face this side of town,
Cause everyone's got his nose in your damn book!
Couldn't the cover be something other than black?
So damned depressing. Anyway,
Come back and be a hero, I'm meant to say,
You rabble-rouser, Dane. Sincerely, Pryce."
ZARA
Manni, it's much too dangerous. Stay here,
Don't go south yet, wait until it's safe!
DANE
Read the letter, my love, the man is falling!
ZARA
All sorts are going to be injured, Manni, not just
The guilty ones – please wait,
We've been so safe up here!
DANE   I've been safe
For twenty years because of my cowardice,
Zara – now I will take the risk of appearing
At Liberty's finest hour!
ZARA   Your big heroics!

Just wait for one more letter! What if there comes
A crackdown?
DANE   No one left to crackdown now –
The Army's full of men who would give their lives
For the memory of the Men of Deed – Petran,
Lopez, Alexin, Suarez – now they know
How these men died!
ZARA   Men who would give their lives.
Why do men always have to give their lives?
Couldn't they give advice, or a helping hand,
Or just give money, maybe?
DANE   My beautiful wife.
I'm going to the Citadel. I'm going for Freedom.
I'm going for you, for us, and I'm going for him.

He points at ZARA

ZARA
Or her.
DANE Or her. Or them.

Exit DANE. ZARA *sits at the desk, leafing through the book*

SCENE IV
Lady Lydia's bedroom, April 7th, '62.

LYDIA, NATALIA, HEIDI, LAZARUS

LYDIA
It wasn't at all like the poem you read at dinner.
LAZARUS
I tried to pick an inoffensive piece,
Lady Lydia, but here that isn't easy.
At least I thought I had a batch of pure
Nature poems but no, each one I looked at
Turned political, right before my eyes.
NATALIA
That's just the air round here, honey. Light
Tends to fizzle out, and music stops,
Ashamed of itself.
HEIDI   All things are political
When people value their own emotions higher
Than other people's emotions.

[83]

NATALIA   Or other people.

LYDIA

What an age to have opened one's eyes.

NATALIA

Mine had got so weary of being wide open
I shut them the one second. Here I am.

HEIDI

I wanted to open my eyes to everything,
Now they won't close.

LAZARUS   Of course.

Because the Age has turned us to her eyes.

NATALIA

He would say that, he's being a poet again,
Instead of the old blues balladeer he started
Turning into. Sing the one you sang.

HEIDI

I wish I could remember as many as you.

LAZARUS

I wish I could remember more than I do.
But this, this is so fresh it stings. I never
Want to do the same thing twice: to do so
Is to accept defeat, but then I never
Made three friends of ladies like you.
And for you I'll sing it again. Which I never do.

Went down to Troublesome Town.
Everyone there wore black and brown
          But a girl like you
          In ocean blue
          Rose up and knew
          What we had to do
Way down in Troublesome Town.

Went down to Troublesome Town.
They built me up and they put me down
          But I knew my song
          And I never went wrong
          Though my hair grew long
          And I didn't belong
Way down in Troublesome Town.

Went down to Troublesome Town.
The face of things had an awful frown

But I cracked a smile
For a little while
North Country style
Was good as a mile
Way down in Troublesome Town.
Went down to Troublesome Town.
One man's head with a paper crown
Turned my way
On a sunny day
And I had to play
So here I stay
Way down in Troublesome Town
Way down in Troublesome Town
Way down in Troublesome Town . . .

HEIDI
When that's in a book, will it say
You made it up for us?
NATALIA   Sounds a bit much,
One poem, three girls. I want a poem to myself.
LYDIA
I'll take the nature one. He does say
It's political, but I don't really see that.
HEIDI
"Way down in Troublesome Town . . . "
You were about to run out of rhymes for "town",
Weren't you?
LAZARUS   No, not at all. There's plenty.
HEIDI   Go on.
LAZARUS
"Brown", "frown" –
HEIDI   No, ones you haven't had.
NATALIA
Well here comes the male race with an idea.

Enter COSKER, GRANCHEV, KALT *and* HAIN

COSKER
What are you smiling about? Thought of something?
Say Goodbye to this room, it's time for a change
Of atmosphere.
LYDIA   When can I see my husband?
COSKER
Miss him, do you?

[85]

LYDIA   Not in the least, but I have
A bargain or two to strike.
COSKER   Lady Lydia,
We're in a much later chapter than you think.
It may be of interest to you to know that the Lord
Has just survived an attempt on his life. Those
Closest to him are either dead or awaiting
Arraignment for conspiracy or treason.
Now I would ride your luck while it's still luck.
NATALIA
Of course, in the New Republic luck is this.
Just like you're a good, compassionate man,
These vermin lovers of poetry, and Gnyss
The victim of a vicious plot. Or else,
It ain't, you ain't, they ain't, and your
All-outliving master is a thug,
A liar, a fraud and a stinking murderer.
COSKER
Of course, either is possible. There is
In free societies such as ours a wide
Diversity of opinion on most matters.
But ours is a clean house: prostitution,
Propaganda and manifold adultery
Spread a wide disease. Are we ready?
LYDIA
Manifold adultery? What?
COSKER
I hardly expect an admission.
HEIDI   Where are we going?
COSKER
Out.
NATALIA Out?
COSKER   Out through the out gate.
To a new land.
HEIDI   Out of the New Republic?
COSKER
To a new land you get to through a Gate.
And this is not a Republic. It is a State.
After the four of you.
NATALIA   Come on, poet.
Room for him in a song of yours. Slave,
One day you may wear a chain too many,
And rattle them till death.

[86]

Exit NATALIA, LYDIA, HEIDI *and* LAZARUS, *then* KALT *and* HAIN

GRANCHEV
What then, do we burn their things?
COSKER   Yes.
We do that then. First,
We do this.

Exit COSKER *and* GRANCHEV

SCENE V
A passageway in the Palace.

MANNI *runs on breathless, still with the camera around his neck. He is lost. Enter from the other direction* ZACARELLI. MANNI *turns and jumps*

ZACARELLI
Don't worry, I'm not meant to be here.
MANNI   No,
Neither am I. I'm desperately trying to get out!
ZACARELLI
What are you, a lost tourist?
You've come on the wrong day.
MANNI   I saw it all,
Oh Heavens, through the lens!
ZACARELLI   I heard it all
From where I was: silence, shooting, laughing,
But no familiar laughs.
I'm on my way to a hideaway. I've got
Equipment there I need and then I'm out.
But these damn Guardsmen everywhere.
MANNI   They shot
Everyone, the polite duke, the attackers!
Then they made arrests, and the only one
Left alive is Victor Emmanuel!
He must have turned to a madman!
ZACARELLI   Maybe he did,
But we'll be dead man and boy if you and I
Don't get the hell out. What are you doing here?
No, tell the grandchildren.

[87]

You don't look like the Court Photographer.
What's your name?

MANNI   Manni.

ZACARELLI   Mine's Zacarelli.
I'm a professional . . . what, I don't know what.

MANNI
Mr Zacarelli, how can we get out?

ZACARELLI
Only one way, the only way I know,
The only way no one would want to stop us,
And only you and I can make it there.
Over the wilderness.

MANNI   The Given-up Lands?
But they go on forever, you can't breathe,
It's all gone bad and no one ever comes back!

ZACARELLI
What do they tell these boys? It's forty miles
The narrowest track across.
And I memorised the way. Without the kit
I've got in the hideaway, I'm with you, Manni,
We haven't a chance, but with it –
We do, and it's the only one. This place
Has gone to Hell and back and gone again.
No place for either Captain Crack's best man,
Or Zacarelli's best boy. Now follow me.

As they make to leave, they almost collide with DAMSEL *and*
TESSEL. DAMSEL *seems to be sleepwalking, or drugged*

TESSEL
Good Heavens, the Star Pupil! And who are you?

ZACARELLI
It doesn't matter. We're going, and you should too.

DAMSEL
Manni, Manni, Manni, you're in the dark
But look at his eyes. Manni, you're in the dark
But look at his eyes.

MANNI   What's wrong with Damsel, sir?

TESSEL
I've no idea, I found her like this – drugged,
Or sleepwalking, running away with things . . .

MANNI
Damsel, listen: it's Manni.

ZACARELLI   Manni, come on,
The Guards are coming.

TESSEL   Who are you, sir? You look
   Unfamiliar to me. You realise
   That anyone unable to explain
   His presence here in the Palace at this time
   Is under grave suspicion of at the least
   Complicity –
ZACARELLI   For God's sake shut up!
   Beginning to have an inkling while the whole
   Picture fries away!
   Power has boiled over in this Palace,
   Now it'll rain on everyone but itself!
MANNI
   You as well, Duke Tessel – you were there –
   It wasn't the plot you thought it was.
ZACARELLI   My group
   Were hired to hit the Grand Duke, not the Lord.
TESSEL
   My God, the assassins, help!
ZACARELLI   That's it, I'm going.
TESSEL
   Guards, a further outrage!
ZACARELLI   Manni, let's go!
MANNI
   I've got to try and help her!
ZACARELLI   No you haven't!

ZACARELLI *pulls* MANNI *off just in time, as* KALT *and* HAIN
enter from the other side

KALT
   Got you.
HAIN   Much as we, etcetera, etcetera,
   Lifetime service, yawn, yawn, respect . . .
KALT
   Venerable personage, however . . .
HAIN
   Unpleasant duty to have to say to you . . .
KALT
   Francis Tessel, we charge you in the name
   Of the one Lord Gnyss, with False Imprisonment
   And the Attempted Abduction of his daughter.
TESSEL
   I'm – I'm doing this on Victor's order!
KALT
   Best to save it, Duke.

[89]

TESSEL   But I found a suspect
   In the assassination – they went
   That way!
KALT   And we'll go this, shall we, Duke Tessel?
HAIN
   Miss, would you come with us?
DAMSEL   You're not Manni.
HAIN
   No indeed I'm not: I'm a brand new uncle.
TESSEL
   Take me to the Lord!
KALT   With pleasure, sir.
TESSEL
   You're letting them get away!
KALT   I'm sure we are.
   That makes it their lucky day, but not yours, sir.

KALT *leads out* TESSEL, HAIN *leads out* DAMSEL. *When they're gone,* MANNI *and* ZACARELLI *creep across with backpacks, holding masks to their faces*

SCENE VI
The Given-up Land.

Darkness

VOICE OF LAZARUS
   This is "The Song of Things To Do Tomorrow":

            Walk till you drop,
            Sing till you stop,
            Cry till you yawn,
            Mock till you mourn;
            Hope till you know,
            Speed till you slow,
            Yearn till you dry,
            Flap till you fly;
            Write till you can't,
            Plough till you plant,
            Grow till you don't,
            Will till you won't;

Tan till you yellow,
Drink till you mellow,
Eat till you fatten,
Fast till you flatten;
Touch while you lust,
Kiss while you must,
Pray while you plan,
Run while you can;
Walk till you drop,
Sing till you stop,
Tell till you lie,
Love till you die.

*Faint green light comes up extremely slowly during the poem,
revealing the dead bodies of* LAZARUS, HEIDI, LYDIA *and*
NATALIA *huddled together on the ground*

But a good third of the rhymes were given to me
by three companions: the Honourable Lady Lydia,
Natalia of the Night, and above all
Heidi the lover of verse. She wouldn't allow me
any old rhyme, she said.
In case you're wondering why we've chosen to stop,
it's the best reason of all. We're going to sleep.
Tiredness came very suddenly over us.
And I only write because I only write,
and never could stop, even when I had to. What
happened to us is written and in our hands.
Perhaps your hands will take it away from us.
The ladies are all asleep, I think. So I wish
I had an idea for a piece, but these will do.
Sometimes you have to leave it, to be honest.
This note for whoever you are . . .

During this, ZACARELLI *and* MANNI *discover the bodies.
They take off their masks and establish the four are dead.
Then* MANNI *photographs them, and* ZACARELLI *finds the
note from Lazarus*

. . . was only really to say
all I really wanted to say was that
all of it whatever was all right
for me because it was all

there was and with these three
ladies who are so kind was that a sentence
I don't know where this is maybe you know
I think these words are going home to my village
they'll wonder where their poet is he is here
how long between these lines you do not know
nor I sight is strange dragons
all pictures now
bird song

MANNI *and* ZACARELLI *pocket all the notes they find on the bodies, put their masks back on, and go on their way*

ACT V

The Palace, twenty-one years later, in '83.

GNYSS *is in his armchair, as at the beginning. His eyes are shut but he does not look asleep. The whitebound edition of his biography is on the floor. Enter* DAMSEL

DAMSEL
    Wake up, daddy, and tell me why I'm the only
    One in the Palace including the servants that nobody
    Tells anything to now!
    The Guards say I can't go out as it's dangerous out,
    And from my bedroom window all I can see
    As far as '48 Boulevard are crowds
    And banners too tiny to read! But I was the one
    You wanted to be your messenger-bringer, daddy!
GNYSS
    Of course I do, Damsel, I still do.
    Bring me a message about yourself this morning,
    Like, were you up early, of whom did you dream:
    Villains, aristocrats or wizards?
DAMSEL   None.
    I dreamt of a flying machine making a ripply
    Shadow over a desert. There were no men.
    So I'm not getting married today, if that's what you mean.
    You see, without any news for me to tell you,
    We run to the tired old topics.
GNYSS   At your age
    Marriage is not a tired old topic.
DAMSEL   Look!
    Daddy, I might have the pick of every single
    Man in the country, how will I know? Well why not
    Go outside the Gates of the Palace and ask them,
    For they're all standing there! So that's how it is –
    They're shouting for me, daddy?
    And Maximilian has utterly changed today.
    I think if I tried to read the Republican Times
    It too would curl up and float away and leave me
    Clueless on my own! Or is it some strange
    Opposite of my birthday, on which the world
    Agrees to go out of its way to make me cry,

And then when I cry puts all the banners down
And goes home laughing? Is that it, daddy?
GNYSS   Sometimes
Agitators stir up trouble, daughter.
Then it spreads and medicine is required.
Colonels Cosker, Henzer and Manolo
Are out there giving it out, or will be shortly.
DAMSEL
I didn't see much in the way of uniforms.
I didn't see anyone running about, daddy.
GNYSS
It's pure, clear medicine.
Down in a dose and the State is well again.
Up and about and raring to go. There is all sorts
Of propaganda on the streets.
DAMSEL   Propaganda?
I learned that word from the girl who disappeared
When everybody attacked us. She said it meant
Something that could be poetry. What was her name?
I was a lover of poetry, if you remember.
GNYSS
Yes, and then your garden and now your horses.
DAMSEL
Well that's a point there, daddy: how do I get
To feed my dears with your people all over the streets?
GNYSS
I'll have Maximilian cut
A wide swathe from here to the riding stables.
DAMSEL
Not with the face he's wearing today, you won't.
GNYSS
Then bring him here. Let me remind him who
Happens to run this Palace as well as this State.
DAMSEL
I jolly well won't bring him here. I'm not one of him,
And you haven't told me the tiniest thing, which is why
I poked my head in here in the first place.
GNYSS   Daughter,
Some kind of anarchic plot about to be squashed
As it deserves I hardly consider worth
Waking you up to see.
DAMSEL   Well you were wrong.
And look I'm awake now, daddy, and –

GNYSS
  Entered the scene without a line, have you, Max?
MAX
  No, not without a line, sir. With news.
DAMSEL
  He could have told it to me, then I could have told it.
MAX
  Duchess, you shouldn't hear it. You should leave.
GNYSS
  How dare you command my daughter to leave! Get out!
DAMSEL
  Something's altered, daddy, he hasn't budged.
  Why should I leave?
MAX   A book
  Has recently, well, yesterday, appeared
  Inside the Citadel, in fact inside
  The Palace Gates. My information is:
  It first appeared in print some ten or eleven
  Days ago in the far North-West of the country,
  And has spread eastward and southward underground.
DAMSEL
  Underground?
MAX   Distributed at night
  By unknown persons. Left at the back doors
  Of bookshops, on the steps of colleges,
  Posted through the porches of great homes.
GNYSS
  All entirely against the Law, of course.
MAX
  It is, but it has happened.
GNYSS   Those responsible
  Will pay in the highest currency –
MAX   Sir.
  The books have been distributed to the barracks
  Of the 2nd, 3rd and 7th Battalions.
DAMSEL
  Do fighting men read books?
MAX   Not commonly, Duchess,
  But they read books with photographs.
GNYSS   Are there many
  Photographs in the books?

[95]

MAX

  Many, yes. I saw a copy this morning.

GNYSS

  Damsel, now, I order you as your father

  To go to your own quarters and pack your things.

  You're off to the Mercury Lakes until –

DAMSEL   I'm not.

MAX

  Duchess, it's certainly better if you go.

DAMSEL

  I'll go, but to my room,

  Not on a mountain holiday while the whole

  Country comes to bits.

Exit DAMSEL

GNYSS

  Max, my friend, the book is entirely lies.

MAX

  Then I'm a believer of lies. For twenty years

  I have been, so I'll go on being.

GNYSS   I need

  To get a message to Colonel Cosker at once.

  He's got to return to the Citadel –

MAX   He won't.

GNYSS

  He won't? He better had.

MAX   He won't. Not he doesn't

  Wish to, but he can't. He's my second

  Item of news, sir.

  You sent him out to deal with the farm workers

  Of Sparfelt County, to force them back to work.

  The book of which I speak

  Appeared among them then, while Colonel Cosker

  And a thousand men were camped by Sparfelt Town.

  He went to deal with a riot, but by the time

  He got there, every rioter had become

  A reader, and ten thousand of them came

  Walking from the Town to meet his platoon,

  Holding banners and shields of the old

  Dukedoms of the region, chanting "Justice"

  And singing songs of Lazarus.

  Most of Cosker's men just melted off

  Into the countryside, and he couldn't have known,

For he met an army of fifteen thousand people
With a shred of officers. By that time
The stately homes were ablaze, and a new battalion,
Under Ivan Petran, the son of the old
Grand Duke, had arrived at Cosker's back.
They saved him from the mob so they could shoot him.
Then they joined their thousand to the thousands.
Manolo's hanging from your battleship.
Your other colonels are either missing or dead,
Or else abruptly loyalist to the memory
Of six murdered dukes.

GNYSS
  I have to get out of here at once.

MAX   Sir.
  That brings me to the final news item.
  There's been a relevant alteration to us,
  In our functions as a personal bodyguard.

GNYSS
  What do you mean? You are among the most
  Trusted men in the land.

MAX   We're the same men.
  But, whereas our former function was a mainly
  Protective one, it is now, I would have to say,
  Preventative. Our orders are: you stay.
  Though we retain our first, protective function,
  It has changed from the protection of yourself
  From some deranged assassin – to your
  Protection from the entirety of the people.

GNYSS
  I'm fast losing patience. Who's that coming?

Enter COLONEL IVAN PETRAN *and a* SOLDIER

  Colonel Petran, I'm hearing lies, lies!

IVAN
  Thank you, Captain Maximilian. Oh,
  One thing. Where's the daughter?

MAX   Gone to her room.

GNYSS
  What business is that of anybody's?

IVAN   Captain,
  Escort her to the library: we have
  Some photographs and a book for her to see.

GNYSS
Tell her it's all lies, Max, all lies!

IVAN
Sit down, Citizen Gnyss.
Private, would you quickly read the charges
While I look out of a window?

SOLDIER   Sir!
"Gnyss, Victor Emmanuel, citizen of the New Republic,
69 years of age, in the name of the National Justice
Committee, you are charged with the following crimes,
committed on or around the 7th April, '62, in or about
this place:—

Case number 559: Alexin, Duke of Whitedale,
conspiracy in the murder of. 560: Fisher, Henrietta,
student, false imprisonment and complicity in the manslaughter of. 561: subject known as "Lazarus", poet: false
imprisonment and complicity in the manslaughter of.
562: Lopez, Duke of Basson, conspiracy in the murder of.
563: Lydia, Lady Gnyss: false imprisonment and
complicity in uxoricide. 564: Petran, Michael, Grand
Duke of the Republic: conspiracy in the murder of. 565:
Polder, Martin, government speechwriter: false imprisonment and complicity in the disappearance of. 566: Suarez,
Duke of Arrowvale: conspiracy in the murder of. 567:
Tessel, Francis, Grand Duke of the Republic: false
imprisonment and complicity in the disappearance of.
568: Ulrich, Duke of Glanford: false imprisonment and
complicity in the disappearance of. 569: Valdez, Natalia
Maria, courtesan: false imprisonment and complicity in
the manslaughter of. 570, 571, 572, 573: two male, two
female persons unknown, suspected mercenaries: conspiracy in the murder of."

IVAN
Ten times over enough.
Citizen Gnyss, we're keeping you here for now
For purposes of stabilising the current
Situation. When it becomes possible,
You shall be escorted to a safer structure.

GNYSS
What are you doing to my daughter, telling her lies?
I never murdered anyone in my life.

[98]

SOLDIER
  "Conspiracy to murder", sir.
GNYSS   Or that.
IVAN
  Private, lead this person away to the corner,
  And keep his face to the wall.
GNYSS   Oh this sounds brave,
  Doesn't it? Brave, don't you think so, private?

The SOLDIER *leads* GNYSS *to the corner. Exit* IVAN

  What's he doing? The predictable thing, I suppose?
  No trial, no chance for the accused to stand
  And bury all these lies? Go on, Colonel.
  Have your dramatic moment. What's he doing?
SOLDIER
  He's gone out, sir.
GNYSS   Gone to get some others.

Enter IVAN, *with* DANE

IVAN
  Remember, sir: what you have done for this country,
  Justice and your profession, these are why
  I grant this interview, but I am the man
  Who has to lead the nation back from chaos
  To lawful rule again. So, if I feel
  The situation outside is out of control,
  The meeting will be terminated at once.
  Were you to go among the crowd out there
  And be recognised, you'd be in no less danger
  Than him, if for the opposite reason.
  A mob's a mob, professor. Five minutes.
  Private, release your charge. That'll be all.

Exit SOLDIER. GNYSS *turns round*

  Citizen Gnyss, this man
  Is Professor Emmanuel Victor Dane, Historian
  Of the Institute of Studies.
  And if I have my way,
  President of the Institute of Studies.

Exit IVAN

[99]

GNYSS

   "Emmanuel Victor"? Well,

There's a coincidence. Do you know my names?

DANE

   I was born in the Year of Revolution, sir,

Remember?

GNYSS   Do I remember '48?

   Oh yes. They should have named you for a hero.

Why weren't you called Petran or, say, Alexin?

A young fellow like you.

DANE   I had no one

   To ask that question, Victor Emmanuel.

GNYSS

   – They're going to do me, Manni. An old man,

Imagine. What do you recommend, old son?

No answer, is there? I thought you could answer

Anything, but you can't answer that.

What would you do, Star Pupil that you are:

Would you allow this poor old feller to live

Alone with books and a bed and a west window?

Mercy's what that's called.

DANE

   Well I believe I would.

But those of us who would, we seldom find

Our way behind the great red leather desks,

Quill in the hand. That's for Colonel Petran.

He looks a just man.

GNYSS   Damnably like his father.

   Why did he bring you here?

DANE   I had a question.

   It bothered me all these years, Victor Emmanuel.

Why did you ask me into your Palace at all?

I didn't mean to be there that day. I didn't

Mean to see what I saw.

GNYSS   You were an example,

   For children everywhere, for my daughter.

Cynical old Gnyss, they said, but I hoped,

If she could meet the best of her own age –

The up and coming young – Now I forget . . .

Did you make friends? She grew and grew, and now

She's beautiful and rides about, fuming

She's still only a Duchess. She's a Duchess.

– But them, they think it was all

Politics, elections, rubbish. Elections?
You don't arrange elections when the people
Are fed a diet of lies by your enemies!
All those ambitious Dukes: they would have poisoned
My people against their Lord.
So I lost my friends to save our country, Manni.
I did, I filled the warehouses and shops,
And everyone in his place – then all those rioters,
Always greedy for more, then other rioters
Corrupted by that criminal few!
And then. This. I have a question for you.

DANE
Hurry, Victor Emmanuel.

GNYSS   I've two.
Why did you write this book?

DANE   Because I had to.
Because the Institute had to, and to refuse
Would have been noted.

GNYSS   You wrote a beautiful book,
With old pictures of Damsel and her mother.
– So why did you wait so long to rip them out
And entertain the children of our State
With shots of wretches gunning down Heroes?
Nice pictures of my dead wife curled up
In the bare arms of a whore, oh very fine!

DANE
Victor Emmanuel, keep your voice down
Or that'll be it.

GNYSS   That'll be it, he goes.
Historians . . .

DANE   I waited twenty-one years.
Because of the consequences. Because of fear.
Fear of you and what the Republic became
After '62. The man with whom
I fled that day, across the infected desert,
He took me to his cabin, far in the North,
And I remained there with him for three years,
Still studying. When I was seventeen
And sure no one was hunting for me, I left
This Mr Zacarelli and travelled back.
The University took me in for Science.
After a time I turned to Ancient Studies
And had the luck to be awarded Honours.

GNYSS

Luck, he goes. Ha-ha, what modesty, Manni.

DANE

I ended up at the Institute as you know.
I wrote your book when they told me to. Then,
I married a girl I met in the far North.

GNYSS

Married? So you should be. What's she like?

DANE

Beautiful, but I would say so, but she is.
A coward had no right to call her wife,
I thought on the night we wed, and ever since.
Three months ago, one Friday,
She told me there were going to be three of us.
I stayed awake all night as the world changed.
The next night all of us were travelling north,
And I wrote your book again in a single week.
I had a friend who knew people who knew
How to print and bind the pages, how to
Get it to towns and cities under the cover
Of darkness in the backs of trucks, carts.
I stayed in the North till now.

GNYSS   Well, Manni, well.

Did you ever think of me as you wrote?

DANE   All the time.

GNYSS

And Damsel?

DANE   Yes, of her all the time as well.

GNYSS

And are you going to be President of the Institute
Of Studies According To Manni?

DANE   Ask my wife.

GNYSS

They're going to need some good men like you.
It's their chaos now and they have to meet it.
If this is what they want with our great people,
Fire and shooting and civil war, so be it.
I gave them peace and pride.
Don't you think at least they'd seek my counsel,
What with my years of experience? But no,
These hotheads will go haywire, you watch 'em.

DANE

Times are going to be hard, Victor Emmanuel.

GNYSS

Yes, if you value life. I've quite gone off it.
Where is that damnable Colonel?

DANE   Shall I get him?

GNYSS

Better than letting him charge in here, ranting.

DANE *rises*

Manni, – I have enjoyed our meeting again.
You've grown and grown as well, and now
You seem a proper Republican gentleman.

DANE

Victor Emmanuel, I hope –
I'll try to talk to the Colonel.

Exit DANE. GNYSS *waits. Enter* IVAN, DANE *and the*
SOLDIER

IVAN

Finished? Take him out. The truck is there.

The SOLDIER *escorts* GNYSS *out*

Did you get the answer you wanted? There's just
One more thing we have to do here. Captain!

Enter MAX, *with* DAMSEL

DAMSEL

Manni, some men are saying you married a woman.

DANE

I did, Damsel, I did.

DAMSEL   She must be clever.

IVAN

Professor, in your book you state that the daughter
Of the then Lord Gnyss, Damsel Caroline Gnyss,
Was seen by you in the company of the Grand Duke
Tessel, and seemed to be in a somewhat
Disorientated state, as if she were drugged.
This certainly is the woman?

DANE   I had no doubt
Whatever that she was ignorant of all
Her father's acts, nor do I doubt it now.

IVAN
　　All right, that squares with what we think. Captain,
　　Take her back to the library for her things.
　　Then we'll smuggle you both through the Rivergate.

Exit MAX *and* DAMSEL

　　That's everything.
DANE　　　　　　　What will happen to her?
IVAN
　　No question of her succeeding, or retaining
　　Any title, but other than that she's free
　　To go where she wants.
DANE　　　　　　Some might go after her.
　　Could she at least receive protection, Colonel?
　　She's guiltless, and she's alone.
IVAN
　　I'll see to it, Professor. In this land
　　The innocent will have no cause to fear.
DANE
　　One other thing: could it be made known
　　That she is safe, and free?
IVAN　　　　　　　　　　　　Made known?
DANE
　　To him – before the time. To him.
IVAN　　　　　　　　　　　　That's one
　　Favour too many, Professor. Let him die
　　Like my father did, with no guarantees.
　　Now let's get out of here.

Exit IVAN. DANE *picks up the whitebound copy of "Gnyss
the Magnificent", and follows him out*

　　　　　　　　　　SCENE II
　　　　　The Danes' home in the Citadel.

DANE *and* ZARA *are eating breakfast.* DANE *is also reading
a book*

ZARA
　　So how come the same Manni is one minute this
　　Fugitive writing his book and perfectly happy
　　With a wife in a single room ten foot by ten foot,

[104]

And the next minute he needs
Five bedrooms, this thing called a dining-room
We breakfast in, a breakfast-room we lunch in,
And three bay windows looking out over the river?

DANE
Yes, but he's just as happy with that old
Wife you mentioned, breakfasting or hiding . . .
Is that the paper come?

ZARA *runs out, then returns with the newspaper*

ZARA
You know what the news is, don't you, Manni?
DANE   Yes.
ZARA
Shall I read it to you?
DANE   No.
ZARA   I didn't want to.

She turns it over

Cold spell coming. The Citadel lost 4–0
But I can't make out what sport. Well that's the news.
That's breakfast and the news.
Shall we go back to bed?
DANE   Hmm, shall we?
I ought to be doing this paper, Zara.
ZARA   Ought to.
We ought to be being kind all over the world
But we're just slobbing about in our own home,
And I don't give a whole blizzard of papers.
DANE
Is that the post?
ZARA   Is that my cue to go
And fetch it?
DANE   No, I'll get it if you want.
ZARA
Well I do want.
DANE   Fine. I need the walk.

Exit DANE, *then returns with a letter*

All that way and only your father again.
ZARA
But Manni, maybe he'll come like I asked him to,
And help when the baby's born.

[105]

DANE   Help?
How, exactly? Don't think I don't want him to,
But what can he do?

ZARA *opens the letter: it's very long*

ZARA
"Dear Zara, of course I'll come,
If only to calm your husband's nerves with his own
Excellent stock of wines. However, I must
Strongly object to your tactics of persuasion . . .

*Her voice blends with the voice-over of her father, who is of
course* ZACARELLI

VOICE OF ZACARELLI
"Describing me, in your view, as 'bound to be
The best grandfather ever' in my case
Probably means 'Father's about to snuff it,
So let's make sure he's among friends when he goes.'
Soon you'll be saying 'He never looked better!' or 'Oh,
He'll live forever, you wait!' – another sure sign
They're picking the old brown casket as we speak.
I've read all the articles, Zara, I'm not stupid.
Three ways to tell a man's on the brink of the big one . . .
One: increasing popularity,
Especially with his offspring. Two: demands
He makes the most of country walks, or avails
Himself of the opportunity to study
A foreign language or two. Three: polite
Enquiries about the origins of his furniture . . .

By this time, ZARA *has put the letter down, and she and*
DANE *have indeed retired to bed, but the voice goes on,
fading out with the lights over the last few lines*

. . . And anyway, how can anyone be the best
Or worst grandfather, when no one ever asked
His permission to make him one, not like being
A father, where one is at least assumed to have known
What he was letting himself and his missus
In for: me, did I ask to be run in this race?
Let alone be informed I won it, even before
It even started. I'll tell you a little story.
I once knew an old man and he always said . . ."

THE BIRTHDAY BALL OF ZELDA NEIN

for DEREK WALCOTT

THE BIRTHDAY BALL OF ZELDA NEIN

Dramatis Personae:

VISCOUNT NEIN

ZELDA, his eldest daughter, 21 today

CLAUDIA, his second daughter

MARIA, his youngest daughter

FLECK, Zelda's secretary and confidant

GLINE, a self-made millionaire

SEWELL, a self-styled poet

BATES, a bouncer

KALLUM, his apprentice

PADGET, an uninvited man

BISON, the Neins' gardener

PALGRAVE, the Neins' maid

The Ball Guests:

LORD LAMPENHEAD OF THE VINES

LADY LAMPENHEAD

THE NINETEENTH DUKE DE VOOR

DUCHESS DE VOOR

MR KRULL

MR KANNISTER

MRS KANNISTER

DR REPPER

MADAME ERRATUM

MISS CHARISMA STONE

MISS ELAN STONE

MISS PANACHE STONE

CANDIDATE O'HALE!

CANDIDATE UBERMANN

TOM KRASHGATE

FLAVIA FULLBRIGHT

PORLOCK KLIPKE

THE BIRTHDAY BALL OF ZELDA NEIN was first presented in the garden of the author's home in Welwyn Garden City, Hertfordshire, on 1st August, 1991, directed by the author and with the following cast:

Zelda	EMILY THOMPSON
Bates	NEIL RICHARDSON
Kallum	DANNY SWANSON
Padget	JAMES HARPER
Gline	CHRIS GILL
Sewell	MATTHEW BELL
Fleck	STEPHEN THOMPSON
Claudia	SARAH PEARCE
Maria	JANE PENNETT
Bison	ALUN MAXWELL
Palgrave	MANDY MAXWELL
The Viscount	JAMES MAXWELL
Lord Lampenhead	BEN KING
Lady Lampenhead	LIZ EVANS
Duke de Voor	SANDY UNDERWOOD
Duchess de Voor	AMANDA SMITH
Krull	DAVID MAXWELL
Mr Kannister	JOE SWANSON
Mrs Kannister	POLLY PRATT
Dr Repper	ROB WALLACE
Mme Erratum	LORNA SKINNER
Charisma Stone	TIFFANY WHILE
Elan Stone	JO WILLOTT
Panache Stone	SOPHIE PRATT
O'Hale!	NEIL TODMAN
Ubermann	MATTHEW CONNELL
Krashgate	JONATHAN DUNHAM
Flavia	LISA SWANSON
Klipke	JONATHAN LOHN
Stage & Lighting	JULIET LLOYD, JONATHAN SHAW, LORAINE UNDERWOOD, JOHN LLOYD, TREVOR WALLACE, CLARE CURLEY, DEREK PALMER, KATHRYN STEVENS
Music composed by	ANTHONY SYCAMORE

The First Act takes place on the evening of Zelda's 21st Birthday Ball, the Second Act three nights later.

ACT I

SCENE I
The gates of the house.

A toast is proposed to ZELDA *by the bouncers,* BATES *and* KALLUM

BATES
  Here's to the daughter of the Viscount Nein!
  Long life and riches! On this night of nights,
  We'd like to wish you –
ZELDA   Let nobody in.
  Unless their names are written down in gold
  Among the hundred listed. Even then,
  Be sure they enter dressed impeccably,
  Whoever they may be. I'm twenty-one
  Tonight, I am of age, I mean to feel
  Special for a change.
  Admission is a privilege, so any
  Ragged or with a name you cannot find,
  Doormen, do as you please.
BATES   Even if
  They're dressed all red and amber as is all
  The rage this April? Do we let them in?
ZELDA
  I want the ones invited and expected,
  Not the people from the magazines . . .
  They wouldn't come this far, and if they did –
  Which of course they won't, the glitterati
  Or what it is they call themselves –
  You'll call me if they do come? which they won't,
  But if they did – but then they're all I expect
  At that enormous firework bash for the blind.
  That's what it says about them. No, I want
  The "Zelda Set", as some refer to it:
  The Kannisters, the Lampenheads, the three
  Sisters Stone, Gline and Sewell, Krull,
  The candidates, the last ambassador,
  The usual. You have your list in gold?
  – And we're too far away for the so-called
  Elite, so they won't come. Any questions?

BATES
> One, and of a simple nature. May I,
> Miss Madame Zelda, be the very first
> To wish you Happy Birthday, many happy
> Returns of it and others, plus success
> In enterprises, popularity
> Among men of significance, and –

ZELDA   No.
> You must be at least the twelfth, and in any case
> I have all those already. So, now,
> Bates – and whatever your name is – begin!
> To work!

KALLUM We're working: nobody is here.
> Nobody of significance, at least.

ZELDA
> Was that a dig?

BATES   Only at me, Miss Zelda.
> Young Kallum is new to this high-level
> Bouncing work, and has a darting tongue.

ZELDA
> I hope you're good at this.
> You don't look very frightening to me.
> I'd like my guests to feel a sense of power
> At passing, qualified, into the house.
> I trust you know the ropes. The way you look,
> A peasant could scuffle his way in here,
> No questions asked.

BATES   We'd not be asking questions.
> A peasant we'd account for pretty sharpish,
> Wouldn't we, Kallum?

KALLUM   Faceless, in the hedges.

ZELDA
> I'm not convinced. Can't you be holding something?
> I had hoped you'd be taller.

BATES   We can try.
> But, with respect, you've not seen us at work.
> First sign of the unwanted – we're like oaks!

ZELDA
> Oaks? You turn to trees to scare them off?
> An oak never took a step to bar my way.

BATES
> Immovable as oaks.

ZELDA   I'm not impressed.
> But then, you're what we've got, and it's too late

To swell your ranks. The guests will be here soon.
. . . I might bring you some cake around midnight.
It's green, with soft icing, and little dwarfs
Trotting around in a ring. It's like a castle,
Turrets and flags and stuff. I don't know why.
Nothing looks like that that I know. Mother
Baked it in the middle of something else.
You know what she's like.

BATES   No?

KALLUM   Well we do now.

ZELDA
A rude man for a doorman.

BATES   I'm sorry, it's –

ZELDA
Why sorry? You're the ones who'll stand and shiver
While we carouse and waltz inside. Oh well.
If I remember, I might bring you cake.
It is the season of goodwill.

KALLUM   It isn't.

ZELDA
On the contrary, it's my birthday.
It's "good" because it's mine, and it's my "will"
To offer cake to whom the hell I please.

BATES
It would please us, Miss Zelda.

ZELDA   You're too familiar.
I offer you cake, but it's a proper job
I'm paying you for: keeping out the . . . scum.
It's made of marzipan.

Music within

The bitches, my sisters!
I told them, I made it clear, until I say,
No cake, no cards, no kisses on the lips,
No candles! Nothing until I say! Nothing
Until all are arrived and in the Hall!
Damn my sisters – it's not their Birthday Ball!

ZELDA *exits to the house*

KALLUM
I wonder whose it is.

BATES
  You're a rude one, Kallum. We need this job, you know.
  We're not the only bouncers hereabouts.
KALLUM
  The only ones paid in green marzipan.
BATES
  That's not true and you know it. That's a bonus.
KALLUM
  Some bonus.
BATES   Yes, and the icing is green,
  Not the marzipan, she never said that.
KALLUM
  Marzipan, marzipan, diet of bouncers!
  Roll up, little dwarfs, have a go at crashing
  Zelda's twenty-first! We'll have you
  Icing-sugared in no time, unless
  Your name's made of gold and we like your face!
BATES
  And if a stranger comes . . .
KALLUM   Out on his arse,
  Prince or peasant. What is this, charity?
BATES
  We're bouncers, and that means inflexible.
  That means we'll bounce as high as boulders!
KALLUM   Sure,
  It's our vocation. You and me were born
  To dress up and prevent. – What was that noise?
BATES
  Early warning, Kallum. Mark my words:
  If someone's on the hill, you'll hear the birds
  Fly up from the forest trail: it means
  People are coming this way – her first guests!
KALLUM
  Only potentially, remember, Bates:
  What it boils down to is how they're dressed.

Enter PADGET, *poorly attired*

  Lost something, pal? Why not ask us for help?
PADGET
  I shall indeed. That's kind of you to say.
  The thing I lost is my way.
KALLUM   In life? Hard luck.
PADGET
  Oh no, in this region I lost my way.

BATES
That's bad for you, my friend, for we're some way
From civilisation here. All these grounds
Belong to Viscount Nein, who's gone insane
And won't allow development.
PADGET   At last!
So this is the mansion of the Viscount Nein!
BATES
Did I say that?
KALLUM   You didn't say that, Bates.
PADGET
You said these grounds belonged –
BATES   Did I, Kallum?
KALLUM
I think you said they didn't, didn't you.
BATES
I wasn't sure.
KALLUM I am.
PADGET   And so am I:
You said the grounds belonged to Viscount Nein.
KALLUM
And so they did, in happier days. Alas,
Then Colonel Zane came riding along and claimed
Everything on spurious grounds.
PADGET
I don't understand –
KALLUM   Property law? No,
It's got me beat, my friend.
PADGET   But yes, you said
The Viscount went insane!
KALLUM   No, Zane's insane.
As far as we know, Viscount Nein is fine.
PADGET
And Zelda?
BATES   In full bloom. It's her birth –
KALLUM
Right!
PADGET Birthright? Oh. How would you know?
KALLUM
We don't. Bates is – fantasising again.
BATES
Er . . . trotting dwarfs! Can't you see 'em in the sky?
Soft and green as elephants, wa-ha-hay!

[115]

KALLUM
  Another brain on the slide. Tragic, innit?
PADGET
  I still don't understand you. Is this not
  The House of Nein? And the twenty-first birthday
  Of his eldest daughter Zelda?
KALLUM   Who?
BATES   Wahay!
  And round up all yon spaniels, for it's late,
  And the green-eyed dining party will surely dine
  And gongs will bang, and –
KALLUM (*aside*)   Shut up, Bates, that's fine.
PADGET
  I think that man's pretending to be ill.
KALLUM
  May that live on your conscience, stranger. Now,
  Get lost.
PADGET   I said, I am. But now I've found
  The House of Nein again after all this time
  My course is clear!
KALLUM   And ours is clearing fairly
  Rapidly, and you can help with it.
  I mean, comply with it.
BATES   Listen, friend.
  We're kidding you, y'see? We're professionals.
  It's just part of our trade to gibe or josh
  Anyone who looks suspicious, or,
  Uninvited, if I may say, like you –
  The truth is this: the grounds used to belong
  To Viscount Nein, but suddenly one morning
  He woke to find the world in a sheet of snow,
  And on a whim invested in it. So,
  The snow melted and he was pauperised.
PADGET
  So what about the daughters?
BATES
  Nobody knows. – Except about the oldest,
  Who soon became a world-class ballerina,
  (Zelda, this is) and moved to the Citadella.
PADGET
  Perhaps this man is ill.
KALLUM   So I've been saying.
PADGET
  Do you expect me to believe your tale?

BATES

I s'pose not.

KALLUM　　Look I've had enough of this.

Guests are walking up, you can hear the birds –

BATES

Early warning, y'see.

KALLUM　　　　– And you, old pal,

Are missing the whole point.

Whether this is the home of Viscount Nein,

Or retirement-home of mental Colonel Zane,

Or an abandoned hovel we've been guarding

Because we're lunatics or the Night Watch,

Is none of your business. You cannot come in

Because you look like that.

BATES　　　　　　　　　You're not dressed up.

KALLUM

And we don't like you. We think you're . . . scum.

BATES

Well I don't mind him, but he can't come in.

KALLUM

In that case then I think you're doubly scum.

PADGET

I mean no harm.

KALLUM　　That makes it two-to-none.

We don't care what you mean, or where you're from.

PADGET (*to* BATES)

Would you at least tell Zelda that I've come?

BATES

That's the least I'd do, if she lived here, son,

But as it is –

Enter GLINE *and* SEWELL, *in proper attire*

GLINE　　　　　　　　Bates! The forbidding Bates!

Weren't you forbidding at the Boathouse Ball

Last May? Sewell, picture him if you will,

In classical posture, mighty on the jetty,

Forbidding a pair of pale newly-weds

From setting foot inside the Boathouse. Why?

They had no documents to prove their names

Were Joseph Carpenter and Mary White!

SEWELL

Oh biblical! Were those their names?

GLINE　　　　　　　　　Of course!

[117]

BATES
It's our job to be thorough, Mr Gline.
In fact, we were about to demonstrate
The blunter end of our profession.
GLINE   Oh?
On whom? On us?
SEWELL   Do we not pass muster?
And I sold shares to buy this tie! Ah well.
GLINE
Don't sell it yet, Sewell: I heard Bates say
Zelda doesn't live here? Doesn't she?
She lived here yesterday. I saw her riding.
SEWELL
Efflorescent beauty!
GLINE   Write that down,
Bouncers: Sewell is a consummate artist,
Steeped in the bubbling arts of consummation!
BATES
I'll need a pen.
GLINE   Haven't you one?
KALLUM   They're joking.
The fact is, we were doing our job, sir,
Preventing this man –
GLINE   There's nobody there.

PADGET *has indeed gone*

KALLUM
Well there was, and he was looking for a scrap.
Said it was Zelda's twenty-first birthday.
SEWELL
Isn't it? I wrote a sonnet, specially!
KALLUM
Her birthday ain't for him.
GLINE   It's movable?
Is it for us, Bates, and your fierce friend?
We are guests, you know.
BATES   Er ... welcome, Guests,
To the House of Viscount Nein ...
SEWELL   Hurrah, the madman!
Is he still ticking?
BATES   ... For the twenty-first
Birthday of Clarissa Zelda May -
Belinda Drummond Overlongie Nein.

GLINE
  Shouldn't you check our invitations, Bates?
BATES
  When you've been bouncing for as long as me,
  Some things are wholly intuital, sir.
GLINE
  I'm sure they are. Let's sally forth and find
  The slurping Queen of the May!
SEWELL   Doubtless already
  Marinaded and blurting out initials
  Of male friends she might like to have had
  Had they not had her first!
BATES
  Might I just say a word?
SEWELL   You might say two:
  In your forbidding function, Bates,
  Who knows what you might do?
BATES   She's in her chamber,
  With Mr Fleck, the Agent, and she asked
  Not to be disturbed until it's time.
GLINE
  Fleck is here?
SEWELL   Oh . . . fun.
  No doubt, final adjustments to the cake.
  He is a master of such things, Fleck.
GLINE   Fine!
  Let's irritate the sisters for a while.
SEWELL
  Where are the sisters, Bates?
BATES   Sitting inside.
GLINE
  Ah, ready and waiting, Sewell. Excellento!
  So long, Bates, and don't forget: Mr Christ
  Is not down on your list, whatever He says.
SEWELL
  Don't crack or crumble, Bates!

GLINE *and* SEWELL *exit to the house*

BATES   Those are wasters.
KALLUM
  I'd like to waste like that.
  Gline made a million off of the Harvest
  Holdings, and that Sewell's not at the bone.

[119]

And they're young, Bates, they've hardly started yet.
What worked for them could work for me and you.
BATES
Nobody works for me, Kallum.
KALLUM   I do,
  Nominally.
BATES   Well, nominally start
  By looking unfriendly, and by looking smart.
  The night's young as well.
KALLUM   I hope some guests
  Feel like using teeth against our fists.

SCENE II
Outside the house.

Enter MR BISON *with an empty wheelbarrow, and* MISS
PALGRAVE *with an empty wheelchair. Oblivious of each
other, they collide*

BISON
  Out of my way, lass. I have this plant
  To plant, on the orders of the mistress
  That it be planted.
PALGRAVE   Excuse me, Mr Bison,
  But I have to take the Viscount to the folly
  And leave him there.
BISON (*peering over*)   He is not in your trolley.
PALGRAVE (*checking*)
  Oh. No he isn't, but he absolutely was.
  It's not the first time he hasn't been.
BISON
  I know that, Miss . . . Palgrave, I know that.
  But what it means is that this empty trolley
  Of yours is insignificant, whereas I
  Have a plant to plant.
PALGRAVE (*peering over*)   It's a small plant
  You have to plant.
BISON (*checking*)   Ah. That is because
  It is not there. It must have . . . fallen out.
PALGRAVE
  You'd better find it. You'd better move your barrow
  Backwards, Mr Bison.

BISON   Not so fast,
  Lassie: you have also lost your charge.
  And this was a small plant. You have lost a large
  Entire homo sapien.
PALGRAVE   Lost a what?
BISON
  Perhaps you had better beat your own retreat.
PALGRAVE
  I don't see why, frankly, Mr Bison.
  If you don't find your plant, the Viscountess
  Will get just like she was with the duckling flan.
BISON
  True, true, we cannot let that occur.
  But who can hazard what our escaped employer
  May do or say? Recently he has said
  On more than one occasion: "Never paddle
  In stagnant waters after a dinner of cheese . . ."
PALGRAVE
  I think we may be both in a bit of peril!
BISON
  On top of that, the Birthday Ball is about
  To commence, and we must both be in . . . positions.
  You to remove the coats, and I to recite
  The long, taxing titles of . . . the people.
PALGRAVE
  That's really the butler's job.
BISON   It is many days
  Since the last reported sighting of the butler.
PALGRAVE
  So in fact we're both in a hurry!
BISON   I suggest
  You look in the Lavender Room for your lost patient.
PALGRAVE
  Oh, thank you, Mr Bison! My advice
  Is look around in the gardens for that plant!
BISON
  Thank you for that . . . advice, Miss . . . Palgrave.
  In the meanwhile, let us both retreat
  The way we came.
PALGRAVE   Yes, let us both retreat
  The way we came.

They wheel their vehicles backwards, and exit

The gates of the house.

Processional music. BATES *and* KALLUM *take up defensive positions at the gateposts;* BISON *and* PALGRAVE *re-enter and wait beside them. Enter, very slowly, in strange, serpentine file, the* BALL GUESTS. *Each time one of them, or a group, reaches* BATES, *he checks their invitations.* KALLUM, *apparently resentful that anyone at all should be admitted, hovers intimidatingly, prodding, looking in handbags.* PALGRAVE *runs up, grabs the cards from* BATES, *and takes them to* BISON, *who reads them out. As he reads,* PALGRAVE *zealously drags their coats and cloaks off them and hangs them in total confusion on a nearby rack. The Procession halts. The* LAMPENHEADS *and* DE VOORS *arrive*

BISON
  "Billiam, Lord Lampenhead of the Vines!"
  And "Lady" . . . er, presumably of the selfsame
  Vines. "The 19th Duke and Duchess . . ."
  I presume also the nineteenth, otherwise
  Another number not on this card . . . "De Voor!"
  Duke of many places I have not
  Personally heard of. However, here they are.
LORD LAMP.
  A gardener for a butler? As you see,
  My dear, the Neins are entirely gone to pot.
LADY LAMP.
  How frightfully frightful-looking the place has got!
  In my day, that was there and that was there.
DUKE D. V.
  One cannot blame the Viscount. Fifty years
  Of that woman I too would have mislaid
  Innumerable marbles.
DUCH D. V.   Three daughters!
  What did they think they were doing? and not one
  A patch on ours, or on me for that matter.
  – Oh Claudia, how extraordinarily nice
  It is to see you!

The DUCHESS *goes in*

DUKE D. V.   The Duchess was just saying

How nice it would be to see her, and it was.
Never far wrong!

The DUKE *goes in*

LORD LAMP.   A gardener for a butler.
  Asking for complications.
LADY LAMP.   In my day,
  Gardeners were located in the garden,
  Gardening. And that was over there.
LORD LAMP.
  A gardener for a butler. I declare!

LORD *and* LADY LAMPENHEAD *go in.* MR KRULL *arrives*

BISON
  "Mr Krull (but do not say this name)."
KRULL
  Imbecile. Read what's written down.
BISON
  "Mr Krull (but do not say –"
KRULL   Sshhtt.
  Has a tall man come through with dark glasses . . .
BISON (*to* PALGRAVE)
  Lassie, has a tall man –
KRULL   Sshhtt.
  Have two women appeared, a lady in red,
  And a lady in yellow . . .
BISON   I'm not in charge of the coats,
  Mr Krull-but-do-not-say –
KRULL   Sshhtt.
  On the 23rd, at a minute to eleven,
  Did you spot me on the bank of the Blue Canal?
BISON
  Indubitably not.
KRULL   Keep it that way.
  What were you doing down there then anyway?
  That's private ground. You'd better watch your step.
  That's all for now. Remember, you never saw me.

KRULL *goes in*

BISON
  I shall not forget I never saw you, sir.
  What an unorthodox man.

[123]

"Mr Erasmus Kannister and Mrs
Erasmus Kannister." That must be confusing
Around the house. And "Dr Repper", the doctor.
MR KANN.
You will look into it then, doctor?
REPPER   Ho yes,
By all means yes. I've got my tools with me.
We'll open you up in no time.
MRS KANN.   And close him?
You will have to close him too.
REPPER   Ho I'll close him.
MR KANN.
I'll be a brand new man, you won't know me.
The Sisters Nein won't know me, but I was a friend
Of a friend of a friend of their father's
Clockmaker. I wonder if they've changed.
MRS KANN.
Never forgets a face, does my Erasmus.

MR *and* MRS KANNISTER *go in*

REPPER
He won't forget the one I'm going to give him.

DR REPPER *goes in.* MADAME ERRATUM *arrives*

BISON
"Madame Erratum, Medium." Medium what,
Precisely, madame?
ERRATUM   Erratum, Medium,
Clairvoyante, Astrologer. What time were you born?
BISON
Early, on Christmas Day, which I recall
Fell on a cold day that day.
ERRATUM   The Goat.
BISON
Precisely correct, Madame. Your powers are quite . . .
Formidable.
ERRATUM   "Stargazer to the Stars"
It says in my column. I was the only one
To predict my marriage to the eight-foot man,
And all the recent deaths by the canal.

MADAME ERRATUM *goes in. The three* STONE SISTERS

arrive, indistinguishable. CHARISMA *is escorted by* CANDIDATE O'HALE!, ELAN *by* CANDIDATE UBERMANN, *and* PANACHE *by* TOM KRASHGATE

BISON
  "The Three Sisters Stone: Charisma Stone,
  Elan Stone, Panache –" oh it's gone – . . . "Stone."
  Plus "The Honourable Filbert O'Hale,
  Exclamation Mark." Oh I see, ahem . . . "O'Hale!"
  There. "The National Strength In Union Party
  Candidate." And "Candidate Ubermann,
  Of the Brothers of the Blue Cravat." Meanwhile,
  You are familiar, but . . . who are you?

KRASHGATE
  Don't mind me, it's cool, I often crash here.
  Don't I, Panache?

CHARISMA   That's not Panache, it's Elan.

UBERMANN
  You told me you were Elan.

ELAN   No, I'm Charisma.

O'HALE!
  You told me you were Charisma.

CHARISMA   I also said
  I'd vote for you. Isn't that enough?

KRASHGATE
  That's cool, let's make music, let's make love.

ELAN
  I don't think much of yours, sister Charisma.

UBERMANN
  You just said you were Charisma.

PANACHE   She's Panache.

The STONE SISTERS *giggle conspiratorially and huddle together*

O'HALE!
  Always a step behind, eh Ubermann?

UBERMANN
  Up till election night, Mr O'Help.
  When the Brothers are in power, this time next week,
  You may find your own self walking in step.

O'HALE!
  Ubermann, I'll wave to you as you take
  Your last walk to the wall.

CHARISMA   You politicians,
Always chatting. But nothing ever gets better.
ELAN
Something got better once, but I forget what.
PANACHE
I remember what, but can't remember why.
KRASHGATE
Governments, who needs 'em? Kids, hi,
Me again, and this is my new assistant . . .

They all go in. FLAVIA FULLBRIGHT *arrives*

BISON
"Flavia Fullbright, formerly Miss October."
Presumably you altered your name to avoid
Confusion with the month of the same name.
FLAVIA
Idiot, I'm a Beauty Queen!
BISON   A Queen?
Is there not already a Queen? Or are you that Queen?
FLAVIA
Do you have the faintest idea who you're talking to?
BISON
I have this card to which to refer, your Grace.
FLAVIA
Blind and mad! Have you seen the cover of FACE?
You're only talking to it!
BISON   Indeed, your highness.
FLAVIA
And the back of FRONT, the autumn issue – guess who?
BISON
That lady looks not entirely unlike you.
FLAVIA
So you see I'm famous.
BISON   Indubitably you are.
FLAVIA
So, how do you feel now, now you've met a star?
BISON
Whelmed, your majesty, extremely . . . whelmed.
FLAVIA (*going in*)
It's me, me! No, not Flora – Flavia!

PORLOCK KLIPKE *arrives*

BISON
Mr – this is a different order of card . . .
KLIPKE
Klipke, Porlock Klipke, making me usual
Tradesman's entrance.
BISON   Are you the last person?
KLIPKE
Always the last person you want to see!
Right, that's quite a popular joke about me!
Envious of my success, you see, Mr –?
Let's try that again. I say "Mr", and you are –?
BISON
I have remembered.
KLIPKE   That'll save some time. So, –
BISON
I have remembered where I left that plant.
I left it in a crate, for safe keeping!

BISON *and* PALGRAVE *run off.* KLIPKE *is looking for his
catalogue*

KLIPKE
Fine, fine. Anyway, Porlock Klipke:
You want it, I got it. So, as I was saying . . .
Oh, there's no one here. First rule of selling:
Never waste your breath. If no one is buying,
Move right on, and here,
I'm closing in on no one, that's clear.

KLIPKE *goes in*

BATES
He'll have some buyers here, if all he sells
Is breath. This lot have bought up everything else.
And that leaves no one nowhere.

SCENE IV
Zelda's chamber.

ZELDA *is sorting through her birthday cards. Enter* FLECK

FLECK
The multitude is in, but, as regards

[127]

Those of whom you enquired:
Sewell is here. And the young moneyspinner.

ZELDA

Gline you mean. He's only twenty-six.
Not bad, eh, Fleck? And Sewell can write!

FLECK   Indeed.
Quite an accomplishment. You must be flattered.

ZELDA

I will be, Fleck. No "must" about it.

FLECK   Quite.

ZELDA

All these cards! All these admirers! Well,
Time to file them, Fleck, I think in order
Of intrigue! This is plainly from the Earl,
I know his symbols. This? His foreign friend
We saw at polo: excellent! This?
That's the dull painter, he can go low down.
And this one, yek, the envelope's disgusting!
Does he expect a star of society
To finger such a thing? To open it?

She flings it away, and resists the vague curiosity that follows

Probably some beggar from the town,
Trying to buy some pity. I suppose he thinks
I'm not in need of some myself!

FLECK (*pocketing the envelope*)   Of course,
Of course, Zelda, I know it well. The poor
Have no monopoly on sadness. We all
Shed tears.

ZELDA   Mmm, and I shed more than most.
I shedded several only yesterday,
Realising my girlhood was gone
So quick – and no achievements to my name!

FLECK

Oh how you talk, when to be born a Nein
Is an achievement quite past compare.

ZELDA

It doesn't feel like one.

FLECK   Only to those
Blessed with its dignity and history.
To us, clawing along, it seems a pinnacle
Quite mountainlike in its, er . . . highness.

ZELDA

All those long words – as if to make up
For the brief Fleckness of your name. Oh Fleck,
You're sweet, but this is not the surest way
To win the prize of my first dance tonight.
There is a way, but it's a secret way.

FLECK

As it should be, on this your special day.
I am delighted merely to be able
To smoothe, facilitate, and generally
Make pleasurable your night. You will need a layer
Of help between your vulnerable self
And the rack of steaming suitors, the likes of Gline
And Sewell, doubtless all desiring your hand
For true love, as opposed to . . . other reasons.

ZELDA

Where is Father?

FLECK   Wheeled about by the maid.

ZELDA

He ought to be out of sight and out of mind.

FLECK

Rest assured he is quite out of mind.
But Zelda, the guests are in, and all below,
Attended only by your undependable
Sisters, probably gossiping of us both.

ZELDA

You think so? I don't think so. They all know
You're just my agent, not necessarily
The one I choose – but not necessarily not!
It could be you, it could be the lyrical Poet,
It could be Gline, whose stake in Harvest Holdings
Was trebled in the war. That impresses me
As much as your old knack of making me
Do what you say.

FLECK   A kind exaggeration,
Unmerited.

ZELDA   I know. Now go down,
And tell them I was rather short with you,
Refused to sign a thing, and slapped your face
For claiming the first dance – say all that
And you may keep your hopes as high as you wish!

FLECK

In friendship I would do this unrewarded,
But, for a birthday girl, as a privilege.

And my hopes, as you term them, are merely these:
That you should dance your dance with whom you please,
And that who pleases you –
ZELDA   What a lovely note
On which to leave the room.
FLECK   I've left the room.

Exit FLECK

ZELDA
But my first partner: who's that going to be?
A secret even from me!
Fleck is a blessing in his loyalty and trust,
(I can trust him to tell me all the inner secrets
Of my blushing sisters!) Well, a birthday girl
Is privileged in all respects, and I
Will dance the first and second and third dance
With the untaken men: Sewell, Gline,
The candidates, the strangers from the coast!
Just to annoy my sisters and the Stone girls,
I'll even dance with the Lords,
Dukes and the recently married – no one will blame me!
Later I will narrow down the field,
And hurdle midnight in the arms of say,
Three, whichever three, I don't care!
I'm twenty-one! I declare
The final choice a choice of luck and wine:
So many might be mine!

Exit ZELDA

SCENE V
The gates of the house.

BATES *and* KALLUM, *in their defensive postures again, notice
that* PADGET *has reappeared, no better dressed than before*

KALLUM
Personally, I don't believe he's there.
BATES
He's there all right.
KALLUM   It really shows a nerve,

[130]

Shuffling up, pretending to exist,
Pretending to be a bona fide guest:
A gross insult, apart from anything else,
To our obstructing selves, isn't it, Bates?

BATES
You can't come in. We did explain all that.

KALLUM
You can try, peasant, or take some good advice
And don't.

BATES   Don't!

KALLUM   There: that's good advice.
Now take a hike. You look like you were shat.

PADGET
I can't deny I don't look the part.
The things I lack –

KALLUM   Doubly irrelevant!
Both that you deny, and that you lack,
Are of no interest. We can see you lack.
You lack to high heaven –

PADGET   But I'm expected.

KALLUM
Expected? Expected?
Expected as you're welcome, which is: not.

BATES
Explain, who expects you?

KALLUM   I do. Shortly
I expect him to be horizontal.

PADGET
Zelda expects me: she asked that I come.

BATES
You're not on our list.

PADGET   You don't know my name.

BATES
When you've been bouncing for as long as me –

KALLUM
Exactly, Bates. You can be on my list,
Peasant, in fact I'll slot you in at the top.
There. Now I'll show you what it's a list of.

KALLUM *advances on* PADGET

BATES
Steady, Kallum. We have to look unscathed.

KALLUM
  Who exactly is going to scathe me, Bates?
  I'm the one doing the scathing here.
  This man's a rind, his shoes outweigh him.
PADGET   Friend,
  I want no troubles. I intended none.
  And you can't strike a man for doing nothing.
KALLUM
  Where's that a law? I never heard of that.
PADGET
  It's only fair.
KALLUM   Oh fine, so it's not law.
  You've got ten seconds to be miles from here.
  Ten!
PADGET   That was the age at which Miss Zelda –
KALLUM
  Nine!
PADGET   I was two years older, so I'm now –
KALLUM
  Eight!
PADGET   That if I did the chosen things –
BATES
  What things?
KALLUM   Seven!
PADGET   Dark and dangerous things!
KALLUM
  Six!
PADGET   I went in search of certain people.
  There was a rhyme, that's how I remembered –
KALLUM
  Five-Four!
BATES   Isn't that cheating?
KALLUM   I delayed.
  Three!
PADGET   And if I accomplished the given tasks,
  Then Zelda –
KALLUM   Two!
PADGET   – Would, on her coming of age,
  Grant me the first dance –

Enter CLAUDIA *and* MARIA, *the sisters*

CLAUDIA   Padget!
KALLUM   One!

CLAUDIA
  I beg your pardon?
KALLUM   Sorry, it's a cough – Whon!
CLAUDIA
  It's Padget! Padget the greengrocer's boy,
  Grown up! How funny.
MARIA   No, it isn't him.
  He was much smaller, and his coat was blue,
  Which I remember because Uncle Boll
  Had one just like it. But a bit bigger.

CLAUDIA
  It is you, isn't it? After all these years!
  Do you still hide in the hedges and read books?
  Please say it's you – or I'll be made a fool!
PADGET
  It's me.
BATES He should have said.
PADGET   It always was.
CLAUDIA
  Thank God! So, what brings you to neck in the woods
  With us? You certainly chose your moment:
  It's Zelda's birthday today. She's seventy-four!
MARIA
  Actually twenty-one, but it's not him.
PADGET
  I'm here especially.
CLAUDIA   Oh. Are you a guest?
  I love the outfit – will you change inside?
  Zelda's upstairs, reflagging an old face,
  But Fleck is here, the poet Sewell, Gline,
  Who made a million on the Corn Exchange –
MARIA
  Just under, actually, but it was close.
CLAUDIA
  Was it just under? But there's blush champagne
  Of course, and a huge cake with soft icing,
  Shaped like a what-is-it? schloss, with little men
  Trotting about, green men.
  And candles to be lit, cards to be signed,
  – There's going to be carousing and canoodling!
  Or will be when her Highness Zelda deigns
  To get the Ball rolling with her first dance.

BATES (*to* KALLUM)
  "Ball rolling" – I like that.
KALLUM (*to* BATES)   I don't like it.
PADGET
  The dance is another reason.
MARIA   Are you Padget?
CLAUDIA
  Of course you're Padget. Don't deny it now!
  I was the one who recognised you first!
  Maria didn't. Won't Zelda be pleased?
PADGET
  Indeed.
KALLUM   I doubt it.
MARIA   So do I.
BATES   No way.
  We were expressly told not to admit
  Even a prince if his dress failed to meet
  Miss Zelda's rigorous constrictions.
CLAUDIA   Rot.
  This is Padget, "constrictions" don't apply.
  He's from the Past, that makes him a surprise,
  And Birthday Balls are all about surprises!
MARIA
  This qualifies all right. What has he done
  To justify admission dressed like that?
KALLUM
  I have to agree there.
CLAUDIA   Oh no you don't.
  You have to shut up and do as you're told.
PADGET
  No need for these troubles, Miss Claudia.
  As I told these two guards: I'm expected.
CLAUDIA
  That proves he's Padget – he remembers me!
  What have you come for, Zelda's hand in wedlock?
  You ain't the first.
PADGET   You mean she's married?
CLAUDIA   Oh,
  Have I hit on it?
PADGET   No, she can't be married.
CLAUDIA
  She's not, but there's a whole paddock of hopefuls
  Pacing about inside.
PADGET   May I go in?

[134]

CLAUDIA
 You may. I'll take responsibility.
MARIA
 In doing so you lack it, Claudia.
 Zelda is strict, and it's her twenty-first.
BATES
 No doubt we'll take the blame.
CLAUDIA   No doubt you will.
 That's why I don't mind doing this at all.
 Andiamo, Padget! Bienvenue!
 Dance up a storm and join the queue!
PADGET (*to* BATES)
 Thank you for your earlier advice, sir.
 I hope you will understand –

CLAUDIA *hurries him into the house*

MARIA   Extraordinary.
 I think he's who he says he is, but still:
 He has a cold, searching look. In fact,
 He always did. An odd thing to recall.

MARIA *exits into the house*

BATES
 There's something wrong when someone dressed like that
 Gets in so easily, and he called us "guards".
 "Bouncers" is our name.
KALLUM   It's not my fault.
 He's got to get out yet. And we're a long
 Mile from civilisation here, Bates.
 His name is Padget. Well,
 We got a name, we got a face. That's good.
 He may still find himself – lost in the wood.

SCENE VI
Outside the house.

A *window opens and* BISON *leans out. Another window
opens and* PALGRAVE *leans out*

BISON
 No trace of the lost Viscount in here.

[135]

PALGRAVE
He's not in here, Mr Bison, I'm in here.
BISON
Ah, there you are. You say he is not in there?
PALGRAVE
He's not in here, Mr Bison. Is he in there?

Both disappear back into the rooms. Enter the VISCOUNT, *carrying a number of brass fire-irons. He seems agitated. He exits.* BISON *reappears*

BISON
I can reassure you he is not in here.
Are you in there? Tell me if you are,
And tell me if you are not.
PALGRAVE (*from off*)   I am not there,
Mr Bison, I have moved down to down here
And found the lost Viscount is no more here
Than he was there and he wasn't, remember, there.

BISON *disappears again.* PALGRAVE *comes out of the house, wheeling the empty wheelchair*

If I can do exactly what I did
The time when he was here I can remember
Exactly when he wasn't.
BISON (*from off*)   He isn't here!
I fear he may be elsewhere entirely!
PALGRAVE
That's my fear as well, Mr Bison.
We may be both again in a bit of peril!
I see you aren't there.
BISON   I am now here!
PALGRAVE
I'll come up now and see if he isn't there.

Exit PALGRAVE. BISON *shuts his window. The* VISCOUNT *appears at the other window, and shuts that too*

SCENE VII
In front of the house.

Enter the GUESTS: LORD *and* LADY LAMPENHEAD, DUKE *and* DUCHESS DE VOOR, KRULL, *the* KANNISTERS, DR REPPER, MADAME ERRATUM, *the* STONE SISTERS, O'HALE! *and* UBERMANN, TOM KRASHGATE, FLAVIA FULLBRIGHT *and* PORLOCK KLIPKE. *They say one or more of these twelve lines, in any order, whenever:*

Well here we are again, in the Tomb of Nein.
All the gang's here, I see, all the gang.
Now what's the time? Must be beginning soon.
This Zelda's quite a girl, she's getting the hang.
I'm wide awake! I slept all afternoon.
High time to hit the high road to the wine . . .
Was that the Lavender Room or the Lemon Room?
Look at that lot: last of a wretched line.
Did you not get my message? I rang and rang.
Oh look, her stones are going to clash with mine.
I see those two are starting with a bang.
Here's to the Viscount Nein on a full moon!

And they always greet each other in the following ways:

GUEST
Lord Lampenhead, I hear the Hunt is on.
LORD LAMP.
Naturally we are dealing with the deacon.
GUEST
You always let the bitches have their fun!

GUEST
You dazzle, Lady Lampenhead, a beacon!
LADY LAMP.
Well, you had your chance in '31.
GUEST
The flesh is willing, but the spirits weaken . . .

GUEST
So what's your secret, Duke? Confide in me.
DUKE D. V.
One wriggles as one can, in these – clutches.

[137]

GUEST
A duke of love and of diplomacy!

GUEST
You glow among your sex, heavenly Duchess!
DUCH D.V.
Hardly a challenge, in this company.
GUEST
A sweetness gracing everything it touches!

GUEST
You must be the notorious Krull.
KRULL
I don't know what you mean. I wasn't there.
GUEST
I'll have you know they're dragging the canal.

GUEST
Repper – and not a stethoscope in sight!
REPPER
Yes, you can die this evening if you wish.
GUEST
But you won't let me – not without a fight!

GUEST
Kannister – and not upon a horse!
MR KANN.
A double-horse, no less. As big as this.
GUEST
I hear you have assembled quite a force.

GUEST
A brand new Mrs K – or is it Ms?
MRS KANN.
It's Mrs Erasmus Kannister – of course.
GUEST
This week it is, my dear, this week it is.

GUEST
So, dear madame, what's in store for me?
ERRATUM
A planet is in your house, and that means nothing.
GUEST
Extraordinary, I was expecting nothing.

GUEST
I'll vote for you this time, Mr O'Hale!!
O'HALE!
Sir, you will not regret it. That makes two.
GUEST
I never forget a friend, Mr McShale.

GUEST
Ubermann, next time I vote for you!
UBERMANN
Felicitations, sir, we shall not fail.
GUEST
That's the spirit. You'll know what to do.

GUEST
Mademoiselle Stone, let me guess . . . Charisma!
CHARISMA
No, I'm Elan. You must want my sister.
GUEST
Perhaps I do, perhaps a change of plan.

GUEST
Mademoiselle Stone! Now you must be Elan?
ELAN
Panache. We're very alike. We like a man.
GUEST
You seem to have changed my mind, like in a flash.

GUEST
Mademoiselle Stone, don't tell me – Panache?
PANACHE
You have Charisma, and I have to dash.
GUEST
No hurry is there, dear, no hurry, is there?

GUEST
You again. You show up everywhere.
KRASHGATE
It's cool, I'm crashing here, I always do.
GUEST
Don't let me keep you. There's a bed in there.

GUEST
Aren't you the woman who doesn't, but used to do?

FLAVIA
No, I was voted the Girl Most Likely To!
GUEST
I'm sure you were and I'm sure you did, too.

GUEST
Excuse me, what exactly do you want?
KLIPKE
It's you who wants, and I've got just the thing!
GUEST
I think perhaps I have some sheep to count . . .

*After a while, a game begins. It may resemble certain games
of our society appropriate to the bearing, social class, and
costume of the Ball guests, but it should be a game we have
never seen before, and its rules should seem arcane, obscure,
even absurd. When this game has produced some congratu-
lated winners and some consoled losers, the* VISCOUNT *leans
out of a window, clears his throat, and delivers the following
speech:*

VISCOUNT
Now, bring all of the pieces and all of the people
Cheerily into the centre and say Hi Ho.
Someone is something tonight she has never been.

Halve the inhabited cake and open the apple
Gleamingly to the elements. Say No
To one who insists he knows the men you mean.

The sons have raced their race and are in the chapel
Breathless while the ball is falling below
Into the gloves of the giddiest white Queen

And never gets there quite. A crumbling couple
Are on the march and no one is in the know
But I and I have seen what I have seen.

I drink a blue inflammable favourite tipple
Nowadays and it makes the garden glow!
But a huge industrial woman comes to clean.

Remember me to the person wearing purple.
Moreover mention me before they go
To those who go. Don't take me to the dean

Before the time. The disappearing ripple
Outripples all of any times ago.
Set the villages down on the village green

With utmost care. Curtain again the temple.
Light again the unshredded paper and blow
Human air to fan the inflaming scene.

Pull each of the grey pieces and each of the people
Wearily out of the ashes and ask Why So?
Someone is something tonight she has never been.

Thank you. Finally, and before I go.

The VISCOUNT *shuts the window and disappears back into
the house. The* GUESTS *applaud and take up their positions
for a deranged waltz. Then they go back inside*

SCENE VIII
Zelda's chamber.

CLAUDIA *is helping* ZELDA *at her toilette*

CLAUDIA
  You'll never guess!
ZELDA   So why the childish game,
  Wasting my special day, Claudia? Tell!
CLAUDIA
  You haven't seen the person for a while,
  And nor had I. He's standing on the landing!
ZELDA
  Oh tell!
CLAUDIA   I'll tell you how the others looked.
  Fleck didn't know him. Fleck went straight outside
  To moan at the poor bouncers, but Gline! oh,
  His mouth was wriggling and his eyes were wide –
  He poured his glass more wine than it desired!
  And Sewell recognised him too, and gaped
  As if a poem of his had arrived!
ZELDA   La Moon!
  La Moon, the one-eared boy? My God, Claudia,
  If you've dragged one like that in –

[141]

CLAUDIA   Not La Moon!
  He's got two ears and he's an old favourite,
  An ancient sweetheart. Is the suspense too much?
ZELDA
  No, Claudia, I don't care.
  He's not invited. Get him out of here.
CLAUDIA
  I would, if he were not, but he is, – or
  He says he is. He says he's expected.
ZELDA
  I haven't seen him for how many years?
CLAUDIA
  Eleven. Oh, you're excited now!

Enter FLECK *in a fury*

FLECK   Zelda!
  Your sister – you! – you have just admitted
  An inadmissible person who as we speak
  Is standing on the landing! – Zelda,
  Your sister has just admitted an –
ZELDA   I heard.
  I am in the same room, and have two ears.
  Who is he? Let's see this mystery stranger . . .

Enter PADGET

CLAUDIA
  You didn't guess!
ZELDA   Of course not. I don't know him.
  The stranger part is that he is a stranger.
  The mystery is how he was let in.
FLECK
  Don't worry, I've been shouting at the doormen.
CLAUDIA
  Thank Heavens, Mr Fleck, that's very useful.
FLECK
  This is your fault, Miss Claudia –
ZELDA   Shut up!
  It's my birthday and this is disappointing.
  I don't know who he is. And I didn't lose,
  Claudia, it was an unbalanced game.
  Why did you let him in?
CLAUDIA   Because, because.

FLECK
Esprit de saboteuse.
CLAUDIA   Up thine, monsieur.
ZELDA
No swearing on my birthday!
CLAUDIA   It's Padget.
ZELDA
So it is.
PADGET Many happy returns,
Zelda! I have come as I promised.
CLAUDIA
See, I told you so.
FLECK
It's Padget, is it? Oh, well, stop the clocks!
Fire a salute, my mistake, I'm sure!
PADGET
Oh not at all, you see I don't know you either.
ZELDA
Fleck, I know this person.
Go and tell the guests I'll be down soon.
FLECK
But this intrusion!
ZELDA   Just do as I said.
CLAUDIA
Just do as she said, honest Mr Fleck:
Can't you see she's hopelessly involved?
FLECK
In Heaven's name –
CLAUDIA   No swearing on her birthday!
ZELDA (*aside*)
Dear Fleck, I shan't be long. I'll sort this out
And follow you down. – Claudia, you go too.
Remember, no champagne, no cards, no candles,
No anything until I'm there!
CLAUDIA   Would I?
After you, honest Mr Fleck . . .

Exit FLECK *and* CLAUDIA

ZELDA
Perhaps – you didn't know it was my birthday.
PADGET
I did, and it still is.

ZELDA
  Yes, I invited friends, about a hundred.
  Perhaps you remember Gline and Sewell?
  Gline's struck it rich with Harvest Holdings –
PADGET   Good.
ZELDA
  And Sewell writes his sonnets to me –
PADGET   Good.
ZELDA
  So . . . now I'm well-known, Padget, you could say
  A star of high society, though I don't.
PADGET
  A star of high society. Good.
ZELDA
  Uh? Perhaps you should have written to me first,
  To say you were about – it's been ten years.
PADGET
  Eleven, all told. And I did write first.
  Perhaps you didn't read my letter.
ZELDA   No
  "Perhaps" about it.
PADGET   Still, I'm sure you remember.
  I've thought of nothing else on my long trek.
ZELDA
  Your what? Is this some kind of birthday trick?
  Damn them, I'm not a girl now –
PADGET   No indeed!
  You are a beautiful woman. I can hardly
  Form words in the face of my good fortune.
  You must be the Princess of all the belles . . .
ZELDA
  I think I'm having one of my dizzy spells.

Enter FLECK

FLECK
  Excuse me, Zelda, but the guests are all
  Gathered and gossiping. I had thought
  This unscheduled intercourse concluded.
ZELDA
  Conclude that you thought wrong!
  Who cares what's being said? – What's being said?

[144]

FLECK
   That an anarchist, desperate and contagious,
   Forced his way in here for purposes –
ZELDA
   Rot, Fleck, get out! You have no right
   To barge in here without a knock – go down
   And tell them I'm on my way – which I am!

FLECK *goes to the door*

FLECK
   They won't wait much longer.
ZELDA   They'll wait a year.
   All of rich society's here.
FLECK
   Starving, needing a drink!
PADGET   Isn't there water?
   Isn't there bread?
FLECK   See, an anarchist!
   I'll say you're on the stairs.

Exit FLECK

ZELDA
   I don't know why you're here, but I must say
   You did arouse my curiosity
   For a good three minutes. Now it's time to go.
PADGET
   After the ceremony?
   You mean: together? Now?
ZELDA   Ceremony?
   What ceremony?
PADGET   The marriage. The fulfilment
   Of the old promise, of course.
ZELDA   What old promise?
PADGET
   You don't remember?
ZELDA   I'd remember that.
   I don't make promises, and when I do
   I keep them.
PADGET   Good. So let's go down together.
ZELDA (*aside*)
   I don't like this. I think this man's a feather

Light of a full pillow.
– Well, Padget, you're a disconcerting fellow
And no mistake! But off you go. You can leave
By the side door. Goodbye, good luck with life!

ZELDA *tries to usher him out*

PADGET
   "Zelda shall be Padget's wife
   On the night when she has lived
   Twenty-one years of her life
   If, in the year before she lives
   The twenty-first year of her life,
   Padget goes, and Padget gives –"
ZELDA
 Gives what? I remember that rhyme.
 Well, one remembers rhymes: life, wife, knife . . .
 Gives what? They were unlikely things.
PADGET   They were.
   "Hazel to the man who hangs,
   Potion to a plaguy boy,
   Hops to the hag on the yellow crag
   And drums to the ghost at sea . . ."
ZELDA
 Yes, impossible things, the worst outcasts,
 I do remember that! What a wild, wild
 Imagination we had in those days.
 So. Are you staying in the region now?
PADGET
   "Zelda shall be Padget's wife
   On the night when she has lived
   Twenty-one years of her life
   If, in the year before she lives
   The twenty-first year of her life,
   Padget goes, and Padget gives
   Hazel to the man who hangs,
   Potion to a plaguy boy,
   Hops to the hag on the yellow crag
   And drums to the ghost at sea.
   Zelda swears on her Father's House
   She shall be mine, or pay the price."
ZELDA
 Was that how it went?
PADGET   That is how it goes.

ZELDA
You came a long way to read nursery rhymes,
Padget. Can you whistle up any others?
PADGET
I can whistle up all sorts.
ZELDA (*aside*)   Oh no, he's short
Many, many feathers.
PADGET   Here I am!
Here I am, on the very night, with you!
Here is the man who travelled far and wide!
Here is the man who crossed his heart for you!
Who gave witch-hazel to the hanging man
And cut him down while he was cursing me,
Who saved the cracked boy with a milk of bindweed,
And scaled the yellow cliff to feed the hag!
Who gave –
ZELDA   Oh my eyesight – what did you give?

Enter CLAUDIA

CLAUDIA
This sounds promising – is it a tiff?
ZELDA
Can't you knock before you come in?
CLAUDIA   I did,
But softly, so as not to disturb the tryst!
ZELDA
I'm on my way! I'll be about a second!
CLAUDIA
Oh that's not it. Take as long as you like.
I'm having my own Ball inventing gossip.
I merely wondered might I open the first
What-is-it, Nebuchadnezzar?
ZELDA   You *know* you can't!
CLAUDIA
Oh yes . . . I'd forgotten. Silly Claudia.

Exit CLAUDIA

ZELDA
You mean you saw the hag?
PADGET   Saw, spoke to,
Escorted her back home to the southern port
That banished her for crimes that never were.

[147]

I lived among the poorest and the most
Desperate of the land.

ZELDA Why? Why?

PADGET

It was a promise.

ZELDA A plague of them on you!

PADGET

Oh? Well, a curse is a promise too.

ZELDA

Padget, I know the rhyme. I do remember.
We were strange children. Everyone said so.
And children'll tell tales, but tales, they're not
Binding, Padget. So, you did all this.
Good, good. I'm sure you feel a saint
And better for it. Thank you. Now, goodbye!
I have a life to lead!

PADGET So did I.

ZELDA

Oh my God.

PADGET You do believe?

ZELDA Believe?

PADGET

That all the tasks were done? You never asked
About the ghost at sea.

ZELDA What was it – a drum?
You gave him a drum? Of course you did! I bet
He's banging away in the sunset even now,
Ghastly grin on his face! Yes, Padget,
The pal to spooks and lepers – Padget the Good!

PADGET

I did my best. I promised you I would.
And here I am. What game are you playing with me?

ZELDA

No game, Padget, I came down from my tree.
We all did. I'm leading another life.

PADGET

One girl, one life, one woman, one wife.

ZELDA

No! A girl! And in the old days, Padget,
I used to say – "goo-goo!" and "bow-wow-wow!"
I don't expect to be held to them now.

PADGET

But they weren't promises.

[148]

ZELDA This promise I made,
Or . . . might have made . . .
PADGET You made it. I was there.
ZELDA
Or . . . might have made.
PADGET Mind you sustain the truth.
ZELDA
But it was long ago, and we were young!
We only have your word –
PADGET No! Your word.
You said you knew the rhyme. You know you did.
ZELDA
Don't tell me what I know, old friend. I said
All manner of things these one-and-twenty years.
Goo-goo! Bow-wow-wow! I'm ninety-nine!
Amazing – was that me? Is she insane?
PADGET
No, not insane but playing a strange kind
Of dangerous game, Zelda, I think: you can't
Wish away a promise.
ZELDA What promise?
Refresh my memory, I don't recall a promise.
I was only a child – you were only a child –
Tonight I double both of you with years,
You nobodies on swings!
And as for you, Padget – perhaps you lied.
PADGET
I cannot lie.
ZELDA You're at it again tonight!
Claiming I knew the rhyme – I didn't know it!
This isn't a play – you can't turn back the pages
And prove I said I knew it – which I didn't!
PADGET
I hope you know the real truth, Zelda.
ZELDA
Breakfast with your hopes! Lunch with your hopes!
Prove that I knew the rhyme and you can stay.
Fail, prove without proof, and I shall feed you
To the doormen like the leftover you are!
FLECK (*from off*)
Shame and sorrow on me but I must
Perforce intrude! Urgent business, Zelda!
PADGET
Are these terms like your promises, Zelda?

[149]

ZELDA
    A promise is a promise is a promise.
    Which I didn't make. I'd keep it if I had.
FLECK (*from off*)
    In the name of . . . all important things, I demand
    Admission to this room! I have a letter
    Expressly and directly to deliver
    By manumission into your, er, hand!
ZELDA
    So where's your proof? If you could ever prove
    I said these words, –
PADGET   Or wrote them?
ZELDA   At that age
    I doubt I wrote them.
FLECK (*from off*)   I'm starting to open the door!
    You leave me with no choice!
PADGET   You would accept
    A written proof?
ZELDA   Of course. You think I'm mad?
    I do believe what I see, not what I'm told
    I did by others. I go by my own eyes.
    I never doubt what's right in front of me.

FLECK *bursts in with the letter* ZELDA *discarded earlier*

FLECK
    Then you will see this letter, Zelda!
    I am not a man to intrude, but urgent business –
ZELDA
    That letter's dirty, I didn't want to see it.
FLECK (*aside to her*)
    A ruse, merely, to satisfy myself
    This vagabond has not trespassed upon –
ZELDA
    Well he has! We're finished here. Claudia! Maria!
FLECK
    Sir, what have you done?
PADGET   What must be done.
    Zelda, this postman has arrived in time.
FLECK (*apoplectic*)
    What?
PADGET Read your letter.
ZELDA   Claudia! Maria!

FLECK
Did you call me a postman?
PADGET   Read your letter.
Isn't it why you ran into the room?
FLECK (*flummoxed*)
Of course, but –
PADGET   Read it aloud.
FLECK   But –
PADGET   Read it aloud.

FLECK, *somewhat intimidated, opens the letter*

FLECK
              "Zelda shall be Padget's wife
              On the night when she has lived –"
ZELDA
No!

FLECK *drops the letter as if it were infectious*

FLECK   Disgusting! It's a riddle-rhyme of – lust!
A pervert and an anarchist commingled!
Sir, prepare to fight!
PADGET   For what? With whom?
FLECK
Er . . . for Honour, and with others!

Exit FLECK

PADGET
You find such furious people nowadays,
Even where the riches are.
ZELDA   Padget,
Our little play is over, understand?
Thirty men are here for my hand,
And won't take kindly to your fantasies.
PADGET
I know about that many men too,
Humans. They will not know what to do,
Should you negate this promise.
ZELDA   What do you mean?
Claudia! Maria!
PADGET   Your sisters seem fine.

ZELDA
We're not all in the cuckoo clock with you.
What people did you mean?

Enter CLAUDIA *and* MARIA

CLAUDIA
All Hell's breaking loose, and it's called Fleck!
He shouted Help! and fell down the stairs,
But no one picked him up.
ZELDA   It doesn't matter.
CLAUDIA
So when's the honeymoon? You'll need a parson!
ZELDA
Be quiet, Claudia – how many guests are here?
MARIA
And witnesses.
ZELDA   What?
CLAUDIA   Nearly a hundred.
ZELDA   What?
MARIA
You'd need witnesses, not just a parson.
ZELDA
What?
CLAUDIA   Ninety, say – oh, sorry, ninety-one!
The guest of honour!
ZELDA   About to make his exit!
PADGET
Honour?

PADGET *picks the letter up and shows it to* CLAUDIA *and*
MARIA

                    Is this the seal of Viscount Nein?
CLAUDIA
Of course. I'd recognise those ugly monks
Anywhere. And I know that handwriting . . .
          "Zelda shall be Padget's wife
          On the night when she has lived
          The twenty-first year of her life
          If, in the year –"
ZELDA   Let me see that!

ZELDA *snatches it and reads*

[152]

CLAUDIA
  Padget, you old oddball, a contract!
  In Zelda's hand! How did you pull that off?
MARIA
  It's no time to mix metaphors, Claudia,
  But it is her script. Or at least it was her script
  When she was young. Mine had a kind of slope.

ZELDA
  There's nothing wrong with this.
  Of course I wrote this! Of course I agreed
  To be his wife if this was done – of course!
  But do you really think he did these things?
  Do you really think he can prove he did these things?
  Plucked the villain off the very gibbet?
  Risked his blood on some encrusted brat
  And fed the witch on the cliff? Nobody ever
  Would do such things – these are the poisonous people,
  The outcasts, the forgotten, the dead souls!
  Why would he do all that and only for me?
CLAUDIA
  It sounds implausible . . .
  But perilous, and brave! I'm almost jealous!
MARIA
  I'm in the dark. If these things are so hard,
  So unspeakable and in general really nasty –
  Why did you make him do them?
ZELDA   For a joke!
MARIA
  Sealed only with the seal of our father . . .
ZELDA
  You think I planned to marry *him* tonight?
MARIA
  The seal of our forefathers . . .
ZELDA   Shut up!
  It doesn't mean –
CLAUDIA   This was a mad, mad action!
  That document's a promise, which to break –
  The seal is sacred – we would all be cursed!
ZELDA
  But only if he really did these things!
MARIA
  A timely point.
ZELDA   Any could wander in,

Pretend he did these things, grab my hand
And all my fortune – it doesn't mean he really
Did them, does it?
CLAUDIA   But if he proves?
ZELDA   He can't!
CLAUDIA
  Can you?
MARIA Can you?
PADGET   I arrived with nothing.
  I hoped and I believed you would. You did
  When you were young.
CLAUDIA   That's not enough, it seems.
ZELDA
  It's not. My hand's at stake. I won't believe
  Where I can't see.
PADGET   I'll have to go away,
  And come back to this place another time.
  When I next come I'll bring what you can see.
  You will believe.
ZELDA   Impossible! Insane!
  The Ball begins tonight!
  Wait for him to prove what can't be proved?
CLAUDIA
  He's proved you promised him your hand, Zelda,
  And on our ancient seal. It's not his fault
  His marbles rolled away in the meanwhile.
  But how can you endanger our old House
  Denying the word of a Nein?

ZELDA *considers*

ZELDA   Three nights.
  Three nights we'll wait for what – ribbons and scraps
  Of "evidence" you think you can muster.
  If I am satisfied, I am – your wife.
  If not, you will regret your reappearance:
  Associates I have will escort you
  Quickly along a zigzag path somewhere
  You know no one. You should have stayed on the cliff
  Or haunting the seven seas with your – shipmates.
PADGET
  This was the last I hoped.
  To bring the evidence you are asking for.
  But I hope –

[154]

Enter GLINE, SEWELL *and* FLECK

FLECK   Eleventh hour! The sides are even!
GLINE
  Padget, you always were the droning sort,
  But we're getting rather jumpy back inside.
  Perhaps you could go home and/or to hell.
SEWELL
  I'm sure your togs won't seem so out of place
  Down there, and there'll be books to read.
PADGET   Friends,
  I have to go. I promise I'll be back.

The suddenness of this takes the suitors by surprise: they
stand as if paralysed, and PADGET *exits unscathed*

GLINE
  Oh do, do, do! And bring a friend!
FLECK
  Outrage on outrage! I can't comprehend –
SEWELL
  Let's start the Ball, we're dropping hours behind!
ZELDA
  Nothing is starting! No blush champagne,
  No cards or candles, nothing. No – kisses.
  You'll have to tell the guests.
FLECK   But how much longer?
ZELDA
  Three nights.
FLECK   Three nights???
GLINE   Three nights?
SEWELL   Three nights?
ZELDA   Three nights.
FLECK
  Who on earth is that man?
GLINE   We know his name.
  We'll have him sorted out.
SEWELL   What happened here?
ZELDA
  He must be left alone. At least, for now.
  In three nights he'll be back and then we'll know.
  In three nights we shall drink champagne, and laugh
  About that man, and I shall make my choice
  And I shall dance.

FLECK/GLINE/SEWELL   What are we waiting for?
ZELDA
For me. That's all you need to know. For me.
If you have hope, you'll stay, for if you leave
You leave your hopes to another man. That's all.
Sisters, Fleck: what you know, forget.
Sisters, tell the guests of my . . . whim.
"Typical Zelda", they'll say. Don't mention him.
Fleck, tell the two doormen. Double their wage.
That's all. Now leave me here.
Good riddance to who goes. To you – good cheer.

The MEN *hesitate, then exit slowly*

CLAUDIA
Don't worry, Zelda: you won't see him again.
And this gives you your chance to find the man
Who really cares.
MARIA   Meanwhile, what of the cake?
I doubt our mother will have time to bake
Another – shall I wrap it?
ZELDA   Let it be.
Three nights, all this will be a memory.

Exit the NEIN SISTERS

SCENE IX
Outside the house.

Enter LORD LAMPENHEAD, CANDIDATE UBERMANN,
CHARISMA STONE *and* MR KANNISTER *from the house*

LORD LAMP.
Extraordinary behaviour of the Neins!
UBERMANN
I doubt there's room for them in our new plans
For everything.
CHARISMA   Will there be room for me?
UBERMANN
Wear the Blue Cravat and wait and see.
MR KANN.
Anyone seen my wife? She's about so high.

[156]

UBERMANN
Then there'll be room for her.

MR KANN.   Oh. Why?

LORD LAMP.
And you, my dear, who did you say you were?

CHARISMA
It doesn't matter. The Ball is over, sir.

ALL 4
WE WON'T BE TREATED LIKE THIS. WE'RE
   GOING THEN.
WE MAY NOT COME AGAIN.

Enter DUCHESS DE VOOR, PORLOCK KLIPKE, MADAME
ERRATUM *and* PANACHE STONE *from the house*

DUCH D.V.
Always hard to be outshone, I know,
But no excuse for telling us all to go.
I cannot help my looks.

KLIPKE   But perhaps this can:
Tested only on an orangutan,
And yours for a song.

DUCH D.V.   Who is this appalling man?

ERRATUM
Hmm, twilight. Another prediction of mine
Eerily come true.

PANACHE   Is it a sign?

DUCH D. V.
Does it explain the ludicrous Family Nein
Expecting us to wait three nights for a Ball?

ERRATUM
Saturn has gone, and that means nothing at all.

PANACHE
And nothing happened! Maybe there's something in it!

KLIPKE
Just like this catalogue – have you got a minute?
I haven't sold a thing today.

ERRATUM   You won't.

DUCH D. V.
You may find this amusing, but I don't.

ALL 8
WE WON'T BE TREATED LIKE THIS. WE'RE
   GOING THEN.
WE MAY NOT COME AGAIN.

Enter DUKE DE VOOR, MRS KANNISTER, ELAN STONE
and CANDIDATE O'HALE! *from the house*

DUKE D.V.
  I say, what evil timing, and I'd just
  Discovered I knew you somewhere in the past . . .
MRS KANN.
  Duke, what's done is done. Now we must find
  The encumbrances we failed to leave behind.
ELAN
  So were you serious about your offer?
O'HALE!
  A junior post to start with, and then after,
  Depending on your eagerness, Miss Stone,
  You could become surprisingly well-known.
ELAN
  I always saw myself in a top position.
O'HALE!
  I do believe you've made a wise decision.
  We'll make a date together . . .
DUKE D. V.   Candidate,
  Do a duke a favour. I do hate
  Having to leave so early. Dear O'Hale!,
  When you win power, throw the Neins in jail.
ALL 12
  WE WON'T BE TREATED LIKE THIS. WE'RE
    GOING THEN.
  WE MAY NOT COME AGAIN.

Enter LADY LAMPENHEAD, FLAVIA FULLBRIGHT, TOM
KRASHGATE *and* DR REPPER *from the house*

LADY LAMP.
  In my day this would never ever happen.
  Balls began at eight and ended at seven.
FLAVIA
  When I was Miss October, in October,
  I couldn't find a single servant sober.
LADY LAMP.
  In my day people knew their place.
KRASHGATE   Hey chicks,
  Cool it, we could crash at the doctor's digs,
  Couldn't we, doc?
REPPER   You may get quite a surprise.

KRASHGATE
Yeah, we could watch the sunrise.
REPPER   What sunrise?
LADY LAMP.
In my day Balls began when the sun set.
KRASHGATE
In my day we took everything we could get.
FLAVIA
But my day was a day they'll never forget.
REPPER
And my day hasn't even started yet.
ALL 16
WE WON'T BE TREATED LIKE THIS. WE'RE
GOING THEN.
WE MAY NOT COME AGAIN.

Enter KRULL *from the house*

KRULL
There will not be a Ball. It's just as well,
For I was never here. Perhaps you'll tell
That to the men who stand at your open door
Taking out my photograph once more.
        Remember you never saw me.

I am not one of these nor one of you.
I vote for neither the scarlet nor the blue.
I have no information to impart,
Nor plot nor plan nor sabotage to start.
        Remember you never saw me.

I am the one you always fail to place,
The never blurred but never circled face,
The one no one remembers having known,
Who leaves no man alone but leaves alone.
        Remember you never saw me.

One will have been invited and left last.
Two will attempt too much and too fast.
Three will be standing cold on the fourth day.
And the uninvited blow this world away.
        Remember you never saw me.

ALL
WE WON'T BE TREATED LIKE THIS. WE'RE
    GOING THEN.
WE MAY NOT COME AGAIN.

Exit the GUESTS

ACT II

The gates of the house.

Three nights later. BATES *and* KALLUM *sit at the threshold.*
Suddenly, BATES *leaps up to confront a shadow!*

BATES
    I told you once – I won't tell you again!
    You can't come in, you don't exist – so there!
KALLUM
    So where.
BATES So nowhere! It's my joke again.
KALLUM
    Tell it again in an hour.
BATES   Oh no, I wait
    Till the timing's right, and – oh, I see.
    Your sarcasm again, Kallum. Well,
    You think of a way to pass the time.
KALLUM
    Three nights! Three nights waiting in the cold
    For that rag-and-bone. This never happens!
    These Balls are thrown by the great families,
    The Lampenheads, the Wantzes, the de Voors,
    And nothing happens! Well, the usual happens.
    But when it comes to the old, heirless Neins . . .
    Something happened here, and it doesn't fit.
    Something small, and dirty, and I hate it.
BATES
    At least she doubled our wage, don't forget.
    And offered cake –
KALLUM   But gave none, gave none.
BATES
    Nor to her guests, insulted and long gone.
KALLUM
    No cake, no cards, no candles, no champagne –
BATES
    No clocks, no cabbages, no complaints, no crime –
KALLUM
    No Kallum and no –

Enter ZELDA, *rather bright-eyed and dishevelled*

[161]

ZELDA   No!
No nothing till it's time! It's the third night.
BATES
It's colder than the second or the first.
ZELDA
I wouldn't know. I'm sitting in the heat.
Has there been any signal, any light?
Whispering? Has there been anything?
BATES
Not since the last invited person left,
Miss Zelda. It's been a quiet afternoon.
KALLUM
It's not so bad a job, minding a door
When nobody's expected to attempt
To open it, except to go away.
ZELDA
You don't expect him.
KALLUM   I expect the moon
Will join us for a hand of poker soon.
ZELDA
Well you don't know the circumstances.
KALLUM   No.
One day it'd be interesting to learn
Exactly why we stood here so long.
Not that I mind so much:
Maybe you'll employ us to guard a pebble,
Or have a tortoise followed, or observe
The sea, and tell you how it spends its Sundays.
ZELDA
Witty in the cold, Mr Doorman.
But if he comes, you tell me instantly.
We must be ready for him, whatever he brings.
Then I can make my choice. Nobody knows
What my choice will be! Of course
That's no concern of yours, it couldn't be you.
But many remain behind!
BATES   The Kannisters
Never came back, I'm afraid. Nor did the doctor.
The Candidates came back but changed their minds.
We don't know why that was.
ZELDA   So who remains?
BATES
Mr Fleck, Mr Gline, Mr Sewell.
ZELDA   My,

Clairvoyance. Right, I'm going inside. Do you
Have knives? Don't answer that. I'm going now.

Exit ZELDA

KALLUM
  A filthy interruption, to be sure,
  This "master" Padget, shrank her to a girl.
BATES
  "Have knives"?
KALLUM   To cut the birthday gateau, Bates.
BATES
  You'd think they'd have their own.

BATES *sees the uninvited shadow again*

                  Who goes there?
  Persistent shadow! Guest without a face!

KALLUM *unsheaths his knife and stabs the "guest": they both
watch its demise*

KALLUM
  Enough of you. Gatecrash a hotter place.

SCENE II
Outside the house.

*A white light goes on in an upper window, silhouetting what
appears to be the Viscount. Enter* PALGRAVE, *holding many
blankets. The light goes out. There is hissing from all sides.*
PALGRAVE *panics, and runs back into the house*

SCENE III
The conservatory.

There is a great cauldron of wine. Enter FLECK, *who hovers
near it with a capsule*

FLECK
  "In vino veritas" – there's truth in that,

A superficial truth appropriate
Exclusively to frequenters of fleshpots:
But this – the thing itself! No tendency
To quaff and leak confessionally, no!
A bright compulsion, biological
And irresistible as sleep itself!
One sip's enough to fuse one to the truth,
To make deceit, exaggeration, falsehood,
Expansion, understatement, hazarding
And all the slick crew of the not-quite-so
Impossible to verbalise. One sip:
The tongue's a restless stallion, unstabled,
Unreined by thought! Out tumbles the heart,
And all that organ's secrets and desires
Heap nakedly in sight of every man,
Or woman . . . Two remain:
The scribbler and the speculator, both
Fluttering round the woman I require
Like bugs at a streetlamp. Once the vagabond
Stumbles back and is hunted down for his pain,
Two – and I – remain, and I will offer
A good luck drink to my rivals: they will sip
And out will trickle the truth: they want her money.
They want the moonshine Viscount's money. Zelda
Will hear and make her choice: what choice is there?
A parasitical poet, a very
Maggot of the marketplace – or I,
An honest servant? – This drunken duet
Of fawning suitables will taste a wine
Of veritable edge. Thus she will hear
Their true desires: her money and her money.
The rest is choosing one from one – no choice!

He laces the wine

Your health, true lovers! Here they come – reaction!

Enter GLINE *and* SEWELL, *somewhat the worse for wear*

Still about, my honourable friends?
GLINE
Some question, Fleck, you dead-o'-night. Of course.
Somewhat amused to see you hanging on.
Presumably for cake? You're rather gaunt.

[164]

SEWELL
Devour it, Phantom Fleck! I'm sure it can't
Quite have rotted.
FLECK   Ahem. No cake until –
GLINE
We know, we know, we're all obedience.
Though in Servility mere amateurs.
FLECK
Implying?
SEWELL   Oh, in Implication gods!
FLECK
I mean –
SEWELL   And in our Meaningfulness masters!
FLECK
You must think me a fool.
GLINE   A fool? Must we?
What deeds of yours make this obligatory?
FLECK
I didn't mean –
SEWELL   And should have meant? Too bad.
We must think you a fool.
FLECK   I am no fool.
I am a trusted man, an honest friend,
A problematical foe.
SEWELL   Oh that's rich!
All sorts of men are fools, it's not just fools.
FLECK
I note your life of scribbling has equipped you
With a range of quiddities.
SEWELL
Multisyllabic man! Neglected sage!
No man trusts you like I do, or is more
Honest in assessment of your worth.
No man would be so loth
To have you for a foe, for I value most
A life unproblematical.
GLINE   Hurrah!
Let's make a trio to be reckoned with!
FLECK
You would be well advised. May I then suggest
A drink to our most wise association?
SEWELL
The wine's forbidden, Fleck.
FLECK   In point of fact

She gave no word concerning the wine here:
Champagne is the proscribed beverage.
GLINE
    Bending the rules, friend Fleck? That's unlike you.
    That's more like us!
FLECK (*filling his glass*) Let me propose a toast
    To honest gentlemen, to bachelors!
SEWELL (*doing likewise*)
    How bibulous of him! Oh well, I'm game.
GLINE (*doing likewise*)
    To arms, to arms! And legs and eyes and brain!

Enter CLAUDIA *and* MARIA *before they can drink*

CLAUDIA
    Caught at the lip of disobedience!
MARIA
    A contradiction, certainly. A shame.
CLAUDIA
    Unutterable naughtiness, poet.
SEWELL
    It didn't reach my lips. It was a bet.

He throws his wine back, as does GLINE

GLINE
    Nor mine. There, with the fish. I didn't drink.
FLECK (*doing likewise*)
    Nor I. I don't. Or seldom. Just a prank.
    A therapeutic action, –
CLAUDIA   Mr Fleck,
    Much as I love your discourse and your voice,
    I play the messenger who drives it hence:
    You're wanted in her room.
GLINE
    Wanted somewhere, Fleck? Is this a first?
FLECK
    Why am I required?
CLAUDIA   A recurring question.
    Perhaps she requires some long words about things.
FLECK
    Brisk in obedient agency, I go.
GLINE
    Just time for a quick syllable or ten.
    Why not just go?

FLECK   No time to answer that!

Exit FLECK

SEWELL
  So why is he required? Is Padget come?
  We're ready when he does.
CLAUDIA   No, Zelda thinks
  It's time to sign some documents. In case.
SEWELL
  In case of what? (*aside*) Damn peasant, I've a thirst.
  My patience wants the vinegar-sponge.
GLINE   Yes,
  When Fleck begins to hanker and lunge
  For things forbidden, we can't last long.
  So . . . how's the cake?
MARIA   Quite hard. Greener than ever.
  There may be problems with the colourants.
GLINE
  Hmm, the colourants.
CLAUDIA   He's teasing you.
SEWELL
  Not at all: he has a share or twain
  In sugar cane. He knows his colourants.
  Now Claudia, attend: I need a hand.
CLAUDIA
  Doubtless another Zelda poem.
SEWELL   It is,
  A lyrical birthday ode, to a delayed
  But nevertheless significant milestone.
CLAUDIA
  Millstone, more likely, if she told a lie.

SEWELL *shows his poem to* CLAUDIA

GLINE
  So what did Padget say? You can tell me.
MARIA
  A secret, I'm afraid, Mr Gline.
GLINE
  Oh, call me William.
MARIA   "Mr Gline" is proper.
GLINE
  "Mr William Gline, Millionaire

[167]

Proprietor of Harvest Holdings, Inc."
Is proper, dear, but –
MARIA   Harvest Holdings?
Is that the grain-distributor?
GLINE   It was.
I'm turning it around to make it more
Cost-effective. What did Padget say?
MARIA
Good day, goodbye, and something in between.
CLAUDIA (*reading*)
        "A lover's kiss is an exotic fish.
        Her name a large unnecessary hat.
        Her soul a soup-spoon, her desire a dish,
        And I love Zelda, true as this is that."
Is this a section?
SEWELL   No, a complete ode.
MARIA
A complete ode of something, certainly.
CLAUDIA
"A lover's kiss is an exotic fish"?
MARIA
Do you find that cost-effective, Mr William?
SEWELL
Think of a salmon – soft and pink, delight!
One might devour a thousand, three a day,
Utopia! Ah, that will dull the desire.
GLINE
A fishy explication.
MARIA   Excellent!
You made a pun on fish. Let me think.
CLAUDIA
"Her name a large unnecessary hat."
A Zelda-cap? Did Uncle Boll wear one?
MARIA
Homburgs, he wore.
SEWELL   What's in a name? It means.
After the flush of knowing a beloved name,
It doesn't matter – yet it still exists.
GLINE
Cap that, Maria.
MARIA   Exactly my "porpoise"!
CLAUDIA
"Her soul a soup-spoon"?
SEWELL   That's – I don't recall.

[168]

Alliteration, like "desire a dish".
Surreal, you'll agree.
CLAUDIA   Surreal Sewell!
And rhyme as well!
SEWELL   Scholastically noted,
My dear, who knows? You could most prove critical.
GLINE
In the name of love we see great art prosper.
SEWELL
No art intended, Gline.
GLINE   None taken, Sewell.
MARIA
No sign of a fish yet.
GLINE (*aside to* SEWELL) But here's a net,
Sewell: these girls are green, and Zelda turns us
Rotten with delay.
SEWELL   A windfall?
It may amuse us while we wait for Fleck
To bore our lady rigid.
GLINE   Don't forget:
At the brink – turn back.
SEWELL   – Claudia!
Art is making me giddy! Your acumen
Has shaken Zelda out of my thoughts: my poem
Is now a poem to you.
MARIA   Too many syllables.
GLINE
Maria, your mathematical sense has quite
Ravished me! We'll see solicitors,
They'll lend solidity to our late love!
MARIA
Extremely late. Presumably a jest.
GLINE
Presumption? Possibly. A jest? Never!
CLAUDIA
Maria, a moment . . .

CLAUDIA *and* MARIA *go aside*

SEWELL
Too easy. Let's reward ourselves with a taste
Of what's forbidden.

SEWELL *dips his finger in the wine, and licks it*

[169]

I'm a shallow liar.

GLINE
  I beg your pardon?

SEWELL   Sorry? I don't know –
  What did I say?

GLINE *does the same*

GLINE   Who gives a shit. I hate you.

SEWELL
  What?

GLINE What?

SEWELL   Better leave the wine
  For later . . .

CLAUDIA   Mr Sewell: you have eleven
  Other Zelda poems: would it be possible
  To change –

SEWELL   The Z is stiffened to a C.
  A new school is begun.

CLAUDIA   Consider me
  Its brightest pupil!

GLINE   What a brave foursome!
  Maria, we must peruse a catalogue.
  You'll need a wardrobe.

MARIA   I've got a wardrobe.

SEWELL
  But should we not start out with a first kiss?

GLINE
  Perfection, Sewell: etiquette *parfay*!

CLAUDIA
  Oh yes, it sounds correct, and not amiss!

MARIA
  It sounds like neither but let's, anyway.

The SUITORS *advance, make to kiss the* SISTERS, *then pull away*

GLINE
  Confounded interdiction!

SEWELL   Woe is me!

GLINE
  No kisses on the lips!

SEWELL   Alack the day!

CLAUDIA
  You twisted us! They twisted us, Maria!

[170]

MARIA
 The wardrobe was arousing my suspicions.
CLAUDIA
 Yes, they dote on Zelda, for her name,
 Her firstborn privilege, rich as they are.
GLINE
 Children, a harmless game! Are you angry?
SEWELL (*aside*)
 Vixen, of course they are. Did she believe
 I would adjust my works to slot her in?
 O Philistines, O World.
CLAUDIA   Let's leave them here.
 I need some air. So, carry on together!
 Dart your dual tongues at one another!
 Come on, Maria.

Exit CLAUDIA *and* MARIA

GLINE   Women, women, women!
 Their moods outchange the English weather.
SEWELL   Gline.
 My patience, which was stretched, is now knotted.
 Zelda must choose tonight.
GLINE   And choose she shall.
 (*aside*) Perhaps the man most patient, and most cool . . .
SEWELL (*aside*)
 Perhaps who most delays is most the fool . . .

Exit GLINE *and* SEWELL

SCENE IV
Outside the house.

Enter BISON, *wheeling an empty wheelbarrow. Although
there is a sinister commotion in the hedges, and a strange
apparition in the windows, he remains oblivious to both, and
exits, whistling an old tune*

The gate of the house.

BATES *is restless,* KALLUM *dozing*

BATES
What time is it? What time is it?
KALLUM   Too late.
Midnight if anything. He's too late.
BATES
No, you slept. You over-estimate
The time you were asleep. Perhaps it's ten.
KALLUM
I'm glad you woke me up to tell me perhaps
It's ten, Bates.
BATES   It means he's got two hours.
We must be fair.
KALLUM   Quite right, Bates, very fair.
Or else the birds will file complaints, the trees
Embark on litigations, and the stars
Report us to some other stars. Oh yes,
We must be fair.
BATES   I see you need more jokes
To cheer your mood.
KALLUM   Like I need elephants
To shine my shoes.
BATES   Think of our bonus.
KALLUM
I'm thinking, I'm thinking – all that cake!
Here comes another idiot patrol.

Enter CLAUDIA *and* MARIA

BATES
Miss Claudia, Miss Maria.
CLAUDIA   Thank you, Bates.
We are accustomed to distinguishing.
BATES
What tales of revelry and junketing?
CLAUDIA
None. The men grow sick
With lust in the delay. We needed air.

KALLUM
Have it. We're done with it. Our blood has stopped.
MARIA
Unlikely, but this is some fahrenheit.
BATES
Certainly a night to make or break.
And how's Miss Zelda?
CLAUDIA   Zelda jaws with Fleck.
She spent the day with father collecting pebbles.
KALLUM
Time'd be better spent finding his marbles.
CLAUDIA
What did he say?
MARIA   Probably bouncer-talk.
I think I know who's coming.

Enter GLINE *and* SEWELL

GLINE
The Neins start to dispopulate their House,
Sewell! Is this the next act on the bill?
A presentation at the Court of Bates?
CLAUDIA
We so missed your company these moments,
We came to ask the whereabouts of vipers:
One trails money like a mild disease,
And one excretes small tumuli of verse.
Have you seen them, doorman?
KALLUM   Yes, in the wood.
SEWELL
Oh really. That a habitat of yours?
KALLUM
Of course it ain't.
SEWELL   Keep a civil tongue.
KALLUM
A civil tongue, sir, or a servile one?
GLINE
Woh, dictionary bouncers! Brave, brave!
Democracy of syllables – Fleckism!
CLAUDIA
We hoped for noblemen and we got reptiles.
GLINE
And so of course you come to Bates for breeding!

[173]

SEWELL
  Your judgement is polluted by our jest.
CLAUDIA
  Which one? The love, the lack of it, or both?
BATES (*to* MARIA)
  I don't know how you upper classes cope,
  So many sarcasms making a web.
MARIA
  Indeed it puzzles us.
GLINE   Our kiss, of course!
  Zelda's interdiction against lips
  Applies under her roof. Beneath the stars,
  Maria, we are free to –
MARIA   Man-fatigue.
  I was in conversation otherwise
  Engaged.
GLINE With whom? With Bates?
SEWELL   A famous wit.
KALLUM
  Don't do him down.
GLINE   I beg your pardon?
KALLUM   Beg?
  Oh grandchildren, I heard a rich man beg!
GLINE
  You must be drunk.
CLAUDIA   A pity your pretences
  Lack that excuse.
MARIA   Disturbances! Listen . . .
SEWELL
  Disturbances of what – of molecules?
MARIA
  Of course, but those would be inaudible.
SEWELL
  A walking faculty of chemistry.
BATES
  I heard something.
GLINE   Probably your voice,
  Or that of your offensive vice-bouncer.
CLAUDIA
  Suffer him to work, you rich man.
GLINE
  I suffer, I suffer!
KALLUM   Oh, a prophecy?

[174]

CLAUDIA
  That's forward of you.
SEWELL   Forward? On the block,
  With the axe raised!
KALLUM   The axe made of what?

Enter PADGET, *properly attired, carrying a black case*

PADGET
  Is this the mansion of the Viscount Nein?
  I do believe it is.
  You show surprise, and that surprises me.
  I promised I would come and so, I have.
  I hope I have enough now to prove
  The claim I make.
SEWELL   We do too, for your sake.
PADGET
  No. I'm hoping *you* believe, for your sake.
  Otherwise you may wake up tomorrow
  Places you did not expect to be,
  With people you did not expect to know.
GLINE
  What does he mean?
SEWELL   It's not her birthday now.
  There's no reason to be here, peasant.
PADGET   Oh?
  But you remained.
CLAUDIA   You have to let him in,
  Doormen, Zelda said so.
SEWELL   Zelda's sick.
  And it's contagious.
KALLUM   That's a lie, by the way.
GLINE
  Outrageous!
BATES   Welcome to the House –
GLINE   Enough!
  Another word, you'll never bounce again!
  Now, in my capacity as friend
  To Viscount Nein, and to his eldest daughter,
  I challenge this late guest to pay a fee
  In reparation for our wasted time!
  I could have made a million, and he
  Composed an entire epode. A thousand pounds!
SEWELL
  Double, treble that!

Enter FLECK

FLECK   Contrariwise,
  Lust-merchant, strike it out!
GLINE
  Oh God, a verbal forest come.
CLAUDIA   Oh Fleck,
  Water down these quarrels with a dull
  Dilution of long words.
FLECK   No call for such.
  Circumlocutions are superfluous.
  She spied him from the window, and she nodded.
  He is admitted. Doormen, part.
GLINE   Oh . . .
  Flecking Hell.
FLECK   You have your evidence?
PADGET
  If need be, yes.
FLECK   In that?
PADGET   If need be.
FLECK
  Ladies, escort him in.
  Conduct him to the Trophy Room, to wait.
CLAUDIA
  Poison outside, and who knows what within?
  At least we have one promise kept. Come through.

CLAUDIA *and* MARIA *escort* PADGET *into the house*

GLINE
  Why this smooth access, Fleck? Have you given up?
SEWELL
  We all desire the ultimate full stop
  Be put to this pretender.
FLECK   Follow me,
  Into the Lavender Room to hear of a plan.
  We may soon see the last of that man . . .

FLECK, GLINE *and* SEWELL *exit into the house*

BATES
  All sins accounted for, deadly and venal.
KALLUM
  They'll cancel out to nil.

He could have brought a gospel for his proof,
They'd pulp it back to its original
And pay him off.
BATES   So. We're finished here.
KALLUM
Not yet. If we can hover above the heat,
We'll profit, I should think, at the collapse.
BATES
A profit here would prove a loss, perhaps.

SCENE VI
Outside the house.

Four are silhouetted in a window. Enter PALGRAVE *with the empty wheelchair. She looks up at the window. The light goes out. There is more hissing from the bushes.* PALGRAVE *crouches down and tries to cover her eyes and ears at once. Enter* BISON *with the empty wheelbarrow*

BISON
Is it not Miss – Palgrave yet again?
PALGRAVE
Yes, M-Mr B-Bison – but look up there!
There are four people up there and none of the people
Is anything like the Viscount!
BISON   Nobody, lassie,
Is anything like the Viscount. I daresay
In another civilisation somewhere,
And at another time entirely someone
Was something like he is but one could not
Locate one here or, indeed, locate one . . . there.
PALGRAVE
There!

The light is on again, but nobody is there

BISON   I feel you may be mistaking a light
For a person, Miss – Palgrave. An easy mistake
To make but . . . misleading.
PALGRAVE   But also the bushes
Are whispering and hissing in the most
Disturbing way, Mr Bison!

[177]

BISON   It's only the wind,
  As I always say: it's only the wind. There,
  Said it.
PALGRAVE I don't want to work here any more!
  Everything I find I lose, and everything
  I lose I find is always coming back!

Four are silhouetted in another window, only for a moment

  There they are!
BISON   Where?
PALGRAVE   There! They're not there!
  See?
BISON No.
PALGRAVE   I'm going upstairs to pack,
  Mr Bison. I had a good time, but you can't work
  With people who are never there when you see them!

Exit PALGRAVE *to the house*

BISON
  I do concede that might be a drawback.
  I too have had my fair share of working
  Long hours for long invisible persons.
  I think it may be time to wheel my belongings
  Into another garden . . . altogether.
  Only the wind, or not.

As BISON *wheels his barrow off, the light goes on again, and
we see, in silhouette,* PADGET *set upon by* GLINE *and*
SEWELL *as* FLECK *looks on. The light goes out*

SCENE VII
The conservatory.

ZELDA *stirs the cauldron of wine*

ZELDA
  Zelda shall be Padget's wife,
  If she wants to, if she wants to,
  Zelda shall be Gline's and Sewell's

If she wants to, if she wants to,
Zelda shall be Fleck's and no one's
If she chooses, if she chooses,
Zelda Nein is twenty-one
An age ago, an age ago. Those stars,
There they are again!
I saw those stars forming a perfect Z.
They didn't wheel themselves into an N
While I was watching: N is for No Choice,
Z is for Zelda's Choice! Freer than air,
Freer than threats and promises, and as free
As day, light, life. Free as this.

She dips her finger in the doctored wine, and sucks it

Ha! I broke my own promise! We're doomed!

Enter FLECK

FLECK
The nerve! Unspeakable! He is without!
ZELDA
Well bring him in.
FLECK   I mean he came without!
Without a shred of evidence – unproven!
ZELDA
I don't believe it! Why would he come back?
FLECK
That's immaterial, ma chère! His game
Is over and his due payment near!
Bring him, fellow bachelors!

GLINE *and* SEWELL *haul* PADGET *in*

GLINE   Voilà!
We caught the rogue aping a gentleman.
SEWELL
One up from his monkey costume, Gline.
FLECK
Clarissa Zelda May Belinda Drummond
Overlongie Nein:
'Tis the trimestral night pursuivant on
This man's initial claim, sans precedent,
Anarchic and perverse and downright – wrong.
And – but here he is, he can speak for himself.
Master Padget. Let us have your proof.

[179]

PADGET
There are no proofs against such men as you.
GLINE
Whining, Padget? Show your evidence!
SEWELL
Your documents, your affidavits, Padget!
PADGET
Zelda, I had everything you asked for.
Everything in writing, as you desired.
These three men, for purposes I do not
Understand, knocked me down and stole them
After your sisters left.
ZELDA   Where are my sisters?
FLECK
I thought it meet to keep them out of here.
ZELDA
Tell them otherwise. Get them. Go!

Exit FLECK

GLINE
I don't believe my ears – did he just say –
SEWELL
That we attacked him? Slanderer!
ZELDA   The papers,
Where are they now?
GLINE   They never were. He lies
In desperation. His tale's ludicrous.
SEWELL
Spellbind us again: what did we do?
PADGET
You knocked me down and stole the things I had.
Then I smelt you burning them.
GLINE   Woh,
A fiery chapter! Aren't we the end?
PADGET
All that's left is where I stand and you stand.
SEWELL
Oh iron proof, the bells!

Enter CLAUDIA *and* MARIA

ZELDA   Claudia, Maria,
What did Padget have when he came back?

MARIA
A case. Like father used to have. A case.
CLAUDIA
A document case.
SEWELL   I saw no such thing.
CLAUDIA
Well, that's because you're a bloody liar.
ZELDA
Claudia!
MARIA No, it's true, Zelda. He is.
And so is William.
GLINE   True. My name is John.
ZELDA
Maria, did you see the documents?
MARIA
I saw a case. Is your name really John?
ZELDA
So where's the case?

Enter FLECK *with the case, which he reveals to be empty*

FLECK   Before your very eyes!
Null, and void.
SEWELL   Padget believed his charm
Would quite suffice. Ha! It's a vanity case.
GLINE
I never said he didn't have a case.
It looked easy to carry. No wonder.
CLAUDIA
Oh, Padget, you're a twister too. Oh no.
MARIA
I bet he's not called Padget, either.
FLECK   Well,
We are concluded on the formal side.
What remains is a matter –
ZELDA   These documents.
FLECK
Zelda, ma chère, we had just proven –
ZELDA   Shut up!
Sit on your chère, sir. I saw the contract.
Three nights ago I saw it.
CLAUDIA   Yes that's true,
It did exist!

FLECK   A trick of the light, ladies.
This man is clearly an illusionist.
ZELDA
I saw the contract. I recalled the rhyme.
FLECK (*aside*)
Are you insane as all the Family Nein?
You want to vindicate this man?
ZELDA   I'm scared.
If I believed I saw a thing that wasn't,
Surely – nothing is.
CLAUDIA   How dare you flash
These questions at her? I saw it too!
GLINE
Zelda, the crux is this:
There is now no evidence that this
Uninvited rambler ever wrote
Or said or did or saved or understood
Anything. He is merely unwelcome,
His shadow-play is lit from all sides
By lamps of truth. Now you are twenty-one
And I, your humble servant, proffer my arm.
SEWELL
Too soon! Unproffer it, jump back again.
FLECK
And I must deal – well, we must deal – with him.
SEWELL
Simplicity itself.
ZELDA   Stop – all of you!
As Mr Gline asserts, I am twenty-one
And the three nights are gone. Now I can choose
My partner for the first dance of the Ball,
And everything can start again.
CLAUDIA   Some Ball,
Sister: a ring of suitors and a ghost.
FLECK
Zelda, suspend your choice a while. A toast
Before you choose, wine for we bachelors,
And may the best man win!
GLINE   At it again,
Vinicultural Fleck?
SEWELL   What about him?
GLINE
Tongue-tied, Padget?
SEWELL   Where are your papers?

ZELDA   No!
  No wine before my choice is made.
PADGET   Zelda –
  It's time for me to go. I had a place
  To take you to but this is what has happened.
  Now I must bring it here.
FLECK   Enraging man!
ZELDA
  I will not dance with you.
  You are an advocate of nothing much.

PADGET, *who was leaving, pauses.* FLECK *has not realised*
ZELDA *is addressing not Padget, but him*

FLECK
  Yes, sir, begone!
ZELDA   You are a sheaf of things.
  You are a dull addendum. A shortfall.
FLECK
  A game, I think. Are we begun?
ZELDA   You are
  An unbeginning, an unending joke.
  You are a place we probably won't visit.
FLECK
  Zelda, ma chère –
ZELDA   I wave my hand through you,
  Fleck, my space, my freckler of white sheets,
  Spinner of policies – what does it mean
  Wherever I write my name? What does it do?
  How many nothings do I owe to you,
  Ink-dribbler, expediter, agent Fleck?
CLAUDIA
  Ha, ha, an avalanche of fact!
FLECK   Clearly
  A ruse of some description –
GLINE   Jolly fine
  Acting for a ruse!
ZELDA   Moneyed gent:
  What more do you believe your fortune means?
  Dead weight accumulated, roundabout
  Of gold, dream of zeroes upon zeroes:
  Show me money, then I will tear it.
GLINE
  Then I won't show it.

[183]

ZELDA   Then I won't believe it.
Value, Mr Gline, what is your value?
GLINE
Zelda, this test –
ZELDA   Is over and you failed.
GLINE
Damn you, there's plenty other fish.
MARIA   And snakes.
SEWELL
Zelda, this my fortune's undeserved.
ZELDA
I don't agree with that.
SEWELL   I'm humbly yours.
By process of elimination –
ZELDA   You
Proceed to yours, your fortune, well-deserved.
SEWELL
But I've a sonnet here!
ZELDA   Show it to me.

SEWELL *produces the sonnet.* ZELDA *snatches it*

ZELDA
I see nothing.
CLAUDIA Nor do I.
MARIA   Me neither.
SEWELL
You have it upside-down.
ZELDA   Oh no I don't.
I see nothing like this, like this, like this.
This is an abstract poem.
SEWELL   Then let me recite . . .
"A lover's kiss is –"
ZELDA   Whatever you say it is.
It doesn't mean you get one.
FLECK   I cannot
Permit this comic jest –
ZELDA   No jest for miles.
My choice is he who came with nothing, who has
Nothing but can now have the nothing
I'm fast becoming. Padget . . . will you dance?

Exit ZELDA *and* PADGET, *slowly, arm-in-arm. There is a
very long pause*

[184]

FLECK

I'm at a loss for words.

CLAUDIA   Obviously not.

"Zelda Padget"? Mother will go mad.

MARIA

I hope so, then she'll get on well with father.

CLAUDIA (*to the* MEN)

See you later, at the wedding Ball!

Second and third and fourth ain't bad at all!

Exit CLAUDIA *and* MARIA

SEWELL

A plague of Neins – a culture gone to seed!

GLINE

Resenting my success – envy indeed!

FLECK

A joke, a test, my friends – nothing to heed.

She knows it'll get her talked about all week.

She wants to know which one of us will wait,

And, speaking personally, –

GLINE   A clerk in hell!

Sewell, I'm sick of this professional.

SEWELL

Seconded, Gline. Let's split the odds between us,

Scuttle Padget, let the better man win.

FLECK

What do you mean?

SEWELL   It's late, Fleck. Go home.

FLECK

I count this house my home.

SEWELL   Then you miscount.

FLECK

Do nothing hasty, fellows, I have a plan –

SEWELL

Good health, Fleck!

GLINE   Cheers, and down the hatch!

They duck FLECK's *head in the cauldron*

Champagne for us, now Fleck has corked the wine!

SEWELL

Cork has flecked the wine? Champagne for us!

[185]

FLECK
I drank the wine. I cannot tell a lie.
I talk too much. In fact I am a prat.
SEWELL
Now Fleck has got a handle on the facts,
We mustn't miss our chance. Once the peasant
Has met with a sad accident – quite possible –
Then you and I are left in the Grand Final.
My bet's on you.
GLINE   Oh no, she has a weakness
For fine words. You should approach her first.
SEWELL
With your advantage you are modest, Gline.
Go straight to her and offer the globe.
GLINE
I wouldn't dream. Go, serenade her stupid.
SEWELL
Bribe her bedward, merchant, with a backhand.
GLINE
Sewell, dribble stanzas till she swims.
SEWELL
Gline, dazzle her blind with tacky gems.
GLINE
Oh, pen her in the arbour with your lays!
SEWELL
Crap your gold and fertilise her days!

Enter CLAUDIA *and* MARIA

CLAUDIA
My noble gentlemen,
As you now know, our sister made her choice
And is now dreaming of her wedded bliss
Under the stars with Padget. You, therefore,
The extraneous males, are invited to go home
And, if you so desire, collect some cake
On leaving.
MARIA   Wrapped in tissue that's provided.
The cake, that is, not you.
GLINE   A further test?
FLECK
Two plus two plus minus two is two.

CLAUDIA
What's wrong with Fleck?
MARIA   Nothing, two's correct.
SEWELL (*aside*)
Another test? I've had enough of this.
Gline, we won't be going out dry-lipped!
GLINE
Carriages at once!

SEWELL *grabs* CLAUDIA, GLINE *grabs* MARIA

Your mother's spitting image!
CLAUDIA   Home to Hell!
I use my mouth to bite with, not kiss!
MARIA
Vicious Gline, mad John, uncaring William!
Three times a villain!
GLINE   Three strokes of luck!
CLAUDIA
Your real self! – Do something, Fleck!
FLECK
Fighting has broken out but I am not
Personally involved.

Enter BATES *and* KALLUM

BATES   Assault and battle!

GLINE *and* SEWELL *release the sisters*

GLINE (*to* BATES)
Back away, you oaf! I have friends!
KALLUM
Not here, not there – write postcards to 'em all!
SEWELL
Since when have bouncers had the rights of entry?
BATES
Since screams were heard by bouncers.
CLAUDIA   Thank you, Bates.
(*to the* SUITORS) Your absences are urgently required.
KALLUM
Enforceable, if necessary.
CLAUDIA   No,
Noble Sewell is a man of sense,
And sensible of Bates's strength, and yours.

SEWELL
  And of a House diseased, maniacal.
  Come on, Gline, let's get our coats. Bouncers,
  We'll settle this at a more even time.
KALLUM
  By all means try.
BATES   We're only doing our job.
GLINE
  Of course, of course, hard labourers of the world.
  Come on, Sewell, let's talk virginity:
  How it both sharpens and blunts desire.

Exit GLINE *and* SEWELL

CLAUDIA
  Have you a knife?
BATES   I think they've gone.
CLAUDIA   The cake.
BATES
  In that case, yes.
CLAUDIA   Then follow us inside.
FLECK
  I want a big piece, all for me.
CLAUDIA   You do?
  Well then, you come too.

Exit CLAUDIA, MARIA, BATES, KALLUM *and* FLECK

SCENE VIII
Outside the house.

*By now there is a great deal of strange disturbance in the
windows and in the bushes of the Nein Estate: lights going
on and off, silhouettes appearing and disappearing, the sudden and brief laughter of invisible persons.* BISON *and* PAL-
GRAVE *come out of the house with many suitcases and exit
at a run*

SCENE IX

ZELDA *leads* PADGET *into the conservatory*

ZELDA
  That was the first dance but not the last.
PADGET
  There is no more to do here.
ZELDA   Not for you.
  How long have I left the other men inside?
  An hour? Half of an hour?
PADGET   Halve again.
ZELDA
  I wonder if that's enough. I think it's enough.
  Now you can go.
PADGET   Go?
ZELDA   Right back in the forest,
  Padget – don't pretend you thought I'd thrown
  A celebrity and a millionaire away
  For you! You are the end, you are a puzzle,
  Padget, with your memories and rhymes,
  But I am the Viscountess of all the Games
  And make my choices as I choose to make them!
  Now wasn't it all a scene they'll never forget?
  How I shocked a hundred guests with a poor
  Peasant! Did you see their faces? Padget,
  You should have seen them . . . Now, that's long enough.
  Goodbye to you and your promise of love!
PADGET   Love?
  I never mentioned love.
  Nobody has ever mentioned love.
  The promise never mentioned love for you,
  Not on my part, nor between us two.
  Love makes no appearance in this place.
  I have never met love here. I have never
  Met love anywhere. I do not love.
  I keep a different kind of faith.
  I made an undertaking. An oath.
  I kept a promise. You did not. So.
  Now you must take what has to come to those
  Who snap what they have sworn in their own names,
  So cut ties of blood. There is a price.

ZELDA No!
  Padget, you old mystery, it was only
  Another charade, and I was acting too!
  Stay, sit at my right – I'll . . . come with you!

She makes to leave but enter GLINE *and* SEWELL

GLINE
  Whore, where's your father?
SEWELL Out at night?
  Let's join him, Gline!
GLINE Where are your father's guns?
ZELDA
  My father's sleeping!
SEWELL Fine! We'll wake and ask him.
  In the Madhouse of the Neins only the mad
  Will tell the truth. Come on, Gline: a-hunting.

Exit GLINE *and* SEWELL

ZELDA
  What's coming to an end? Oh Padget, come back!
  I'm wrong, wrong, wrong, I retract it all! I
  Unsay, undo, uneat, undrink, unlie!
  I'm ready to be true, and good, and – true . . .

Enter BATES *and* KALLUM, *eating cake*

BATES
  The path of true love never did –
ZELDA You two!
  The gentleman ran off – I want him stopped!
  He said I broke the promise but I hadn't
  And I don't mean to, so it's not fair! He went
  By Giles's Path, and walking fast: where it bends,
  The sudden marshes – you should catch him there –
  Don't injure him, don't let him go – I need
  To see the gentleman and tell the truth!
  Now hurry: I'll be waiting here. We'll stand
  Together at this spot in half an hour!
  You haven't moved!
KALLUM Brr. A dangerous night.

ZELDA
  Gold! I quite forgot – one second!

ZELDA *runs out*

KALLUM   So.
  A task not unexpected, finally.
  Have you your knife?
BATES   There's cake inside.
KALLUM   Not that.
BATES
  Oh. Persuasion? Making him return?
KALLUM
  Have you got ears? She said she wanted him
  "Stopped", she and I understand each other.
BATES
  She said "Don't injure him."
KALLUM   "Don't let him go"
  Is what she said. And "Don't leave an injury" –
  For any to see.
BATES   She needed to see him!
KALLUM
  She said "the gentle*men*" – the two peacocks.
BATES
  She said they'd stand together at this spot,
  In half an hour.
KALLUM   She said *we'd* stand together,
  Me and her and you, for requital.
BATES   Oh.
  Well I do know Giles's Path. But it seems a shame.
KALLUM
  Work is work, Bates. Black or white or grey.
BATES
  Indeed. Well he was the uninvited kind.

Enter ZELDA

ZELDA
  Gold, now run, by Giles's Path!
BATES   Lady, –
KALLUM
  Come on, Bates, we've got a job to do!

KALLUM *and* BATES *take the money and run*

ZELDA
I'll give him what he wants, whatever he wants!
I'll try to understand whatever he means!

Enter CLAUDIA *and* MARIA

CLAUDIA
Zelda, alone out here? Where's Padget?
The men for miles around are turned bestial.
ZELDA
Promises to keep. He's gone away.
MARIA
And the men you hired?
ZELDA   Gone to bring him back.
CLAUDIA
Don't lie to us! Promises were broken
And on our name itself: now there's chaos!
The gardener has gone, and all his plants
Have moved at least a yard away from the house!
MARIA
The maid left a note but it was blank.
Mother cannot find father, and we cannot
Find either father or mother!
CLAUDIA   The forest is wild
And glowing, Zelda, and Fleck uses only
Single syllables! Nobody should have gone.
ZELDA
Well they all did.

Enter FLECK *with the remains of the cake*

FLECK   Here I come, with the cake.
CLAUDIA
Where are the others, Fleck?
FLECK   I like cake.
I am not liked as much as I'd like to be.

Enter GLINE *and* SEWELL, *armed*

CLAUDIA
Heavens, a shooting party!
MARIA   Father's guns!
GLINE
Tally-ho, we're bouncer-hunting, girls!

SEWELL
  Your father needs some fresh heads on his walls!
  We asked politely and he said "Platoon."
  "All present!" I replied, and he said "Full Moon!"
GLINE
  We'll catch you at some other Birthday Balls!

Exit GLINE *and* SEWELL

CLAUDIA
  We've got to stop them!
MARIA   How?
  They are men, and have decided what they want.
CLAUDIA
  What if they kill the bouncers?
ZELDA   Then there'll be
  No bouncers, but we don't need any bouncers.
  Nobody's coming now.
MARIA   At least the cake
  Hasn't gone to waste. Sisters, a bit?
FLECK
  I think I'm going to put my face in it.
MARIA
  Fleck is getting curiously candid.
CLAUDIA
  Zelda, what happened to Padget?
ZELDA
  He left. I don't know why. Maybe he hates us.
CLAUDIA
  But the first dance! Didn't he fall in love?
ZELDA
  Of course he did! I'll be a Viscountess
  One day. But you can ask him
  Yourself when they catch up with him. They will.
CLAUDIA
  Not if Gline and Sewell get to them first.
MARIA
  Claudia, listen – those were human cries!
CLAUDIA
  Heavens, yes, but whose?
ZELDA   One out of five.
FLECK
  Leaves four, which is divisible by two.

CLAUDIA
  A breaking branch? Or was it another cry?
  A crack of something?
MARIA   Not a surprise in a wood.
CLAUDIA
  Or was it a shot? We ought to go inside.
MARIA
  It wasn't a shot. But then, we may be needed.
  They're not my cup of tea, but they are people.
ZELDA
  Or were people.
CLAUDIA   Zelda, what have you done?
ZELDA
  Lived longer, three days longer.
MARIA   Now it's quiet.

The SISTERS *huddle together as the lights fade. Suddenly
there is a bright light in an upper window, and processional
music begins. The* GUESTS *of the Birthday Ball of Zelda Nein
are promenading past the window, in silhouette. The music
stops suddenly and the lights go out. The* SISTERS *wake*

CLAUDIA
  It's been an hour.
MARIA   No more than half an hour.
CLAUDIA
  Perhaps they're all in a glade, gossiping
  About our father and not dissimilar sister.
MARIA
  That would explain the quiet. As would death.
FLECK
  My name is Fleck. I'm cold. I want my mother.
CLAUDIA
  Poor agent, all his syllables dispersed.
  Fleck, you conversationalist of yore,
  Go to the Peppermint Room and look for the Viscount.
  Anything could come, we are undefended,
  And the forest seems alive.
MARIA   It is alive.
FLECK
  I'll go to the Peppermint Room and look for the Viscount.

Enter BATES, *breathless, shocked, caked in mud*

BATES
  Various horrors! Am I among the Neins?
CLAUDIA
  It's Bates!
ZELDA   It isn't Padget.
MARIA   Whatever happened.
CLAUDIA
  Whatever happened?
ZELDA   Did you earn your money?
FLECK
  This man is covered in mud. I find that funny.
  I'm off to the Peppermint Room to look for the Viscount.

Exit FLECK

BATES
  Every time it was Padget it wasn't Padget!
  But every time it was! I didn't reckon
  You meant for us to waste him, lady, but he –
  Kallum, my underperson, he thought you did –
  Want for us to waste him! We went quick,
  Chockerblock as you said! and down by the Giles's
  Just where the sudden marshes are we saw him,
  Padget, and I say "Stop there, stop there, young 'un!"
  But it's too late, Kallum draws and jumps him,
  And "Done", he says, and it's over in a matter!
  Body – drops, floats onto the swamp,
  And turns and it ain't Padget but it was Padget!
  Before, I mean. When it sank it was the poet.
  Few bubbles, and that was that.
CLAUDIA
  Sewell, oh no.
MARIA   He was gunning for them, remember.
CLAUDIA
  Even so.
BATES The other comes out of the trees,
  Pounces on Kallum, shouts, "Die in the shadows,
  Padget!" but it was Kallum, it weren't Padget!
  They fought and started to sink, and both shouting
  "Die, Padget!" "Die, peasant!" and fighting,
  Sinking and fighting, sinking and fighting! I tried
  To get between – but the millionaire and Kallum –
  And they were gone, and ladies –
  He would have been a credit to all bouncers,

[195]

Ladies, but he couldn't move in the end
With all his fighting, and then – well that's the story.
And the rich man went too. Which reminds me.
Lady, here's your rather muddy money.

BATES *throws it down and falls to his knees*

I must apologise for my –
ZELDA   Sir . . .
We are sorry you lost your friend.
BATES   But it ain't all!
People all round the marshes, all small –
Dwarfs, old women, horrid, gnarled cases,
Gentleman with a cord around his neck,
An admiral you can see the moon right through,
A lad whose skin – oh ladies,
But lots, a manifold! Many, many
Manifolds! Not one in proper attire,
But there's jackets everywhere, jackets and hats,
Greatcoats and gowns of satin hanging
In all the trees or spread on the swamp like, ladies,
Lily flowers! A terrible infrestation!

Enter FLECK

MARIA
The death has loosened his mind.
CLAUDIA   Or coloured it in.
BATES
I wasn't seeing things! I was seeing – things!
And they were moving up the hill not down it!
CLAUDIA
That means towards –
FLECK
              "Padget goes and Padget gives
              Hazel to the man who hangs,
              Potion to a plaguy boy,
ZELDA (*joining in*)
              Hops to the hag on the yellow crag
              And drums to the ghost at sea.
              Zelda swears on her Father's House
              She shall be mine, or pay the price."
CLAUDIA   They're alive
Oh heavens, in the forest.

MARIA   And heading here.
CLAUDIA
  We'll all be scared to death!
ZELDA   No, Claudia,
  It's me they're coming for.
  What did you do but get born to a House
  Without an heir, without a future, with nothing
  Left but a past, and money? It's me they want.
  To break me for I broke a girl's promise.
  That's the compassion of Fortune, to pick me
  Blindfold, out of a bag.
  Now for the ghost and hag, and the suffering,
  But maybe one thing. Maybe one thing.
  We could, whatever we do, show a – kind face
  To whatever comes, sickly, hungry or cold:
  We have a house, we have all the grand food,
  We have all the heat and light a thousand'd need.
  If every moth and fly comes fluttering here
  To our one lamp we'll let it shine, open
  The gates and doors to them all, open the curtains
  In all the vacant rooms – the Apricot Room,
  The Lime-and-Silver Room and the Black Room,
  Shine the light on the pool and allow as many
  In as come, however, whatever, where from –
  And live among them now as well as we can.
CLAUDIA
  Zelda, Maria, come!
  We'll change the House of the Neins to a huge home!
MARIA
  And show the golden basin to this one.
  Come on, sir. Your bouncing days are done.

CLAUDIA, MARIA *and* BATES *exit to the house*

FLECK
  It seems to have got warmer. I am not sad.
ZELDA
  And nor am I. I'm ready. From the wood
  Come what, come anything, I will be ready.
  If I am cursed I'll vanish cursed, but vanish
  At my best, be a – loss to the new world.
  The old days are over.
FLECK   It is today.
  My name is Fleck. I have some words to say.

[197]

ZELDA
  Say on, you strange man. Now, work begins.

Exit ZELDA

FLECK
  Three hours pass as I stand here. Fresh winds
  Blow from the north. I hear the sisters at work.
  I hear the noise and rustling in the dark,
  But three more hours go by, and the dawn comes up.
  The noises lessen, lessen, lessen, and stop.
  Whatever was held against this House has passed.
  Nobody comes from the wood. Not even a ghost.
  The light is pure blue, and the night is gone.
  I have my bowtie on.
  When morning comes they find him in his chair.
  The Viscount Nein is dead. There is no heir.
  There are no men for miles around but me
  And old Bates. And we will all take tea
  Before we go wherever we go. Soon
  The wine will have worn off, I know. By noon
  I'll be a different man, a new man.
  I hope to be a good one if I can.
  My name is Fleck. I'm me.
  And in I go to breakfast.

Exit FLECK *to the house. Lights fade*

LAST CROSSING OF ISOLDE

for ANTHONY
AND
HELEN SYCAMORE

LAST CROSSING OF ISOLDE:
Author's Note

The works upon which this play is based are Gottfried von Strassburg's 13th Century verse 'Tristan' (the last sixth of which was never completed) and Thomas of England's earlier 'Tristran' (of which, by a miraculous coincidence, only the last sixth exists, so that the two fragments form a relatively coherent whole). I have tried to combine the ironic tone of Gottfried's wonderfully humane and secular poem, with the actual plot of Thomas's religiously orthodox, less imaginative work.

A reader would benefit from some familiarisation with the Gottfried/Thomas version of the legend, which is also, incidentally, the version drawn upon most by Wagner for his own 'Tristan und Isolde'.

The precocious Tristan, born in Parmeny (probably somewhere in Northern France) is abducted from his kingdom in childhood by some Norwegian sailors. After a series of adventures, he becomes the favoured knight in the court of King Mark of Cornwall, fighting his battles, controlling his barons, running his errands. One such errand finds him sailing to Ireland to woo – on Mark's behalf – the beautiful Princess Isolde, known, like her mother before her, to possess supernatural healing powers.

The Irish court, in deference to various acts performed by Tristan, reluctantly surrenders the even more reluctant Isolde, and she sails ruefully to Cornwall with her cousin and maidservant Branwen. Isolde's mother has entrusted Branwen with a love-potion, which, when drunk, will cause Isolde instantly to fall in love with King Mark – but disaster strikes when the ship berths in a cove. Branwen and the crew have left the ship to swim, leaving behind Tristan, Isolde, the love-potion, and a young servant who, in ignorance, offers them the potion when they ask for wine. Tristan and Isolde fall ecstatically in love.

For years, they continue an adulterous passion under the nose of the naïve King Mark at the Cornish court, but finally, even the King sees what is happening, and Tristan is banished. He goes to the Castle of Karke (in Brittany), where, finally despairing of ever seeing Isolde again, he marries her namesake Isolde of the White Hands, whom he does not love. When he is mortally wounded fighting a giant (Estult), he realises that only Isolde (the Irish) can save him, with her dual powers of healer and lover. He calls to his bedside his young friend Cardin (brother of Isolde of the White Hands) and begs him to go to Cornwall, abduct Isolde and bring her to Brittany in disguise. Cardin must not take longer than forty days, and when his ship is in sight of shore, he should hoist a white flag if Isolde is on board – but a black one if she is not, so that Tristan can die in the knowledge that she will never come. He admits he has never loved Cardin's sister. But she, Isolde of the White Hands, has overheard everything . . .

This scene is where 'Last Crossing of Isolde' begins.

Thomas's story does mention the French merchants on Cardin's ship, employed to conceal his actual mission. Captain Clement, his cabin-boy Valentin and the English amateur actors who stow away on board, are my modern additions to the tale.

LAST CROSSING OF ISOLDE

Dramatis Personae:

ISOLDE, the Fair Maid of Ireland, Queen of Cornwall and England, lover of Tristan

TRISTAN, of Parmeny, banished from England, now Duke of Brittany

ISOLDE of the WHITE HANDS, Duchess of Brittany, wife of Tristan

CARDIN, her brother, a young duke

CAPTAIN CLEMENT, a mariner

VALENTIN, his cabin boy

HENRI RAVAL, a French troubadour

YVETTE, his girlfriend, in his troupe

GUIDO, a Spanish musician in Raval's troupe

THE COUNT OF CLUBS, an old man in Raval's troupe

FOL OF ROL, a wit in Raval's troupe

HENRY ORMOND, an English amateur actor

MRS MARGARET ORMOND, his wife

ELINOR, their elder daughter

KARA, their younger daughter

DR VOGEL, a family friend of the Ormonds

BRANWEN, cousin and companion of Queen Isolde

A YOUNG LOOKOUT

ACT I

SCENE I
The Castle of Karke, Brittany, one morning.

TRISTAN *lies in the dark. Light up suddenly on the face of*
ISOLDE, *the* FAIR MAID OF IRELAND, *elsewhere on the*
stage

TRISTAN
  Isolde!

The face disappears

       Isolde? – Isolde.

Morning light slowly up. Enter ISOLDE OF THE WHITE
HANDS

WHITE HANDS   Lord,
  You called my name again. I was asleep
  But it fell clearly, as if a light through woods
  And here I am. If you call from sleep
  Or cry in the day the same will happen: I.
TRISTAN
  What, did I say "White Hands"?
WHITE HANDS   You said my name.
TRISTAN
  Why would I say "Duchess of Brittany"
  Either asleep or aloud? You are always there
  In that room, in your ducal quarters, here
  In this castle, in Brittany . . . in Brittany.
WHITE HANDS
  It was my name.
TRISTAN   If you will always come
  Why should I cry?
WHITE HANDS You cried out "Isolde".
  You cried out "Isolde" and I woke.
TRISTAN
  I cried out Isolde and *you* woke?
WHITE HANDS
  Woke to help if help was needed, Lord,
  Your fever high or the blood pressing again,
  Or only to talk. Of Brittany, of the days.

[205]

TRISTAN
   What's to say of the days. I lie here,
   And in them I get worse.
WHITE HANDS   Brittany prays.
TRISTAN
   Prays? Why prays? For this? – Oh listen to me,
   Half a man again, stirring, sweating,
   Cursing. Duchess of Brittany,
   Forgive all this, this battering through to day,
   Making me this, this wretched – half a man.
WHITE HANDS
   I understand – the fever – I understand.
   It was a dreadful wound.
   It wasn't healed by the twelve finest doctors?
TRISTAN
   Healed by six, unhealed by six. They work
   In even teams, lady, one to sew,
   The next to rip, the third to sew again,
   The fourth to shake his head and rip and so on
   To the twelfth, who tears and leaves.
WHITE HANDS   I'll bring another,
   A thirteenth who will close the sore forever.
TRISTAN
   Spare me the thirteenth doctor. He would find
   An immortalising draught, get me to drink it,
   Then getting a next opinion bleed it out.
WHITE HANDS
   Are you bleeding, Tristan?
TRISTAN   Yes, Isolde –
   Duchess of Brittany: breakfast your dark eyes.

*He throws off his fur covering. The white sheet beneath is
speckled with blood, near the wound in his groin*

   Scientific knowledge is a blessing.
   Observe the sweet activities of colours:
   The white loses faith in white. It lets,
   Lamely, the angry little redness dart
   And dot at will. The white, displaced,
   Glad to be free of the pain of a pure white,
   Holidays in my face. And the question is,
   And easy as hunting trees, from where did the colour
   Drain and the only answer to that is: Tristan.

WHITE HANDS
  Doctors, my Lord, doctors –
TRISTAN   Speed the journey.
WHITE HANDS
  Oh Tristan.
TRISTAN   Right the second time.
WHITE HANDS   Tristan,
  Let me lie here too in the night. I know,
  I know there can't be married love between us
  While you lie fevered, pale, uncured but Lord
  There's other love than that.
TRISTAN   There is other love.
WHITE HANDS
  It could be healing love.
TRISTAN   Some other love
  Could be healing love, yes. Science
  Has shrugged and got his coat and made excuses
  And headed for Germany, but we can die
  Intoning songs and making the wild guesses.
  Dress me in iris, nail a clove of garlic
  Solemnly to the bed and back away;
  Bring every mumbling crumbling clairvoyante
  From the one sea to the other to do their long
  Ludicrous work. – Ah, White Hands,
  Forgive me again. This mind lurches and runs
  Clumsily away amusing itself. You
  Merited better.
WHITE HANDS   Merited?
TRISTAN   Those white hands
  Are perfect white. They shouldn't have to meet
  The soiling hues of dry-brown, hot-yellow
  Leaking from this hull.
WHITE HANDS   But I believe,
  Tristan, I believe. It isn't a guess.
TRISTAN
  Then do believe. Perhaps this will recover.
WHITE HANDS
  You shall, and I shall be your lover then
  As you desired when we were married. – Cruel,
  The poison of a giant I never saw,
  A giant you defeated, should have spun
  A barring web the very night of our wedding.
  A tipped dagger!
TRISTAN   Duchess, yes, it's cruel.

WHITE HANDS
But there is other love. I'll fetch you a new
Sheet, Tristan, and burn this into the air.
TRISTAN
For me to gulp again at a longer hour.
WHITE HANDS
Try to be still, think of the light things
There are: think of the clear light, –
TRISTAN   Isolde:
When you come back, do so with your brother
Cardin. Leave us together
To chat awhile; to talk nonsense awhile,
Jumble my mind from this – talk
Brittany gossip, fool the slithering minutes
Before they catch my eye and stop and burn.
WHITE HANDS
I could talk for you, fool them, Tristan.
TRISTAN
You, Duchess, have earned an hour of freedom
From this fuming, beached hulk of a knight.
I mean it, go, walk on the sand – my love.
Bring Cardin, leave him here.

WHITE HANDS *kisses* TRISTAN's *brow, and exits with the*
white sheet

TRISTAN
Tristan again. Not anything but Tristan.
. . . Tristan, is it? Heights of the morning, Tristan.
We're bringing you two choices now, Tristan.
You are a princely hero: may we set them
Down in this castle now? So, Tristan,
Here is the first: we have called it a beautiful day.
A leopard sun is blazing on Brittany,
The green hills, the glittering sea, the red
Stone ramparts of Karke. This is your part
In this our beautiful day – you will love a girl
Who is far away and married to the king
Of a country that would hang you downside up
Were it to see your smiling face, then laugh
To see you equally grinning to the end.
But lord, you are safely melted to your bed,
In Brittany, where you will swallow and hurt.
Choler and bile you will ship, turn into a curt

And churlish invalid, scorning a wife
Wholly innocent of the one matter.
This isn't all, Tristan, it'll hurt, Tristan.
The days will think of lengthening and they will.
You will be most heroically, nobly ill,
Prayed in vain for, witch-doctored and mourned
While still in open pain and sighing "Isolde"
In earshot of a blank, caring face.
Your hands will be: one, ice;
The other as if it lately shook the Devil's.
You feel you may die here.
Tristan, we offer you all of this, Tristan,
With our first choice. We call it a beautiful day.
– All quiet, it seems. The second choice is simply
What it says: a second, a second of seeing
What's not remotely there: a face. And that
At the gate of night. Two choices: light
And everything you see? Or the jailing dark
And the one thing that isn't. Take your time,
Tristan, for we are standing here, Tristan.

Enter CARDIN *and* WHITE HANDS

CARDIN
    Good morning, Lord. It isn't hard to find me.
    I await the fast-approaching news that the fever
    Is dead as Giant Estult and his six brothers.
    Or as Dwarf Tristan, whose fault the fever was.
TRISTAN
    No fault of his, we helped him for his name,
    Nor ours the brothers were too strong for him.
    All dead now anyway, but us, and the poison.
CARDIN
    I'm sorry, Lord. I should start the day again!
TRISTAN   For pity's sake do not.
CARDIN   But you seem better.
TRISTAN
    I seem alive. Your sister,
    My seeing her in the morning holds a glow
    Briefly to this face and a colour pulses.
    But Cardin, tell the truth of your two eyes:
    Am I not scarily white?
CARDIN   That – is the case.
    Blanched, Lord, yes. Though it's also

A light that shames me, since I was at hand
When you were dealt this –
TRISTAN   When I was dealt this hand.
Cardin, cut your sister free of here.
CARDIN
Isolde, your Lord wishes you away.

While CARDIN *speaks,* WHITE HANDS *makes to leave, but
changes her mind and hides, listening*

She suffers your ordeal. She aches to know
What you will do: whether you mean to die
Inconsolable, for the deep reasons,
Or turn monk, be lost to her that way.
She loves you and does not know what I know.
TRISTAN
If any do, you are not Cardin.
CARDIN
None do. I am. We are alone in Brittany
With that.
TRISTAN   I always was alone in Brittany
With you, young friend. Without you I would long
Have withered or been waylaid by some hireling
Smarting for I lopped his Head of State,
Or by a giant wading with his grudges.
CARDIN
Those words are torture. I was there when this –
TRISTAN
Yes, and here I am. Had you not been,
Tristan, Dwarf Tristan, Giant Estult
And his six brothers had cosily expired
In one scarlet minute. But I live.
And what is more, Cardin, I choose to live.
CARDIN
You choose? Then it must be!
TRISTAN   It must be.
I do not like the choices given me.
CARDIN
Given?
TRISTAN   The real is hell, the other unreal.
I choose to live. I choose to heal. Now,
Listen. If you don't I may yet die.
You – are tied in the act that may save me.
You have your secret.

CARDIN   You told me: like a coin
  Deep at heart but evergreen, with a blinding
  Light on one face and on the other written
  "Isolde, the Fair Maid of Ireland".
TRISTAN   A coin?
  Did I say that? Then friend, become a great
  Bank of secrets now, a hoard, a whole
  Treasury. You have to go to England.
CARDIN
  I have to –
TRISTAN Have to stay silent a while.
  There is a world of people not to tell.
  Your sister's duchess of that world as well.
  My two old friends at Karke: these must be
  Grand Dukes of the Unawareness. One
  Is Curvenal, my old tutor; the other
  The captain of my flagship. Either
  Is too well-known in England, or, more exactly:
  Cornwall.
CARDIN She is Queen of Cornwall.
TRISTAN   "She"
  Does not exist, and you said nothing then.
  And nothing now. I'm telling you the simplest
  First and the most difficult last.
  You murmur while I tell you I may live.
CARDIN
  Forgive –
TRISTAN Find a captain unknown.

Enter CAPTAIN CLEMENT, *elsewhere on the stage, in other*
light

  Unknown at court, unknown at any court;
  A man apparently without a past,
  With no obvious mark but that of a life
  Passed in the main at sea,
  Unknown, even, to me,
  Who'd seem in his very eyes to possess a secret
  Certain to die with him: a whole lifetime
  To last silent as you last this minute.
  Find an unknown captain of a silence
  Infinite, Cardin. And find a boy.

Enter VALENTIN, *who stands by the* CAPTAIN

None of the Breton lads, let the Captain choose
A boy inland, afraid and mutely loyal
As he himself is dumbly knowledgeable.
These two alone to man from experience;
My flagship sails itself. But you need others
For other purposes. Some young and strong
Dissemblers, jongleurs, actors – take
Actors: there is a troupe from deep in the woods
To the far south-west. Curvenal saw them play,
Said they could change to anything, be any,
Jump: in a second, King, in a second, Villain,
In half a second a pitiful crawling creature.
They were seen travelling lately in Parmeny,
But never were further north and are mostly young.
Pay them into your crew. They must be strong
Enough to crew a ship, or can act that too.

CARDIN
You've mentioned them and so has Curvenal.

TRISTAN
Find them, Cardin.

CARDIN   One is called Raval.

Enter RAVAL, YVETTE, GUIDO *and* THE COUNT OF CLUBS

TRISTAN
Whatever they are, turn them into merchants,
For you are crossing the sea to land at Cornwall.
This is all you know so far, and all
They'll ever know, whatever they may guess.
But guard them in your service, Cardin:
I love such players, and, whatever happens,
Do set them free in France.

Lights down, and lights up immediately on RAVAL'S
TROUPE

SCENE II
The harbour at Cornwall, thirty-five days later.

Enter FOL OF ROL, *with a sack*

FOL
Are we arrived or are we about to leave?

This Corny-wall's the same, cold and lonely;
No change there, Raval, and the air's foul.
You all look the same; I expected that.
YVETTE
What's he bleating on about?
FOL   The hull!
The hold, the hull, the – where-everything-is!
The keep, the depot, amis – our merchandise!
RAVAL
You saw it, Fol? It's quite impressive, hein?
YVETTE
Which particular reptile's chosen tonight
To travel north up him? What's eating him?
FOL
It all looks the same! The merchandise!
A week in Corny-wall, doing deals with pigs
For birds, silk, plate, wine, and Raval –
Our merchandise is all exactly the same!
RAVAL
The same, yes. Exactly the same, no.
CLUBS
It's nearly exactly the same.
RAVAL   Thank you, Clubs.
And now give me a moment.
YVETTE
– What are we waiting for?
RAVAL   Unsplitting the hair.
Fine, that's better. Friend, Fol-de-Rol,
Fol of the beautiful lowland town of Rol,
Let me explain. A week ago tonight,
You may remember our mournful-looking employer
Shunting us off that boat to trip over
On Cornwall, England, the North. And there we were.
I, your leader, pushing my crates of plates
Made in Tours, Yvette and her Spanish falcons
Caged and clearly spawned in the worst fleshpots
Of the white south, and Guido, who'd know about that,
Positively loaded down with vino,
And positively throbbing with the prospect
Of ripping off the Cornish something rotten.
You, of course, had special dispensation
To forget about being a merchant and try and steal.
But I forgot the Count of Clubs.

[213]

CLUBS   Blue silk!
  I was a merchant selling a blue silk!
YVETTE
  Still are, Clubs, we're only halfway home.
RAVAL
  With us so far, Fol?
FOL   I recall all that,
  Raval, but now I look in the – holding hull, –
RAVAL
  And see the following?
  Cracked plates from Tours, damaged silk
  Of a colour not unakin to blue and a choir
  Of dago hunting birds. Is that it?
FOL
  That's about it.
RAVAL   And you reckon Time has stopped,
  Turned around and tiptoed off embarrassed.
FOL
  I was taken aback, –
YVETTE   We bought the things we sold.
RAVAL
  Well, Clubs saw a blue silk he found nostalgic.
  Couldn't place it, had to buy it, bought it
  Off a Corn. No doubt the discerning gent
  Who bought my crockery, re-enamelled and sold it
  Yesterday to Yvette.
YVETTE   It looked different.
  At least I flogged those birds.
RAVAL   Dangerous words.
GUIDO
  Pardonne, Yvetta. A romany say they is flightless
  Dancing kind of birds.
YVETTE   You didn't buy them.
GUIDO   No.
  I did. And then they flies a bit, and then
  They comes back to the cage and I close them.
RAVAL
  You up with us so far, Fol of Rol?
FOL
  I'm with you: plate for birds, birds for wine,
  Silk for silk. What did you get, Raval?
RAVAL
  Drunk, but I deserved to by this time.
  What did you steal, felon of a Fol of Rol?

Look familiar, Guido?

YVETTE   Bloody hell.

RAVAL

Splendid, we have homing wine as well,
And all are safely back. Apologies, Fol:
Our merchandise is all exactly the same.
Right the first time.

YVETTE   We ain't merchants, Henri,
We're troubadours. What are we doing in Cornwall?

RAVAL

Ah-ha, up jumps the Cat-Killer. Clubs,
Read that thing we signed.

CLUBS (*reading*)   "A . . . contract.
A: Be Like A Merchant . . ."

YVETTE   I know, I know.

CLUBS

"B: Ask No Questions . . ."

YVETTE   I said I know.

CLUBS

"C: Give No Answers . . ."

YVETTE   Look, I know!

CLUBS

"We, the Undersigned . . ."

YVETTE   I bloody know!
Okay, one question: where is Mr Be-Like,
Mr Ask-No, Mr Give-No, our employer?

RAVAL

That's the Captain, isn't it? Ask him.

CLUBS

"B: Ask No Questions."

YVETTE   Thank you, Clubs.
I think I won't. That's Captain Gives-Me-The-Creeps.

RAVAL

Monsieur told us to load the boat and wait.
We did, we are.

YVETTE   We don't have to wait down here,
Dearest, why don't we board?

GUIDO   Is warm there.

RAVAL

Fine by me. I was waiting for Friend Rol.
Now we're established as the lowest point
In the history of mercantile affairs,

Let's get on the damn boat and drink our wares.
Captain, we're going up! Or barking up,
Or, anyway, –
CAPTAIN   "Embarking" is the word.
YVETTE
It spoke.
RAVAL Please tell Monsieur that all my group
Is come aboard and merchants through and through.
CAPTAIN
I took you for them.
YVETTE   You were paid to.

YVETTE, FOL, GUIDO, CLUBS *and* RAVAL *exit on to the ship*

VALENTIN
Captain, sir, is it time to luff the painter
And anchor down about and star b'daft?
CAPTAIN
I do believe it is.
How maritime you are for a mountain boy.
VALENTIN
It is all you, sir, Captain.
CAPTAIN   Off you go.
And finally check, if I may use land-language,
The twin finest cabins are fit for a Queen,
So to speak. And lock on either side.
And check the landing-boat for another boy
Stowing away like you did. One is enough.

Exit VALENTIN. CAPTAIN *looks off in the other direction*

Everything I have ever expected happened.
And this, as they clamber down that Cornish wall
Towards the ship I captain is the one
Of which I am most sure. The blood they spill
In stumbling over the rocks is sure to be blue.
I know you, I know you.
They've helped each other down: they see the ship.
They'll need a boat to get 'em across the bay,
And there it is. The man
Is happy things have gone as planned, whatever
Things, whatever plan. He pushes away.

Enter VALENTIN *from the ship*

Exhausted the possible work, or just exhausted?
Check those cabins again.
VALENTIN   The landing-boat!
CAPTAIN
What of the landing-boat? You can't have found
Yourself in it again, Valentin: you can't
Stow away on a boat you have a job on.
You are a cabin boy. You have a cabin.
VALENTIN
I looked in the landing boat –
CAPTAIN   The skimmy.
VALENTIN   – The skimmy.
And there I found – I found it's full of a family!
CAPTAIN
It's what?
VALENTIN (*to offstage*) You must come down and see
                                   the Captain!

Enter ORMOND, MRS ORMOND, ELINOR, KARA *and* DR
VOGEL *from the ship*

Here, sir, you must come!
CAPTAIN   What on earth is this.
ORMOND
Ormond. Ormond H. Ormond M.
Ormond E. Ormond K. And Vogel.
VALENTIN
He says his name is Ormond.
CAPTAIN   Valentin,
Go and check the cabins eleven times.

Exit VALENTIN

My stowaway discovers an entire
Clan of stowaways. Did you expect
To last these six or seven days at sea
In that?
ORMOND We were rather hoping to come to some
Arrangement, vis-à-vis, anon, monsieur.
CAPTAIN
I'm not a Frenchman.
ORMOND   Ah, an Englishman!
CAPTAIN
Nor that: I am a mariner.
MRS ORMOND   How super!

[217]

ORMOND
  Margaret, quiet.
MRS ORMOND Girls, that's a mariner.
ELINOR
  Kara, that's a mariner.
KARA   Uh-huh.
ELINOR
  That means he's been at sea.
KARA   How super for him.
CAPTAIN
  What are you, Master Ormond, that you cram
  Your brood into my landing-boat? Escaped?
ORMOND
  Escaping, Captain Sir, but not the Law.
  Escaping an old way of life for a new.
MRS ORMOND
  But just for a little while.
KARA   Already too long.
ORMOND
  We are an ordinary cultural family,
  Tolerably wealthy, not unlike
  The neighbours or the neighbours' neighbours. But
  With one extraordinary exception. Me.
MRS ORMOND
  Mr Ormond's a playwright, and we act.
ORMOND
  Tell him, Margaret.
MRS ORMOND We do the Tales of Arthur.
ORMOND
  We did the Tales of Arthur.
CAPTAIN   Arthur the King?
ORMOND
  A tolerable title, but not ours.
  We've kept the entire town on the edge of its seat
  With "The Beautiful Tale of the Love of Arthur
  (King) and Guinevere (Queen)" – that's Mrs Ormond –
  "Including the Huge Exploits of the Loyal
  Lancelot, a Knight", a play by Ormond,
  H. H is for Henry. And that's what we did.
CAPTAIN
  You're strolling players.
ORMOND   No. Not strolling.
  Players, yes, but up until now immobile.
  Known and loved in our town.

[218]

CAPTAIN   Then a small town.
ORMOND
  A tolerable size.
KARA   A tiny dump.
ORMOND
  Finally, and not without regrettings,
  I plucked the best idea out of the air,
  The ripe idea, and here we are: travelling.
  We heard of a giant festival in the hills
  Of France, for many actors, many playwrights, –
  Not your clever-clever, when-will-you-pay-me,
  Juggling prancing troubadours, but serious
  Actors, writers, lovers of the Arts.
CAPTAIN
  You mean you are not paid. Not at a Court.
ORMOND
  How do you know that, sir?
CAPTAIN   For one thing,
  You stowed, or tried to stow, across on my ship.
  And for another, I know some troubadours.
ORMOND
  I trust we have not offended.
KARA   "We"?
CAPTAIN   No.
  I've never seen an "act", nor care remotely
  Whether such stuff is paid-for or indulged.
  As to your stowing away, you tried and failed
  And there's an end, there's a – curtain on that.
  So this is all of you.
ORMOND   I'm afraid yes.
  Dr Vogel and I – not a medical doctor –
  We are our only men now, hardly enough
  To mount my latest spectacle of love.
  If I am to do Tristan, and he the King, –
CAPTAIN
  What?
ORMOND We will need a Rivalin, and a Gandin.
CAPTAIN
  You're making a play of people who are alive?
ORMOND
  A risk, I know, but Art, Sir Mariner, Art!
CAPTAIN
  Art be quartered! Now I can see the thing.
  That's why you stowed away: you're scarpering.

ORMOND
  No, not at all. How could our play insult?
  "The Beautiful Tale of the Love of Mark (King)
  And Beautiful Irish Isolde" – that's my Elinor –
  "Including the Huge Exploits of the Loyal
  Tristan, a Knight", a play by Henry J. Ormond.
  It's a similar play to the first but contemporary.
  It deals with the great story of our times.
CAPTAIN
  What if the story was still unfolding?
ORMOND   No,
  This is the Tale of the Irish War and the peace
  Engendered by the marriage, plus a few
  Incidents of the Hero slaying the giants,
  Irishmen and dwarfs and what have you.
  There are limits to how topical one can be,
  Even for a modern writer like me.
CAPTAIN
  Rumours cross the oceans.
  Why did your Tristan leave for France so quickly?
  Is that in your happy act?
ORMOND   He came from France,
  Did Tristan, out of Parmeny. We do not –
  I am sorry, sir – believe the rumourmongers.
  Those, there always are. We came through Cornwall
  Researching our new work and we ignored them.
CAPTAIN
  Valentin!
MRS ORMOND It's a nice ship, isn't it, girls?
ELINOR
  Looks good and strong.
KARA   Wet, dark, creaking.
CAPTAIN
  Playwright, you make ready. Valentin!
  (*to* ORMOND) Can the women cook and you pull a rope?
ORMOND   Of course!
  We are an ordinary modern family.
  Not afraid of work, are we, Ormonds?
ELINOR
  We're not!
KARA *We're* not, no.
VOGEL   And nor is the Vogel.

Enter VALENTIN

CAPTAIN

Good. Valentin, that landing-boat is a charm.
It brought me you, and now it brings me these
Ordinary Ormonds. They are players.
They played in a town but now they'll cross the sea
With us to France, and not in the skimmy. Show them,
– Show them to the hull. You can sleep among
The silk and china plates and the caged birds.
The wine'll be down the trouba – the merchants.

ORMOND

Troubadours?

CAPTAIN   This is a merchant ship,

Master Ormond. So, it is full of merchants.
Take your chance. I am ordinary. I want
A playwright on my ship.

ORMOND

The immensity of our gratitude –

CAPTAIN   Is big.

No words before I change my mind. Go aboard.

ORMOND

Thank you!

MRS ORMOND Thank you!

KARA   And the nightmare went ahead.

CAPTAIN

Show them, Valentin, quickly. Then:
Check and lock the cabins. Go, go!

VALENTIN *leads the* ORMONDS *and* VOGEL *off, on to the ship*

Too much has happened now for this to be Chance.
Actors are everywhere on the "Esperance",
The flagship of a hero unseen
For many months in Brittany. Then there's him,
Cardin, the desperate oarsman: it is clearly
Him, and the ladies hooded. That was likely.
But I need a wind to catch the hoods – there,
The blondest banners! Cardin, better be quick
To cover their heads! Now, now, I know them.
He knows I know him, Cardin,
But thinks I have been at sea forever, as if
That would make a trusting
Infant of me in an adult world of scandal.
As if there was no love in the sea.

[221]

SCENE III
The Castle of Karke, as at the beginning.

TRISTAN
  The thing you see is dead. Imagine me
  In England, Cardin: in England is the life
  Of Tristan: here is the name, and the armour.
  She is the life, she is the life, tell her
  She is I. Am I her?
  Maybe. Who can know what crawls in the months
  In the dark maze of intrigue, distrust.
  I saw a baron's face in a red room.
  I gave you the ring?
CARDIN   You did.
TRISTAN   There is no chance
  She'd fail to recognise it. Say when you can
  "Remember the Garden; remember the vow then."
  Later, say – (*he coughs*)
  "Remember the Cave, remember the brook, the orchard.
  Remember the vow in the Garden." And Branwen,
  Her cousin I know you loved and love –
CARDIN   Tristan –
TRISTAN
  She'll not come without Branwen when she comes.
CARDIN
  I'll bring them both with me. That is a vow.
TRISTAN
  In forty days. More, and then I'll know
  Tristan died in England as well as France.
CARDIN
  Forty days from when I leave your side,
  Tristan, Lord.
TRISTAN   All my health is with her.
  "Remember the Cave". And remember all sufferings
  Either for either, since we drank what we drank
  One evil, embroiling day.
CARDIN   Drank, Lord?
TRISTAN
  I couldn't love your sister, Cardin. I hated

[222]

Her name, "Isolde", an ugly, painted name.
I couldn't touch her.

CARDIN   I knew before, remember.
The day she fell from her horse in the white-water.
It lapped her higher, she said, than a man had.
And that included you. You know I knew that.

TRISTAN
Isolde, Isolde, Isolde is all, all.
If she doesn't come with you she wouldn't come.
If she doesn't, neither is still alive. She –
Nor I. Your sister, tell nothing. She has no name.

CARDIN (*to himself*)
She has an unhappy one.

TRISTAN   In forty days
Imagine us together, my health, standing,
Healing here! And Branwen at the window,
The whiteness draining back into sheets of light,
The blood returning with hurrah, hurrah! Cardin?

CARDIN
Tristan?

TRISTAN   Take a white flag.

CARDIN   You have told me.

TRISTAN
And a black one too.

CARDIN   I have vowed, so the black
Had better stay behind, it has no function!

TRISTAN
Hoist the white flag when you see the land.
Hoist the black one if the bark is empty,
Phantom, come to an end.

CARDIN   That needless black
Would indicate my death. It would be indeed
A ship of phantoms with an unknown captain.

TRISTAN
Hoist the white flag when she's standing there
Beside you as you hoist it.

CARDIN   It will be.

TRISTAN
Have her comb her golden hair. I will see
The flag, the ship, and say: "Away over there,
Isolde is standing, combing her golden hair . . ."

CARDIN
Yes.

TRISTAN   You have the ring I gave you.

CARDIN   Yes.

TRISTAN
  For forty days, she is a healing-woman.
  Cloak her, Cardin, hide her well. Hide her.
  A light on this is war at the very least:
  All England on your Brittany, to the death.
  Though I'll be long gone then and rotten, I wish
  Not a single Breton, Cornishman or Irish
  To die for me again. That's the very least.
  Deeper hurt is the final shame of the King:
  What that would do to him, and the Court to her
  If by a horror they snatched her alive. Deeper
  Is that. Deeper than that is the death of love,
  And then the death of night.
CARDIN   None will come.
TRISTAN
  And none of those, should light expose the whole,
  Is more than an irritant against one glimpse
  Of a ship with a black flag.
CARDIN   Tristan of Parmeny,
  Hero of England, Beloved of Brittany:
  All is understood. In forty days,
  Less, less, but forty I will be here,
  The cousin too, and the blinding face on the coin.
TRISTAN
  Cardin, until that minute, the crowning of Love
  And start of life, and end of this – pain –
  God be with you, honest, gentle man.

They embrace. Exit CARDIN

  Tristan, we have brought you a third choice, Tristan.
  We don't want you to take it, Tristan, it's so
  Dazzlingly light we fear it, Tristan, we go –

Enter WHITE HANDS, *from where she was listening*

WHITE HANDS
  Honest, gentle Lord, husband, Tristan.
TRISTAN
  Uh? Duchess of Brittany, yes, I'm alive.
WHITE HANDS
  My brother told me breathlessly on the way
  He'd bring a brilliant doctor over the sea,

[224]

A healing-woman. You cannot imagine how
That makes me feel. I imagine you've changed your mind
About doctors.
TRISTAN   This is the best there is,
Lady, a healing-woman.
Ancestrally a wood-spirit, I was told.
WHITE HANDS
A wood-spirit, I'm sure, and in forty days.
TRISTAN
Cardin told you?
WHITE HANDS   Quickly, and ran ahead.
TRISTAN
Good, he's gone. Leave me now, my lady.
WHITE HANDS
Very good. I shall start to number the days.

Exit WHITE HANDS. TRISTAN *lies back, in pain*

SCENE IV
The harbour at Cornwall again.

CAPTAIN
Here, Monsieur, here: I thought you were lost!

Enter quickly CARDIN, ISOLDE OF IRELAND *and* BRAN-
WEN, *all hooded*

CARDIN
Raise the anchor at once, Captain! A lookout
Seems to have marked us for smugglers, I heard him
Whistle – quickly, aboard and raise the anchor!
CAPTAIN
The merchants are all aboard.
CARDIN   Fait accompli!

Exit to the ship CARDIN *and* BRANWEN, *supporting* ISOLDE

Come on, Captain – home to Brittany!

The CAPTAIN *slowly exits on to the ship. Lights down on*
TRISTAN, *sleeping*

[225]

ACT II

*The "Esperance", below deck. The first night of the
return crossing.*

*There are three tables, Left, Right and Middle, but not much
space between them. There are about twelve seats, or such
as have been improvised by the passengers. The Left table is
vacant. The* CAPTAIN *sits alone at the Middle, though it is
set for four.* RAVAL, YVETTE, FOL, GUIDO *and* CLUBS *are
huddled around the Right, supping, merry. There are stairs
leading up to two closed cabin doors: Cardin's, and that of
Isolde and Branwen*

RAVAL
You take the boy on for his potage skills,
Eh Captain? If so, throw him overboard.
YVETTE
His potage with him.
CAPTAIN   He makes what he makes,
Merchandising seamen: now there's a team
Of abler cooks on board.
RAVAL   He means your birds,
Yvette.
YVETTE No birds of mine.
GUIDO   They is my birds,
Squarely-fairly, Senorita Yvetta.
FOL
Good, I'll give you a plate of Tours for them,
Guido, then we can eat them on it.
GUIDO   Eat?
No!
RAVAL Captain, why'd we hang about so long
And leave so sudden now?
YVETTE   Cue the Count of Clubs . . .
CLUBS
"B: Ask No Questions."
CAPTAIN   Let me see that.
(*reading*) That's what it says, although it also says
"Be Like A Merchant", and, except in terms
Of what, how much, and how, you drink, you weren't.

CLUBS
He knows we are not a merchant!
YVETTE   We know he knows
We're not a bloody merchant: it makes no odds
What the helmsman knows, we're at sea now,
Ain't we, out of England and the fog.
Who are we going to meet to sell to here?

Enter ORMOND, MRS ORMOND, ELINOR, KARA *and*
VOGEL

... Apart from these ten people ...
ORMOND
This must be the dining room, dears.
KARA
Food and men doesn't make a dining room.
ELINOR
Kara, don't you like life on a boat?
Look, there's a little table set for us.
ORMOND
Those must be the merchants over there.
Sit down, Ormonds, Dr Vogel. I'll
Attempt a bridge-building exercise.

The ORMOND PARTY *sits.* RAVAL'S TROUPE, *especially*
YVETTE *and* FOL, *giggle at everything they do or say*

VOGEL
Hmm, good solid wood. Oak, I think.

ORMOND *starts introducing himself to everybody*

ORMOND
Ormond.
RAVAL   What does he mean by "ormond"?
CLUBS   Ormond!
ORMOND
Henry Ormond!
YVETTE   Ha, he's a Henry too!
Raval, I think he's saying his name.
ORMOND   Right!
And you are?
FOL   Oh we're merchants.
RAVAL   Henri Raval.

[227]

ORMOND
  You're a Henry too!
RAVAL   Er, yes, an Henri.
ORMOND
  Captain, would you do the honours?
CAPTAIN   What?
ORMOND
  And you are?
FOL   Look, we're merchants, right?
YVETTE   Yvette!
  And this is Fol of the lowland town of Rol,
  Guido the wine-seller, and the Count of Blue Silk!
  Okay? So, who the hell are you and yours?
ORMOND
  Merchants, ah-hah, yes. We saw your wares.
  Lovely birds.
GUIDO   Gracias.
MRS ORMOND   Lovely silks!
YVETTE
  What?
CLUBS   I'm the merchant selling the blue silk.
KARA (*to* ELINOR)
  Better class of person at sea, don't you think?
RAVAL
  Henry Ormond, pleased and rather alarmed
  To make your acquaintance as I am, I am
  Nonetheless your servant.
FOL   And a merchant.
CLUBS
  He knows we're not a merchant.
YVETTE   They don't know.
ORMOND
  And I, you, yours, and so, sincerely.
  Let me introduce an ordinary
  (With one exception) cultural family
  Ormond (with one Vogel, Dr, not
  In fact a medical doctor), all devoted
  To dramatic and theatrical high arts.
KARA
  All, with four exceptions.
MRS ORMOND   Hush, Kara.
  Your father always says: among strangers
  You must be an ambassador for your country.

[228]

KARA
   If Daddy's the ambassador for England,
   I'm glad we're off to France before they send
   The French Armada.
VOGEL   Have a bread roll, Kara.
RAVAL
   You are all actors? This is a rich surprise.
ORMOND
   It's nice of you to say so. There's Margaret,
   Elinor, my eldest, and Kara:
   We call her Miss Contrariwise.
YVETTE   Oh, why?
ORMOND
   Well it all began –
RAVAL   Let me do those "honours"
   Properly. Yvette is mon amie.
ORMOND
   But she's a girl.
RAVAL   Yes sir, she's a girl.
ORMOND
   Hmm.
YVETTE It means we sleep together.
MRS ORMOND   Kara, Elinor,
   All the merchants sleep together. That's nice,
   Isn't it?
ELINOR I expect they discuss their trades.
YVETTE
   I'm not his woman; I'm his friend.
RAVAL   Mais oui,
   Yvette's my special friend.
MRS ORMOND   That's very nice,
   Mrs Effort, I've got a special friend
   In the next lane. We press flowers together.
YVETTE
   That's nice, Mrs Almond, that's what we do.
RAVAL
   This is Fol of Rol. You won't believe this.
   But he ran out of a black forest to the south
   One sunny day. He looked about eighteen,
   But plainly reared exclusively by wolves.
ORMOND
   This is astonishing.
RAVAL   It isn't over.
   This wolf-cub came to town and spoke perfect

Kaiser's German, King's English later,
Norman, Breton: seemed entirely unscathed
By his ordeals.

ORMOND   He looks a normal man.

RAVAL
He is a total man. Oh, and the stars!
Wolves, they say, see stars in the day: not him,
Not Fol of Rol. Not a trace of his lupine
Origins . . . This is Guido, a dago.
He thinks "dago" means like "one of the boys".
And this is the Count of Clubs. He's getting round
To answering questions put to him last year.

CLUBS
"C: Give No Answers."

RAVAL   He plays our grotesques.

RAVAL *realises what he has said*

ORMOND
I thought you said you were merchants.

RAVAL   Ye-es, he plays
The grotesques, like – er, castanets – oh fuck.

MRS ORMOND
Girls, that's a Breton word meaning "It's late."

KARA
Oh fuck then, isn't it mother.

MRS ORMOND   Kara!

ORMOND   Captain,
You did say "troubadours", didn't you?

CAPTAIN   Sit
Down, Master Stowaway Ormond.

Intimidated, ORMOND *sits*

No one did my "honours".
I, whatever you are, am Captain Clement
Of the "Esperance". The boy who brings your food
Is Valentin, a stowaway like you,
Master Ormond. These men and the woman
Are on a contract, a simple one – here.
It says they are to play
The parts of merchants on a trip to Cornwall.
They all signed, and ably played the parts
Of the drunkest dimmest traders there could be.
They also signed to ask no questions.

And give no answers. What it doesn't say
Is that they mustn't listen to the sounds
A mariner makes. Mariners make sounds.
Like . . . Everybody on the "Esperance" is a player
Except the boy and I.
These people are troubadours. These, English actors
Acting a play of Mark, the King of Cornwall,
And his Queen. And the Parmenian hero Tristan,
Who suddenly went abroad and for all we know
Died abroad. A story for our times,
Of, and in, our times. I let them aboard
Partly out of a mariner's
Humanity, and partly to meet their fellows
In the so noble art of playing another.
The man who wrote this contract is also
The man who swears I'll pay for my transgression
In letting this family on. None of us knows
What he is, except he scowls like a Breton,
Nor who the hooded women were he brought
Out of Cornwall tonight. All else we know
Is that they would not dine . . . But these were sounds
A mariner made: waves, merely, and salt.
Now I have done some "honours".

Exit CAPTAIN

FOL
So much for our contract. You know, I liked
Having a contract. He goes and makes it worthless.
Cheer me up, Clubs, play a Strassburg tune
On the ol' grotesques.
ORMOND   I do hope
The Captain isn't turning in. I'd hoped
To talk marine talk with him: topsails,
Yardage and the like.
KARA   But you've never
Been to sea, daddy.
ORMOND   It was my hobby,
When a boy. Be nice to use that jargon.
MRS ORMOND
Is he a typical Captain, do you know?
YVETTE
He's an oddball Captain, Mrs Almond.
I call him Captain Gives-Me-The-Screaming-Abdabs.

[231]

He didn't say a word on the first crossing.
Now he suddenly comes on like a statue
Sprung to life.
KARA   Who was he on about?
What man? What hooded women?
RAVAL   He means
(*pointing*) Him, who hired us out for more red gold
Than we could carry. He keeps himself up there.
YVETTE
Raval is saying we don't know why we're here.
FOL
I ain't seen any women, hooded or bare.
CLUBS (*to* FOL)
Did you say Strassburg then?
FOL   No. Shut up.
KARA
Well ... "Fuck".
MRS ORMOND   That's a Breton word, don't use it!
ORMOND
Is it a Breton word?
ELINOR   Now I know five.
RAVAL
Well well, Family Ormond, what we do know
Is that we're all in the business. Where do you play,
Tintagel, is it? Arundel? Whose Court?
YVETTE
Hardly be Tintagel. The man said
They're playing a "Tristan" – couldn't do that there.
RAVAL
Good point.
YVETTE   Imagine! Here we are, King Mark,
This is what you need: a play of "Tristan"
Cheer you up no end! So where's the Queen?
She coming along to watch?

The ORMOND PARTY *is offended, but is not sure why*

ORMOND
Why ... would it offend to play my work
In Cornwall?
ELINOR *to* MRS ORMOND   Were they rude about the King?
ORMOND
Why would it offend to play "The Beautiful
Tale of the Love of Mark and Beautiful Irish

Isolde, Including the Huge
Exploits of the Loyal Tristan, a Knight"?

FOL *giggles*

RAVAL
  "Including the – " would you mind
  Trundling that whole title by me again?
YVETTE
  It'll help to pass the time to Brittany.
FOL
  Brittany, mon Yvette? To the world's end!
ORMOND
  There's some misunderstanding.
RAVAL   Fol of Rol,
  Will you behave? We're with some English people.

FOL *giggles again*

ORMOND
  The answer to "The Court of whom do we play at"
  Is "None at all": we are not hired to play.
YVETTE
  You aren't hired?
FOL   Must mean they do it for nothing.
ORMOND
  We do do it for nothing.

RAVAL'S TROUPE *is struck dumb*

MRS ORMOND   For the love.
ELINOR
  And for the company.
KARA   And for the hell.
VOGEL
  We play in the village hall.
  A cricketer told me we were the first to do this.
RAVAL
  What's . . . a "cricketer"?
VOGEL   Oh. I don't know.
  I think he was the first to do that.
ORMOND
  We haven't moved from our town until now.
  This is a new venture for us.

RAVAL   Yes . . .
  Haven't moved, you say?
ORMOND   But look at us now,
  On our way to the Festival in the hills,
  With all those actors! A strolling player told us
  All about it. Someone like yourselves.
  Won't you be going there?
RAVAL   We'd thought of it.
  We have a date in Germany.
ORMOND   Ah, Germany.
KARA
  He's never been to Germany.
MRS ORMOND   Kara.
KARA   But really.
ORMOND
  Ambassadors, that's how we see ourselves.
  A celebration of these modern times,
  Symbolised in a tale of royal love
  Uniting nations.
FOL   Must be another Mark,
  Another Isolde, Tristan, another England.
RAVAL
  Quiet, Fol.
GUIDO   Tristan? We do a Tristan,
  I play a harp, you see, and everyone clapping!
ORMOND
  You've done a Tristan too?
RAVAL   Er, well, many
  Years ago, just a roundelay or two.
FOL
  Raval's embarrassed, he had to neck with Yvette
  In front of all those ducs and comtes and dauphins.
YVETTE (to the GIRLS)
  That's how we began.
ORMOND (to RAVAL)   So you played the King?
  That's the role of Vogel. We're short of men though.
  Mercer and young Gates wouldn't leave the town.
KARA
  I mean, who would? All that coming and going.
ORMOND
  I myself played Tristan. Who played yours?
RAVAL
  I seem to have forgotten. It's many years.

[234]

GUIDO
  You, Raval, is Tristan – Yvetta Isolde!
  And me the harp, and another, he 'ave a beard,
  He left us now, he play the silly English
  King who don't see nothing!

an icy pause

RAVAL
  Thank you, Ambassador Guido, the Voice of Spain.
KARA
  It's late, isn't it?
ELINOR   Kara, that man's from Spain.
ORMOND
  Now, it dawns. Now, I understand.
  Disbelievers from a different land.
  A King: make fun of it. Love: make light of it.
  As long as it's funny. Troubadours do it.
RAVAL
  Do not slight a profession, Mr Ormond.
  Remember, ours is our work. We eat with it.
ORMOND
  Trampling down the truth while you're about it.
FOL (*aside*)
  Pompous English idiot.
RAVAL *to* FOL   Ta gueule.
  I mean, we haven't the luxury to believe
  Everything our town criers tell us.
ELINOR (*to* MRS ORMOND)
  Does he mean Tristan's affair?
RAVAL   Even she knows!
  She's young but she has ears, Mr Ormond.
ORMOND
  Put a man in a room and there is truth.
  Two, there's doubt. Three, there's a rumour. Four, –
RAVAL
  The Beautiful Loyal Family of Ormond,
  Suppliers of white paint to the world!
ORMOND   Margaret.
  In case you're falling behind,
  We're just establishing that this is a group
  Of anti-English gypsies
  Spreading lies about the Court at Cornwall
  And certain old rumours of Lord Tristan.

RAVAL
  Fine. Let me help the Count and our Spaniard.
  Guido, Clubs, this is an English family
  Of amateurs, who actually believe
  King Mark married Isolde and they lived,
  Still live, happily happily ever after,
  Exchanging happy informative belles-lettres
  About love, loyalty, and Tristan,
  Whom they do not remember. Or – barely.
ORMOND (*standing*)
  Barely be damned! Stand up, strolling player!
RAVAL (*standing*)
  Where? Here? Let's fight for the love of it!

CARDIN's *door bursts open and he stands there. All freeze,
shut up.* CARDIN *doesn't retire again until* ORMOND &
RAVAL *resume their seats*

YVETTE
  That was the man the Captain meant, Kara.
MRS ORMOND
  A nobleman, I think. Henry, perhaps
  We all ought to go to bed now. It is late.
ORMOND
  I believe I heard our crowned heads insulted.
RAVAL
  See, he believes everything he hears.
MRS ORMOND
  Mr Raffle, you know that everyone does say
  How lovely a couple the King and Queen do make.
FOL
  Not in our wood, they don't.
MRS ORMOND   Have you met them?
FOL
  No, no, I haven't. Have you?
MRS ORMOND   No,
  But I'm an English woman, so I know.
FOL
  Well I'm French and the French reckon your Tristan's
  Alive and well and living in Brittany,
  Just this channel of water away from you,
  Waiting.
VOGEL Well. Nobody knows a thing.
  Hearsay. Guesswork. One thing. Another thing.

Arguing like that won't change a mind.
We're all aboard. Beginning. Middle. End.
YVETTE
What sort of doctor are you?
GUIDO   Is the Captain!

Enter CAPTAIN

CAPTAIN
What was the storm here? I was trying to rest.
The boy is trying to steer the ship. You,
English sir, are a stowaway: you have
No rights whatsoever to be anything
But thrown into the sea. Do you know that?
With all your brood.
RAVAL   That, we would not permit.
CAPTAIN
Not – permit?
RAVAL   Captain, this is a private
Brouhaha that boiled over the pan.
No more. A professional quarrel, or, in his case,
Amateurish.
ORMOND (*standing*) That's it!
MRS ORMOND (*fiercely*)   Sit down, Henry!
VOGEL
An international quarrel, Captain Clement.
In international waters, I might add.
CAPTAIN
I might add merely that this is the "Esperance"
But you can call it "Some Hope".
MRS ORMOND   That's a niceish name.
CAPTAIN
I do not want a quarrel on my ship.
If I hear your voices swelling up again,
I'll deal with you all ashore, where professionals
Are mariners to a man.

He sits and his manner lightens suddenly

                    Listen, listen.
Why do you think you are here? You don't know.
Don't you know a bold stroke of Fortune
The time it brushes you by? You are all actors.
Seize your opportunity, and act.

I told you I was trying to rest. I was,
But unavailingly. I heard exactly
What your quarrel was, and I shall solve it.
ORMOND
One apology solves it.
CAPTAIN   Shaking hands
Solves it, reddening villager. Your Tristans
Are sun and moon, it seems.
ORMOND   Mine is the light.
RAVAL
Yours is all blind heat, Mr Cottage Ormond.
YVETTE
Shut up and listen to Captain Alive-After-All.
CAPTAIN
Merci, unmarried lady. I've a suggestion.
When I say "suggestion", I mean a strong
Recommendation. (*to* ORMOND) Play your Tristan, sir.
I saw your scripts in the hull. The birds were an inch
Short of eating them. (*to* RAVAL) Troubadour, play yours.
I've heard you boast you can think and act in a trice.
Try it against this English husbandman.
He has his people; you your gang. So act.
When I say "recommendation", I really mean
An order. When I say "order", I mean: in five,
Four nights we will be back in Brittany.
If you both play your opposite Tristans I
Will turn you a blind eye each and by Providence never
Dim your view again. The team I judge
The better, for I shall arbitrate and fairly
Arbitrarily – will win the prize.
Which is – it belongs to me – the merchandise.
GUIDO
My birds!
ELINOR   Oh the silks, daddy!
FOL   The rest of the wine!
CAPTAIN
Exactly. Exactement. Sunshine. Moonshine.
ORMOND
If that was a naval order we have to comply.
RAVAL
Who needs a naval order? We say aye!
ORMOND
Then so do we!

VOGEL   Here's me, a humble doctor,
  Ready to act for the Crown!
FOL   Allez le Bois!
CAPTAIN
  Now you are captains too: shake all hands.

CAPTAIN, RAVAL *and* ORMOND *shake hands like serious
sportsmen*

YVETTE
  This is the strangest rising and falling Captain.
FOL
  Good idea, though, keep our thinking sharp.
MRS ORMOND
  What a thing to tell them when we're back!
KARA
  How the nightmare took a different tack.
ORMOND
  Captain, the sides are uneven.
FOL   That's plain to see.
ORMOND
  We need a man: we're down four men to two.
YVETTE
  And up three girls to one, isn't that true?
ORMOND
  Yes, but we need more men.
RAVAL   That's easily done.
  Guido, mon señor. Since this is largely
  The fault of your good memory, would you mind
  Playing for the English? and what I mean
  By "would you mind" is – you are being transferred.
GUIDO (*moving across*)
  And my guitar! Hallo, new friends team!
ELINOR
  Look, we've got the Spanish man now!
RAVAL
  Excuse me, Henry: now
  We are outnumbered six-to-four. We want
  A female in our gang.
ORMOND   That, could take time.
KARA (*moving across*)
  Why? Ciao, daddy, I'm in a new team!
MRS ORMOND
  Is that a good idea?

YVETTE   It's a perfect one,
Mrs Almond, I'll look after your treasure.
Welcome, young lady.
RAVAL   Now we are favourites.
CAPTAIN
Five to five, no favourites. You are even.
I'll toss my German coin. Call it, merchant.

CAPTAIN *tosses a coin high*

RAVAL
Face of a German scoundrel with a beard.
CAPTAIN (*catching it*)
Ill luck, a coat of arms. English captain?
ORMOND
We'll take the stage, of course! Scatter, Raval,
Your minstrels to the stalls and upper circle!
Elinor, fetch the scripts from our sleeping quarters!
We'll begin with the origins of Lord Tristan.
RAVAL (*to* KARA)
Come with me, ma chère, I will explain
The art of the quickfire act, while your father
Builds a village hall in the ship and books it.

The TROUPE *huddle together.* ELINOR *exits and returns
with the* ORMONDS' *scripts. Both teams prepare for battle*

CAPTAIN
Valentin! Valentin!

Enter VALENTIN

VALENTIN   Captain Clement?
CAPTAIN
Knock on Monsieur's cabin. Ascertain
He has all the things he wants. If he does not,
Give them to him. His is the first door.

VALENTIN *goes up to Cardin's door and knocks. It opens
slightly*

Come on, Pride of England, enough practice!
MRS ORMOND
Rehearsal's what we call it.
ORMOND   We will begin

With a monologue delivered by the Narrator.
That's me.
KARA   Why change the habits of a lifetime?
ELINOR
Traitor, Kara!
KARA   All's fair in acting.

Cardin's door closes; VALENTIN *descends*

VALENTIN
He wants to know what the fires are to our left.
ORMOND
"Port".
CAPTAIN   Of course it's a port. That's why there are fires.
ORMOND
"Port" is the word, I mean.
CAPTAIN   Englishman,
Navigate yourself some feet from here
Before some hurricane helps you.
ORMOND (*to* MRS ORMOND)   Even so,
"Port" is the word; that was in my log-book.
VALENTIN (*to* CAPTAIN)
He seems to think the coast should be behind
Or to our right, but shouldn't be to our left.
CAPTAIN
We'll leave Monsieur's maritime credentials
To one side for now, with Master Ormond's.
Merely tell him this:
He doesn't know how fair a wind we have.
The fires he sees are France's, not England's,
For the wind blew us clear across the water
And now, of course, we proceed westerly,
So now, of course, the fires are to our left:
Norman ports. This ought to make him glad.
We are four days at most from Finisterre.

VALENTIN *goes up again, knocks. The door opens and
closes.* VALENTIN *descends and exits*

MRS ORMOND
That means France is very near, Henry.
ORMOND
It does, unfortunately. But "port" was the word.
And nobody's on the "tiller".

CAPTAIN
  Enough, enough! Begin your English Tristan!

ORMOND *takes the stage, clears his throat*

ORMOND
  What would you call a man who went to Cornwall
  Only to learn chivalry and learn well
  From a young King, Mark by name, leaving
  The good Rual behind in Parmeny, grieving?
  Rivalin, Rivalin, you would call him . . .

FOL *giggles*

  What would you call the beautiful white flower,
  The sister to the King, who at the hour
  She first saw Rivalin was doomed to love him
  And praise and curse the shining stars above him?
  Blancheflor, Blancheflor, you would call her . . .
FOL
  Who are these people?
KARA   Shut up, that's my dad there.
ORMOND
  What would you call the babe born to Blancheflor,
  Whose Rivalin had died, who had naught to live for,
  Who died as the babe was born, which had to be reared
  By old Rual, tugging his white beard?
  Sadness, you would call him: Tristan . . .

Polite applause

FOL
  Short on laughs so far.
RAVAL   I wouldn't say that,
  But he isn't the worst I've seen.
ORMOND   *Fourteen years*
  Pass!
RAVAL They do?
ORMOND   *Norwegians come ashore!*

ORMOND'S *team springs to life: he plays Tristan;* VOGEL:
Rual; GUIDO: *Curvenal (as a Spaniard); the* WOMEN: *Nor-*
wegian sailors

  Father Rual, I wish to go to the harbour
  To see the Norwegian ship. May I, father.

VOGEL

Yes, Tristan, but you must take good care
You do not get into difficulties there.

RAVAL

The monologue, ça va. The dialogue . . .

ELINOR

Ho, young man, will you play chess with us?
We are Norwegian sailors!

ORMOND   I will, yes!

GUIDO

Remember to be casual, Tristan.

ORMOND (aside)

That's "careful", Master Gwido.

GUIDO   Careful, Tristan.

ORMOND

Yes, Curvenal, but chess is a fine sport!
And so they passed the afternoon at the port.
But these Norwegians thought the boy could be
Good luck to them, with his ability,
His beauty and his skill.

ELINOR   Ho there, Tristan,
Come on the deck with us: my name is Wystan.
It is much cooler there and we can play
Many games and while away the day!

ORMOND

But while they did, the ship sailed out of port
And Tristan, so absorbed in the fine sport,
And Curvenal as well, they felt no motion
Until they were in the middle of the ocean.

GUIDO

Alas, alack, and woe. I rue the day
We came down to thees harbour to play!

ELINOR

Stop your wailing: put him in the small boat!

ORMOND

And so they did, though Curvenal still called out.
And he was washed ashore, by chance, at home,
And told Rual what misfortune had come!

FOL

Comb.

VOGEL   Alack, alas, and woe, I shall not rest
From wandering to north, south, east and west
Until I find poor Tristan. Oh Curvenal!

[243]

GUIDO
Rual, I shall search the world as well!
ORMOND
We normally take a break there, for general
Emoting: the old ladies take it hard
That Tristan could be lost when still so young.
An excellent opening, team.
YVETTE   Bravo, Mrs Almond,
The quiet Norwegian.
MRS ORMOND   Yes, no lines as yet.
CAPTAIN
Any questions, troubadours?
RAVAL   No questions.
It's a straight account, historical, un peu
Son et lumière . . .
Certainly this is where Tristan came from.
No quarrel with that. Well recited, Henry.
ORMOND
Merci, Henri. Now, we'll continue.
Tristan walked along in a strange forest.
"Cornwall, Cornwall!" was what the birds chorused,
But he was too busy praying and wailing his fortune
To understand their melancholy short-tune.
All at once a hart, a noble hart,
Bounded across his path, and then the start
Of King Mark's Hunt pursuing it with zeal;
But Tristan caught the hart and made a meal!
RAVAL
Permission to join the fray, Master Mariner.
CAPTAIN
As you will, you will.
ORMOND
Oh hunters, I can show you the proper way
Nobly to excoriate your prey
And make it fit for your King, whatever his name is!
For Tristan did not know the King was famous.
RAVAL
Give way, Ormond, we've got a Tristan too.
MRS ORMOND
I think that's fair, Henry.
ORMOND
Brace yourselves, England and also Spain,
For the Great Frankish Fantasy of Tristan!

[244]

YVETTE
You can't be a bad sport when we ain't started.
RAVAL
Me: Tristan. Them: Hunters of Cornwall.

RAVAL'S TEAM *leaps into rapid professional comedy*

You don't do a hart like that, you do it like this.
See? Perfect. Try.
TEAM *Hey jolly good!*
FOL
What a fantastic bloke – let's make him our leader!

YVETTE *plays a running hart*

Anything else you can do? Can you shoot?
RAVAL *Bang.*

YVETTE *drops dead, legs in the air*

FOL
I say, fellows, let's take him to the King!
(I'm the King.) Who's this guy? Looks familiar.
KARA
Looks a bit like Blancheflor, your sister.
FOL
What can you do, son, can you ride a horse?
RAVAL
Is the Emperor one Holy Roman? Of course!
FOL
What about music? Give him a harp, harper.

RAVAL *snatches* GUIDO'S *guitar and plays something simple*
really badly. His TEAMMATES *drop to their knees*

Harper, you're out of a job. Languages, champ?
RAVAL
Breton, French, Latin, Scots . . .
FOL *What else?*
YVETTE
Sprechen Sie Deutsch?
RAVAL *Wie eine Niedersaxone.*
CLUBS
Cymraeg?

RAVAL   *Dim gwell ffordd i lladd ddraig!*
KARA
  Hvad med Dansk?
RAVAL   *Ligesaa godt som Prinsen af Danmark!*
MRS ORMOND
  Kara, where did you learn language like that?
KARA
  Mother, I'm acting!
FOL   *Make this kid a prince!*
ORMOND
  Oh travesty already!
YVETTE   We let you play!
ELINOR
  Oh no you didn't!
CLUBS   *Nos da i chi, Mister Jones.*

CARDIN *opens his cabin door. Silence below. He descends
slowly*

CARDIN
  Captain, send this loud illicit family
  Down into their quarters.
CAPTAIN   Down, Ormonds.

Exeunt the ORMONDS *and* VOGEL, *slowly, sheepishly*

CARDIN (*to* RAVAL)
  Entertainer, lead your actors to bed.

Exeunt RAVAL'S TROUPE

SCENE II
The same, continuous.

CARDIN *is staring curiously at the* CAPTAIN, *who will not
be disconcerted*

CARDIN
  Normandy ports, you say.
CAPTAIN   Or I'm no mariner.
CARDIN (*sitting*)
  A mariner wouldn't run his ship like this.

[246]

CAPTAIN
  Monsieur, it's a small ship of many people.
CARDIN
  The family was let aboard by you.
CAPTAIN
  I have to make a living.
CARDIN   You are working
  For me, on business of which you can know nothing.
CAPTAIN
  I do know nothing.
CARDIN   Four more days, you say.
  I do not want to see
  The actors or the English people again.
  Or hear their voices. Do you understand?
  There's danger if there's anyone from England.
  What was happening here?
CAPTAIN   Oh some charade.
CARDIN
  Keep them below, Captain, if you desire
  Anything for yourself when we're ashore.
  You deserve little already, for a man I chose
  Specifically for his silence.
  Tell the boy to bring some food here.

CAPTAIN *is still for a moment, then exits slowly*

  Four days at the most makes thirty-nine
  Since I saw Tristan. Only a cruel wind
  Can stop us now, only a cruel god
  Harm him with that wind. The wind is strong.
  God Speed to Finisterre.

VALENTIN *brings food, and exits*

                    Merci, mon ami.

BRANWEN *comes out of her cabin, and descends*

BRANWEN
  Is that our supper, sir?
CARDIN   Yes, of course.
  "Sir", Branwen?
BRANWEN   She's sleeping now, but I
  Must eat something.
CARDIN   Won't you eat it here?

[247]

BRANWEN *stares*

So. Take it to her.

BRANWEN *takes the food up to* ISOLDE's *cabin.* CARDIN *finishes his food and wearily ascends to his own.* VALENTIN *enters and turns the lamps low; he exits. Presently,* ISOLDE *comes out of her cabin, with a candle. She is hooded. The* CAPTAIN *is waiting in the shadows, and comes forward*

CAPTAIN
Walking unconscious?
ISOLDE   Aiee! Mother of God!
CAPTAIN
Hush, I am the Captain; don't be afraid.
ISOLDE
I – came to find some water.
CAPTAIN   Water you want?

He gets her some

Here's some water. Sit at the Captain's table.
ISOLDE
No, I cannot.
CAPTAIN   Do, please, sit with the Captain.
ISOLDE
No, I cannot, I wish to sleep.

She goes to the steps. When her foot touches the first the CAPTAIN *whispers –*

CAPTAIN
Highness.

ISOLDE *stops, takes another step. Fractionally louder, the* CAPTAIN *whispers –*

Highness.

ISOLDE *takes another step. The* CAPTAIN *says softly –*

Highness.

ISOLDE *takes another step and the* CAPTAIN *says loudly –*

Highness!

[248]

ISOLDE *stops, descends backwards, turns, and sits at the*
table. She puts her hands to her face and begins silently to
sob

More water? Don't be sad, don't be afraid,
Good lady. All is quiet again at sea.
Hush, hush, all will always be quiet.
Quiet as the dark night, highness.
ISOLDE   Please –
CAPTAIN   Ah,
Hush: I'll not say that again, that I promise.
A shipman's promise, there.
ISOLDE   What do you want.
CAPTAIN
Want? What do I want?
ISOLDE   Or are you sent ahead
From a cruel power? – is it English or German?
I know a quiet torturer: it's always
"Hush, don't cry, my Irish child, and I
Will make everything go away . . ." My God,
My cousin said we were almost there.
CAPTAIN   We are,
We are: what am I, a sailor of Avalon,
Crossing the ocean as fast as a beam of sunlight?
The wind is fair, and we can go no faster.
ISOLDE
What do you want.
CAPTAIN   A way to pass the time.
ISOLDE
Leave it alone, it passes.
CAPTAIN   Leave it alone,
It almost dies. We will pass it together.
ISOLDE
Absurd. I am escorted by my cousin
And the Breton duke.
CAPTAIN   Self-evidently.
ISOLDE
– This was my own fault.
CAPTAIN   It was only water.
Hardly a fault to thirst, Irish daughter.
ISOLDE
I wish I had died of it.
CAPTAIN   Instead – a chance!

Fortune shone you a light on Captain Clement!
See, I told you my name.
ISOLDE   I didn't ask it.
CAPTAIN
  You did, or what I wanted, and what I want
  I will make clear to you some time tomorrow.
  It will be neither difficult, nor painful,
  Nor sorrowful, nor costly, nor for long.
  Even a good return on your water.
  Amazing what a single drink can mean.
  May I escort you to your cabin – Queen?

ISOLDE *rises, her hands raised to ward him off, and she
retreats up the steps and into her cabin. Enter* VALENTIN

  Listening, Valentin?
VALENTIN   To only the air.
  And I think I heard a thunder, Captain Clement,
  Blowing from the east.
CAPTAIN   That would be sad.
  Try to pray, Valentin, before bed.

Exit VALENTIN

  Thunder? – Uncalled-for, that's a fact.
  But there it is. Now is a time to act.

Exit CAPTAIN

ACT III

The "Esperance", below deck, four days later, afternoon.

ORMOND *and* DR VOGEL *are in mid-oration.* MRS ORMOND,
ELINOR *and* GUIDO *are ready to perform.* RAVAL, YVETTE,
FOL, CLUBS *and* KARA *form the audience.* CLUBS *is asleep;*
FOL *is pretending to be. The* CAPTAIN *watches to one side*

*A Storm is raging, thunder and lightning occasional, every-
one leaning one way together as the ship heaves. The lamps
flicker*

VOGEL
  What do you do here in Brittany, son of Rivalin,
  In this green land that people should be civil in?
  I Morgan rule here now: you owe me allegiance,
  As do all knights and barons of nearby regions!
ORMOND
  And Tristan was outnumbered but he was outraged!
  He demanded that a tournament be staged!
VOGEL
  But Morgan laughed, he thought he had him mastered,
  And said: the whole world knows you for a bastard!
ORMOND
  And in a trice a furious battle starts,
  Which ends with Morgan's head in two parts!

ORMOND *bops* VOGEL, *who falls down*

FOL
  Head in two parts, doctor.
VOGEL   Not today.
ORMOND
  Tristan returns safely to Parmeny,
  A hero to his men. (Lightning) *All Brittany*
  Bows before him, but he misses Cornwall,
  And returns there, where all his friends are born well.
RAVAL
  Blank spot there, old sport.

Thunder. CLUBS *wakes*

CLUBS   Up we come!
ORMOND
  Now when the King of Cornwall was a boy,
  The King of Ireland, Gurmun, did enjoy
  Total domination of his realm,
  So Cornwall had a puppet at the helm.
FOL
  A puppet at the helm?
YVETTE   It isn't fair
  If he starts going backwards in the story!
  He's playing for time, Captain Judge.
ORMOND   Not so!
  These seven pages of political background –
FOL
  Seven pages? This isn't "The Flying Dutchman",
  Friend: we have a destination, you know.
MRS ORMOND
  I like the long quiet parts.
KARA   Mother,
  All your parts are long quiet parts.
MRS ORMOND
  I suppose, yes.
CAPTAIN You can't do seven pages,
  Master Ormond: we are trying to take our minds
  Off the storm. Cut to the next killing.
ORMOND
  You jest, I presume.
CAPTAIN   Certainly you presume.
ORMOND
  But this is the whole background to the Queen,
  Captain: I was coming on to the duel
  Of Tristan and Morold, and therefore explaining
  Who he was, Morold, and why they were fighting.
YVETTE (*to* VOGEL)
  Doctor, I think you're going to be hit again.
CAPTAIN
  Skip it, England.
ORMOND   It can't just be violence
  And sex!
RAVAL We thought there was no sex in yours.
CAPTAIN
  Master Ormond, if you don't cut your speech,
  I'll call your enemies up before their time.

[252]

ORMOND
A judge as fair as the weather. Very well,
I shall endeavour to glean . . . for your benefit . . .
Morold was the brother of the Queen,
Isolde of the Healing Powers, the mother (*Thunder*)
Of our Queen the Fair One of Ireland . . . hmm,
That wasn't in the script, this is me thinking . . .
So Morold was Isolde the Younger's uncle,
And the King's Champion . . .

VOGEL   He goes to Cornwall for tribute,
Henry, doesn't he.

ORMOND   That's right. "Brutal Morold",
Yes: . . . *Bullying the Cornish for their bronze,*
The next year their silver, then their gold,
And finally their sons – brutal Morold.

VOGEL
Tremble, Cornish fathers, Cornish sons,
Every son shall be an Irishman's!

ELINOR
Alas, alas, we have so few to give you!

Pause

ORMOND
Margaret.

MRS ORMOND   Oh –
We'll have to draw lots: may your gods forgive you!

YVETTE *applauds;* KARA *joins in*

ORMOND
Cowards of Cornwall, how can you stay silent?
Drawing lots to yield your lads to Ireland!
Battle this red-haired giant so full of scorn!
What are you – Cornishmen? Or men of corn?

RAVAL
Bravissimo, bravissimo!

FOL   Bis, bis!

ORMOND
Marjodoc, will you stand?

MRS ORMOND   *Too scared by half!*

ORMOND
Melot, how about you?

ELINOR   *I'm only a dwarf!*

ORMOND

Then it is I, Tristan the Loyal and Brave,
Who throws my gauntlet at this Irish knave!

VOGEL

Fool, you have no hope! – the giant said.
I shall sail home to Dublin with your head!

ORMOND

We usually break there, to build the suspense.

Polite applause

RAVAL

Unbearable suspense. I wonder who wins.

YVETTE

Well don't bet on the doctor, whatever you do.

FOL

Are there good odds? Are there good odds, Ormond?

CAPTAIN

Carry on, Master Ormond: we believe
We are sufficiently hanging on our cliff. (*Lightning*)

ORMOND

Ahem. *Tristan, God, Right, and Willing Heart*
Are the Four Powers taking Tristan's part;
But Morold had the strength of four, we are told:
Namely, Morold, Morold, Morold, and Morold.

RAVAL'S TEAM *join in the* "*Morold*"*s;* CLUBS *adds another*
at the end

Then they went out to the islet for the fray,
As Cornish and Irish watched from across the bay.

MRS ORMOND/ELINOR

Go on, Tristan, make all Ireland smile!

GUIDO

Heep heep hooray, son of the Emerald Isle!

ORMOND

The battle rages, under the cloudy sky!

ORMOND *and* VOGEL "*duel*"

And Tristan falls – wounded in the thigh!

ORMOND *falls. Thunder*

RAVAL
  It wasn't exactly the thigh.
VOGEL
  Proud Morold steps up, ready to strike . . .
ORMOND
  But Tristan rolls away –

Enter VALENTIN, *soaking wet, breathless*

VALENTIN
  Captain, excuse me here –
  The water dragged the landing-boat from the side!
  It's hanging by a thread, it's over the side,
  It's almost gone!
ORMOND   The lifeboat, does he mean?
CAPTAIN
  All hands on deck at once! Valentin,
  Organise these country people to save
  The skimmy – Ormond, Raval,
  D'you mind awfully taking time off acting
  To save the boat you may require to save you?
ORMOND
  Rising to a crisis!
RAVAL   Allez, allez!

VALENTIN *leads everyone off except the* CAPTAIN. *Lightning*

CAPTAIN
  Try not to die trying.

SCENE II
The same, continuous.

Thunder. CARDIN *comes out of his cabin, and descends*

CARDIN
  What's the clamour above?
CAPTAIN   Lightning and thunder.
CARDIN
  Then may it strike you if you're light with me.
  You'd better be fat with answers, mariner.
  One, the clamour.

CAPTAIN   Lightning struck the lifeboat.
  The actors made a great exeunt, monsieur,
  And struggle into sailors as we speak.
CARDIN
  Will it be saved?
CAPTAIN   Enquire of some entrails.
CARDIN
  Damn you and answer this: why do you hang
  Balefully by here when a near disaster
  Overtakes your ship?
CAPTAIN   The boy can steer.
  I showed him how. There's precious else we can do
  But wait the storm out. She's a strong ship.
  She won't go over.
CARDIN   Why has the land vanished?
  Four days ago you said we could see the coast
  Of Normandy, were good for Finisterre
  In four days at the most. Why aren't we there?
CAPTAIN
  Demand of the soaked tealeaves
  At the bottom of this storm. Sir, we are blown
  Back in the channel, aren't we?
CARDIN   The wind's from the east.
CAPTAIN
  The wind's from the west. It blows us east.
CARDIN   No.
  It's from the east.
CAPTAIN   Are you a mariner, sir?
CARDIN
  I'm a man with eyes and a sun in the sky.
CAPTAIN   Oh?
  You've seen the sun? No one else has these
  Four–five days.
CARDIN   I've seen the sky and the light.
  The wind's from the east, blowing us west. West
  Is Finisterre, and Brittany, and my home.
  We should have been blown in by now.
CAPTAIN   You want
  To be blown in? Or why not swim from here?
  Or why not flap from here?
CARDIN   Why are you lying?
  Those were the fires of England! Why are you sailing
  Backwards up the channel?
CAPTAIN   Do you believe

A man can know exactly where the winds
Will blow from, for how long and how fiercely?
If I had sailed beyond Land's End . . .

BRANWEN *enters above, unseen, and listens*

And this storm had come then we'd now be falling
Puzzled through the stars! What would you ask me
Then, Breton? "Can you get me to Cornwall
And home in forty days now?" I can,
I will – we have a day. If, as you believe,
The great fortuitous storm has hurled us west,
Rewarding my sea-instinct and your dreams
Of saving what you yearn to save – yes!
When the storm drops we will glide
Singing into the Bay of Brittany, early
On the fortieth day.
CARDIN   What – I "yearn to save"?
What do you mean?
CAPTAIN   I'm sorry, I thought you said
The woman was a healing-woman. So,
You don't deny a mariner some thoughts?
I guessed there was some healing to be done
And quickly.
CARDIN   Yes – there is. Captain, I . . .
Do, then, salute your instinct. Early, you say,
On the fortieth day?
CAPTAIN   Early, if it's calm.
Late, otherwise.
CARDIN   It has to be early. You –
Might have explained, Captain, about sailing
East, and so on – I would have seen the point.
CAPTAIN
I like to sail between the tempers, sir.
That's why I let it be. They were the fires
Of England, indeed, yes. So I salute
Your star-knowledge.
CARDIN   There is another thing.
On the first night I demanded of you, Captain,
To stow these passengers either in the hull
Or on the deck – but anywhere but here
Where everything they do is heard.
CAPTAIN   Oh,
Is it that clear?

[257]

CARDIN   Not by word, exactly,
  Though clearly it's a pageant of some
  Scurrilous description.
CAPTAIN   Does it offend
  The healing-lady?
CARDIN   No.
  In fact, and this is the chief of all my questions,
  – Have any spoken to her?
CAPTAIN   I couldn't swear it.
  None has seen her since she stole aboard
  With you. Unless you have. Haven't you?
CARDIN
  Had it not been for her,
  I would have roared each one of you deaf
  For the acting, for this noise, this saturnalia –
  But then my lady said
  "Let them be," – on the second night, this was.
  As if in unison, I heard a shadow,
  No, a whisper behind her voice say
  "Lord, there is something here you do not know."
  I've wondered what it is.
CAPTAIN   Maybe the lady
  Likes to act herself. Or takes pity.
  These are, after all, poor fools: unlike yourself.
  I'm keeping them out of harm's way here,
  Aren't I? Or I was – now they are sailors.
  I ought to go up to them. Subside, monsieur.
  When did you last hear thunder?
  We're near the cape, the sea will calm,
  You'll bring your women ashore and heal
  Whatever would otherwise die. What I know
  About your mission is nothing, but it is more
  Than any passenger knows. I must go up.
CARDIN
  Yes, yes.
CAPTAIN Your sun is behind a cloud.
  Your land is behind the storm, your Breton earth.
CARDIN
  I hope; I'll try to believe.

Exit CAPTAIN. BRANWEN *descends*

BRANWEN
  Trying to spoil the fun again, Cardin?

CARDIN
  To spoil? No, Branwen – do you know what they play?
BRANWEN
  Why, History. Why not?
CARDIN
  Who knows how far they'll go?
BRANWEN   Why not today?
  That would make them almost prophets. Also,
  You and I might see ourselves as we were,
  Mightn't we? And you're not happy with that,
  Little dukeling, are you?
CARDIN   Branwen.
  If she is recognised, if you or I
  Are recognised – the English are on this ship! –
  War follows, international, shame
  Is universal and deep: we will be seized
  Wherever we land. If she is recognised
  We are all dead – we've stolen away their Helen!
BRANWEN
  You and she are dead.
  I'm Helen's chambermaid.
  I'm beneath all politics, all love.
  You beneath them, sweetness? Or above?
CARDIN
  Why do you hate me now? Have you forgotten
  What we had?
BRANWEN   Have I forgotten myself?
  I was what was had, so no, no.
  I have remembered two squires in a forest,
  A manly escort, courtesy of my cousin.
  One said: "Maid, you know too much to live!"
  The other: "Lord, I won't go through with this."
  And this I owe to him.
  Not to Queens in love with dying heroes,
  Not to dying heroes and not to their friends,
  However well-intentioned at a late date.
  Let's see how the actors do it. Perhaps they'll play
  The games we liked to play.
  But here come the dripping stars themselves.

BRANWEN *ascends, and watches, unseen, from above. Enter*
VALENTIN *and* CAPTAIN, YVETTE, MRS ORMOND, ELI-
NOR, KARA, CLUBS *and* GUIDO

[259]

The same, continuous.

CARDIN *takes the* CAPTAIN *and* VALENTIN *aside*

CARDIN
  Captain, what happened?
VALENTIN   The skimmy cracked on the doglight.
CAPTAIN
  We lost the boat. It's not the end of the world
  But never happened before. The good news is:
  The storm rolled on to the north and there's blue sky
  Over the familiar green of – Valentin?
VALENTIN
  The hills of Brittany!
CARDIN   No – I don't believe it!
CAPTAIN
  Try, sir, it's the truth, and the sea's a glass
  In which you now may down your forty days.
CARDIN
  Thank the Heavens! May I go up and see?
CAPTAIN
  By all means. You may have to clamber over
  Three gentlemen, each proving his vocabulary
  Ultra marine.

Exit CARDIN

              Valentin, you said
  You had a word to say.
VALENTIN   If it's one word,
  Captain, sir, it is "cut".
CAPTAIN   How do you mean,
  "Cut"?
VALENTIN "Cut" as in ropes, ropes as in holding
  The skimmy against the starhead side. It fell
  Because the ropes were cut. Almost through
  But not quite through. Still, the word is "cut".
  I shouldn't bear the blame for the boat falling.
CAPTAIN
  You don't if this is true. Now back to work,
  Before the English acting admiral runs us
  Actually aground.

Exit VALENTIN

YVETTE
  Cheer up, Kara, we could still die today.
KARA
  No offence, but we're almost at your country.
  Always the same. I'm getting used to the boat.
YVETTE
  You're on a winning team, ma belle! Why not
  Tag along with us, make real bread
  For all this fucking about and laughing?
KARA   Oh,
  Father would never let me.
YVETTE   Oh, he will,
  It's part of what they do. Or what they want to.
  But it does get lonely.

Enter ORMOND, VOGEL *and* RAVAL

  Here he comes, with the doctor of the ocean.
ORMOND
  I don't understand a word that boy says.
  "Skimmy", "doglight", "mainspick", quite
  Out of another manual, Vogel.
VOGEL
  Well, the ways of the sea, the seven seas.
CAPTAIN
  Attention, players of parts!
  You have all seen the land, it is Brittany
  But some hours still, a night from voyage's end.
  How better to pass your last hours aboard
  The "Esperance" than with your final acts?
  Know that the Judge is holding you neck and neck
  At this time, France and England, both
  Within an ace of the prize.
ORMOND   We come into our own
  From this point on.
RAVAL   Here's where we diverge
  From ancient history into the true-to-life
  (In our case) and to fabrication in yours.
ORMOND
  Monsieur, any divergence
  Will be between your rotten marks and our records.
CAPTAIN
  Whom were you killing, Master Ormond?

ORMOND   Morold,
  The Irish giant, –
CAPTAIN   Consider him buried and mourned.
  I'm sending in the messieurs.
FOL   Ha! About time!
  Wake up, Count, we're on!
CLUBS   Stand up, Belgians!
RAVAL
  Me: Tristan. Clubs: an Irishman's head.
  Yvette: the head's sister and Queen of Ireland.
  Kara: the niece of the head and called Isolde.
MRS ORMOND
  Look away, Elinor, they're using a head.
RAVAL
  Tristan addresses the head:
  Dear Head, I'm addressing you to the Palace
  Of Gurmun, Dublin, Ireland. Call it a tribute.
  No other message. Do not return to sender.
  Yours sincerely, the big bastard-killer,
  Tristan. Post scriptum:
  Not bad for a man with a . . . thigh full of shrapnel.
  Years?
FOL/KARA   *Pass!*
RAVAL   *Time?*
YVETTE/CLUBS   *Flies!*
TEAM   *Tristan –*
RAVAL
  Reckons he's dead unless he can find a doctor,
  So who's the best in the world?
YVETTE   *The Queen of Ireland!*
RAVAL
  Stands to reason. Right, I'm off to Ireland,
  Mark.
FOL   *Well that's a bit dangerous, isn't it, son?*
  They're a little bit cross with you about that head.
RAVAL
  Don't worry, I've an idea!

RAVAL *turns around three times*

                        Ta-da!
  Hello, my name is Tantris!
FOL   *Who are you?*

RAVAL
  I'm Tristan, but I'm in disguise! It works!
MRS ORMOND
  I can't keep up with this.
ORMOND   It's called a "farce".
  Because it's very fast but lacks the truth.
  There are three rules only:
  Respect nothing. Always laugh. Keep going.
  Fill the gaps with sarcasm and lighting.
RAVAL
  Don't blink, Henry, you'll miss the boat to Ireland!
YVETTE
  Who's the guy with that embarrassing wound?
KARA
  Another job for you, mum, by the look.
RAVAL
  May I present myself: my name is Tantris.
KARA
  Tantris, Tantris, Tantris, stupid name.

RAVAL *and* YVETTE *turn their backs and do something
suggestive*

RAVAL
  My, that's better!
YVETTE   *Good old Irish medicine.*
KARA
  Tantris, Tantris, Tantris . . .
RAVAL   *Must be going!*
ELINOR (*to* MRS ORMOND)
  I never learnt any of this.
ORMOND   It's pure invention.
RAVAL
  Missed the boat again! – Back home in Cornwall . . .
  I tell you, Mark, you want a cracking Queen:
  Look at this Isolde, a blonde of blondes,
  Not bad with her hands, just like her mother,
  Wanders about, muttering "Tantristantris";
  Apart from that, get her albionized.
  Yawning, Henry? A dragon's in the wings!

CLUBS *steps into the scene, a truly inept dragon*

CLUBS
  Rao, rao, rao.

ORMOND   That's a terrible dragon.

RAVAL'S TEAM *hits the floor*

TEAM
Help, help, it's a terrible, terrible dragon!
ORMOND
I mean it's an awful dragon.
YVETTE   *An awful dragon!*
RAVAL
It's a mean, terrible, awful, terrible dragon!
ORMOND (*to* MRS ORMOND)
What can one do with these people?
FOL   *What can we do,*
O People of Ireland?
CLUBS   *Rao, rao, rao.*
RAVAL
And the King said . . .
FOL   *Nothing for it, Isolde, my fair*
And eligible daughter: you'll be the prize
For the Dragon-Killer.
KARA   *Thanks, that's just the sort*
Of chap I had in mind.
FOL   *And the second prize*
Is a week in England watching an amateur play!
MRS ORMOND
Just like ours, Henry.
ORMOND   They know that, Margaret.
CLUBS
Rao, rao.
RAVAL   *And Tristan, lately arrived*
In Dublin again, on a Queen-hunt for his uncle,
Can't resist it: he doesn't believe his spunk'll
Fail him, nor expect that a priest or monk'll
Blame him – in any case, a dragon chunk'll
Help with the wooing he's doing the royal uncle.
ORMOND
That's "uncle" twice, if you notice.
FOL   *But there's a Steward,*
Paid-up member of the Royal Guild
Of Fops & Cowards and he's got the hots for Isolde,
And reckons he's in with a shout, because each time
He's in there's a shout –
KARA   *Sod off!*

[264]

FOL   *And he read somewhere*
   That a shout is a Yes.
KARA   *Sod off!*
CLUBS   *Rao, rao.*
FOL
   So he says he'll kill the dragon.
ORMOND
   Judge, I have an objection. There are certain
   Standards under which no act should fall
   In principle, and they, as "professionals",
   Rather than souls infused with dramatic spirit,
   Ought to observe them.
CAPTAIN   Standards? Standards for playing?
ORMOND
   Yes, and I am referring to their dragon.
YVETTE
   What's wrong with our dragon?
ORMOND   He isn't at all frightening.
CLUBS
   Rao, rao, rao.
ORMOND   Will you shut up?
   Not only is he not, but, if he is not,
   How can the onlooking audience form the impression
   That Tristan's act of vanquishment is heroic?
   I know that's not in their brief,
   Nothing so old and dull as the merely heroic,
   But, as I say, there are standards.
RAVAL (*to* YVETTE)   Where do you start?
CAPTAIN
   Have you a fierier spirit, Master Ormond?
ORMOND
   The doctor plays our disturbing parts.
YVETTE   I see,
   He's a witch-doctor. Toss me an apple, Kara.
KARA
   I've known him since I was born; he's a good giant.
CAPTAIN
   But are you a dragon, doctor?
VOGEL   Allow me a moment.
FOL
   Oh fine, so Ormond can just whinge us offstage?
CAPTAIN
   No, this is dragon-practice: a fest of frightening.
   Count, light that fire again.

CLUBS   *Rao, rao.*

CAPTAIN
Doctor, grill the assembled.

VOGEL
Fire and Frenzy, Frenzy and Fire, all Ireland
Shall char and crumble under my breath so violent!
None shall ever destroy me unless he be
Extremely strong and sail from over the sea!

RAVAL
That's not much of a boast. He may as well say
The sun will never come up until the morning.

CAPTAIN
Both are equally close and equally far.
We'll break this up with a boy. Valentin!
When Valentin comes down, both dragons
Do your worst: the worse dragon's the one
That pales him most: that will take the honours.

FOL
What honours?

CAPTAIN   Why, the stage next. Valentin!

Enter VALENTIN

CLUBS
Rao, rao, rao.

VOGEL
Who sees me dies, unless he runs away!
And he will die tomorrow, if not today!

VALENTIN
These are unusual men. What are they doing?

CAPTAIN
They're frightening you, Valentin, are they not?

VALENTIN
Not exactly, Captain. What did you wish?

CAPTAIN
Judgement, Valentin. Tell the assembled
Which of these dragons scares you most!

VALENTIN   Dragons?
I thought this a loon and this an inept poet.
Him I've observed though, Captain. I know this man
Rather a bizarre person and it's honestly not
Surprising he is making these noises.
But this man is a doctor, I believe.
A doctor pretending he's like a dragon I find
Slightly scarier, Captain.

ORMOND   A victory!
  Vogel, a victory!
CAPTAIN   Thank you, Valentin.
  Recuperate at the helm.
VALENTIN   I wanted to say:
  The monsieur stands, staring out at the cliffs.
CAPTAIN
  Thank you, Valentin.

Exit VALENTIN

                    Ormond has won.
  Consider the dragon done, and go from after.
ORMOND
  Ladies, you must find the wounded Tantris!
MRS ORMOND
  Oh yes, yes, *Isolde and Isolde . . .*

ORMOND *lies down, as Tristan wounded*

RAVAL
  Bets on a rhyme for "Tantris".
YVETTE   Pantries? Gantries?
MRS ORMOND
  Daughter, this is the minstrel who was hurt!
ELINOR
  Mother, he's hurt again. Look at his shirt.
  It smells like the blood of a dragon. Let's take him back
  And give him a bath – his skin is almost black!

ORMOND *rises and gets into a bath as he recites*

ORMOND
  And so Lord Tristan was on the Enemy's lands,
  The sister and niece of Morold, whom, with his hands,
  Tristan had done to death. He sat in the water
  Disguised as Tantris, before the beautiful daughter,
  Healed by the skilful mother, who took a splinter
  Out of his thigh –
RAVAL   Mais non, this generation!
  (*to* KARA) Tell your children's children, it wasn't his thigh!
ORMOND
  Out of his THIGH, and the daughter put it inter
  The sword of her dead uncle, and said –

[267]

ELINOR   *It fits!*
This man in the bath will have to rely on his wits!
For now I know he's the man who slew Morold!
Now I'll slay him, if I may grow so bold!
RAVAL
  At last – now, Ormond, why did she spare him?
  Wasn't that a suspicious act of mercy?
ORMOND
  Not at all: we will show how Tristan's courage,
  Cunning, wit and charm save him here
  While Isolde tries to summon the strength to strike!
RAVAL
  Something else was at work.
BRANWEN (*from above*)   No. Someone else.

Shocked pause. All register BRANWEN *as she descends*

  Allow an Irish exile to wheel her barrow
  Into this county fair of rumours.
  I knew one who knew a servant there
  At Gurmun's castle: this is a quarter-baked
  Washerwoman's account. But yours are both
  Being eaten indigestibly raw.
  The cousin of the Princess was there.
ORMOND
  Branwen, yes, but not in the room –
BRANWEN   But yes.
  In the room. You don't look like you know
  All that many servants, sir. I do.
RAVAL
  What did your servants say?
BRANWEN   Not mine, but that
  Branwen, the cousin, stepped between Tristan
  And a naked end at the hands of one who really,
  Truly loathed him. Neither wit nor charm
  Of his, nor sudden mercies of the Princess.
  Only a clear, sighted maid at a time
  Most were blind.
RAVAL   Not a bad story, Ormond.
  You could spin it an hour, an afternoon.
ORMOND
  I don't see what this proves about your so-called
  Scandal – yes, the cousin, but –

Enter CARDIN; *he sees* BRANWEN

CARDIN   You?
  I thought I heard a low, impossible voice –
  You! An actress now?
BRANWEN   A rumourmonger,
  Like all the living world.
CAPTAIN   Why should you care,
  Monsieur, if the healing-woman's maid
  Wishes to join our company of rumours?
CARDIN
  I absolutely forbid –
CAPTAIN   Upon my ship?
CARDIN
  This girl is in my keeping –
BRANWEN   Ha! Am I?
CAPTAIN
  No discord, please! Mademoiselle –
BRANWEN   O'Ronan.
CAPTAIN
  Your keeper has a case. Perhaps it's time
  To close our revels. I've got another game.
  Even the healing-woman and the birds will play.
  (*to* CARDIN) It's called a Masque of Truth. We form a ring,
  We find out who we are, and what we do.
  Perhaps we mime to each other: it's up to you,
  Monsieur, it's you who wishes to trade the drama
  For the dull fact. We could begin with the merchants.
  Look at their mystery contract –
CARDIN (*understanding*)   By all means play –
  The . . . acting game. I have no wish to – spoil it.
  I was – merely – alarmed to see Mademoiselle.
BRANWEN
  Don't fret, Mr Debonair. My tale's as true
  Or false as these, I'm sure.
CAPTAIN   May we proceed,
  Monsieur?
CARDIN   You may – act, while you can act.
CAPTAIN
  I'm sure we shall. The ball was I think with England.
ORMOND
  Very good. Is Mademoiselle on a side?

CAPTAIN
  No, she plays her wild card whenever.
  She doesn't settle for any old story, clearly.
ORMOND
  Well, the upshot was: Tristan was forgiven,
  Thus ending the Irish feud. But the cowardly Steward
  Claimed he had killed the dragon –
CAPTAIN   Skip the dragon.
  Tristan killed it, the Steward lied,
  Was publicly proven false: even we know that
  Who sail between the planets. On, Ormond.
ORMOND
  But the next thing's the marriage.
CAPTAIN   Oh no it isn't.
  The next thing's the voyage from Ireland
  To Cornwall, Fair Isolde
  Plucked from her own people, only her cousin
  With her now, and the go-between: Tristan.
ORMOND
  See, Raval? A go-between the two.
RAVAL
  At first, oui. A go-between at first.
MRS ORMOND
  I don't see how we can do the voyage, Henry.
  You haven't written it, have you?
ORMOND   Of course not.
  It's only a sea-crossing. Nothing really happens.
RAVAL
  I never heard any tales about the voyage.
BRANWEN
  Didn't you. Well then that clips your wings.
CAPTAIN
  I think so too, and if both illustrious teams
  Are suddenly at a loss, I have a solution.
  I myself will form a team, and we
  Shall use our imagination. Allow me . . .

CAPTAIN *ascends to* ISOLDE's *cabin door, and knocks*

CARDIN
  No, no, Captain, I –
CAPTAIN   You wish to play
  The Masque of Truth again? we'll begin with you:
  What is your real mission? Is it –

CARDIN   No –
Do . . . act, do.
CAPTAIN (*descending*) The healing-woman
Is going to present a personal act of healing
Between your weary factions.

ISOLDE *comes out of the cabin and descends, slowly. She sits*

ISOLDE
*I curse the man . . . I curse the man who brings me
Out of my home and everything I remember
To marry me to an alien king. I had rather
Died than set my eyes on him. I had rather
Married the Steward. Mother,
I'll never see you again. Branwen, cousin,
Alone with sailors and this one arrogant lord
. . . Tristan. Mother, I wish
The healing powers you possess and I will possess
Were cursing powers. For I would pepper the sea.
Mother, think of me
Lost on the deck with the man who slaughtered your brother,
My uncle – and has purchased me for his king.*

CAPTAIN
Mademoiselle O'Ronan, will you play
The Irish cousin? the wine can play the poison,

ISOLDE *and* BRANWEN *react sharply*

If you see what I mean.
I myself shall humbly attempt a Tristan.

CARDIN
What poison do you mean?

BRANWEN   I'll be the cousin.

ISOLDE
Branwen, we are wholly lost now.

BRANWEN
Dear Isolde, no. Among so many?

CARDIN
What poison, Captain?

ORMOND   I suspect another slander,
Though the lady is a not-to-be-sneezed-at actress
Certainly, at the sad end of the spectrum.

FOL
What is this, Team Three?

RAVAL   Who cares now.
This sea-captain's rules are made of fish-scales.

CAPTAIN
Irish friend: tell how the cousin guarded
An irresistible potion of true love;
How Queen Isolde, the mother, had brewed it, only
To drink with the Cornish Mark, so that her daughter
Would *think* she loved him at least . . .

CARDIN   This is arrant nonsense.

BRANWEN
Why should I tell all that?
You yourself are happy engulfing the boat
With waves of the disastrous and forgotten.

CAPTAIN   Oh?
Am I?

BRANWEN   They say there was a potion, yes.

CAPTAIN
And?

BRANWEN   Something went wrong.

CAPTAIN   And? And?

BRANWEN
"And? And?" And it got drunk, like this!

BRANWEN *seizes a bottle of wine and exits to her cabin*

ISOLDE (*to* CAPTAIN)
I am sorry, sir, for the conduct of Mademoiselle.

CARDIN
You apologise to him? What are you doing,
Sir? What are you saying?

ORMOND   I'm saying Good night.
And so is every Ormond, Contrariwise
Included. I feel a slander in the weather.
I sense an impending insult.

KARA   Raval is my captain.
It's up to him if I have to go the cabin.

ORMOND
Assuredly not.

ELINOR   Be sensible for once.

RAVAL
Au revoir, my favourite Isolde . . .

YVETTE
Favourite, Henri? Where do I finish?

RAVAL
Here, my favourite Yvette.

ORMOND   Good night to you all.
To defend the name of our Queen we are ready even
To yield the merchandise to these jongleurs.
And Henri, you yourself
Are quite outslandered by this ragged shipman.
CAPTAIN
Stow yourself, monsieur, where you are quietest.

Exeunt the ORMONDS *and* VOGEL

RAVAL
Nothing amuses us
About your script, mon capitan. It is sad:
We do this work to brighten our time not weigh it
Down like this.
CAPTAIN   Then go. There are no jokes coming.
And clearly you'll miss your Ormonds.
RAVAL   It's no game
Without them.
YVETTE   And we're tired, blue and tired.
Come on, Count.
CLUBS   I was thinking it today,
How the millwheel turns. He's sure to play his guitar.

Exeunt RAVAL'S TROUPE. *Later we hear Guido's guitar,*
softly

SCENE IV
The same, continuous.

CAPTAIN
Well, we have an audience of one.
CARDIN (*to* ISOLDE)
Speak aside – what hold does he have on you?
CAPTAIN
No more than I have on you, Cardin of Brittany.
Two things only. One is that I know
Everything. Don't ask me how I know
Or I might tell you. Two, is that I will say
Nothing, if you do just what I say.
CARDIN
Which is.

CAPTAIN   In your case, noble and hired duke,
  Go up on deck and do what you like. Drink,
  Peer in the night for your castle silhouette.
  Work for the cabin-boy. Be my lookout.
  Do what you will but don't – disturb us.
  We're playing this act to an end and need some time.
CARDIN (*to* ISOLDE)
  What do you say to this?
  (*to* CAPTAIN) – You'll know a due reward for this, Captain.
  I hope to be paymaster.

Exit CARDIN

CAPTAIN
  A boy entirely sewn together with hopes.
  He must quite love your friend.
ISOLDE   He does love him.
  For he inspires love and only love
  In hearts that are good. The opposites he engenders
  Are on despicable show before my eyes.
CAPTAIN
  That sounded suspiciously not like acting.
  Will you go on with your scene, or shall I summon
  The various players back to meet a monarch,
  A live royal in the flesh?
ISOLDE   Such as you are,
  Break the heart of hatred and leave only
  A borderless field. An end is my only wish.
CAPTAIN
  By the by, whom do you think is winning?
  The English are very loyal, are they not? though
  You must know only too well, how silly they seem
  Pony-riding in a tale of honest virtue.
ISOLDE
  If I were alive I'd love them for it.
CAPTAIN   The French . . .
  Not exactly taking it seriously, are they?
  They probably think, well,
  It wasn't just Tristan but many a beau at Tintagel
  Over the years . . . they don't really see it either.
  How stories spread and gather!
ISOLDE
  Captain, where is Tristan?
CAPTAIN   He's in Karke.

ISOLDE
  How near to death?
CAPTAIN   Track down Death and measure.
ISOLDE
  From where do you know me?
CAPTAIN   The floor up, and earlier.
ISOLDE
  Why do you torture me?
CAPTAIN   Because it's torture.
ISOLDE
  What is torture?
CAPTAIN   Love without a lover.
ISOLDE
  What kind of love?
CAPTAIN   The only and forever.
ISOLDE
  And is it I?
CAPTAIN   Yes, it is, Isolde.
ISOLDE
  So, that's it, for all your mystery,
  Duplicity and calm, calm lying.
  Your enigma drains away, leaving a brute
  Ignoble stump and that's all.
CAPTAIN
  But it's not all.
ISOLDE   Whatever you say, it's all.
  And for it, you are steeped in all evils.
CAPTAIN
  – Let's play our scene, before you send me away
  Crying "The healing-woman is Queen Isolde,
  A whore in transit!"

He fetches a bottle of water

                  Look, I've brought you some water
  A second time.
ISOLDE   I didn't want it.
CAPTAIN   But look.
ISOLDE
  It's unclean.
CAPTAIN   It's seawater.
  It's lasted twenty years. The day its breath
  Was corked was a hot day. An English ship
  Was sailing home from Ireland with a Princess.

[275]

Tristan was on the ship and so was Branwen.
Branwen possessed a bottle she was charged
At all costs with conserving till Isolde
Could drink it with King Mark, and so adore him.
The ship sailed into a cove so the men could bathe
And cool themselves. Three remained on the ship.
Isolde . . .

ISOLDE   . . . Lord Tristan.

CAPTAIN   And a serving girl.

ISOLDE
Branwen had left the bottle and gone to the cove.

CAPTAIN
The servant didn't know. It looked like wine.
Play the part, Isolde.

ISOLDE   It's – no, no –

CAPTAIN
Play the part.

ISOLDE   Further than evil!

CAPTAIN   Play it!

ISOLDE
– *Bring me a drink, Lord Tristan, I – am thirsty* . . .

CAPTAIN
Lady, I'll call the servant. Girl, some wine!

ISOLDE
I'd rather sleep, Lord Tristan, be – alone.

CAPTAIN
You asked for a drink and here it comes. Drink!

ISOLDE
Home – homesick! Oh, Tristan!

CAPTAIN   Drink it down!

ISOLDE *takes the glass*

ISOLDE
It's s-s-seawater.

CAPTAIN   Drink it, Highness,
(*voice rising*) Highness, Highness –

ISOLDE   Tristan, oh my love!

ISOLDE *drinks, tastes and spits it out*

Uch – it's warm, sweet, it's – it's drunk . . .
Tr – Tristan drank it too. You have to drink.

[276]

CAPTAIN
This Tristan doesn't need to.
He swallowed it for real where he swam.
He was a cabin-boy. The day was as hot
For cabin-boys as Queens and heroes. I stripped,
And dove deep from the ship. I think I'd swum
Ten times bow to stern,
When the ocean from its delicate lapping blue
Seemed to crimson and stir,
Seethe, crackle my skin and I gulped for air –
All went dark and I must have floated for hours,
Dreaming. When I paddled back to the ship
From a green cove the current had tugged me into,
I glimpsed you both on the deck, staring down
Oblivious, unable to blink or move.
And I stared back your love.
All three were stuck. You didn't want to see me.
Do have the decency to tell me truly:
Didn't your cousin come back, see what had happened,
And in her remorse void the poisonous flagon
Back in the sea? Or why would I
Have lived since like this?
Tracking, trailing, disguising, spying
Tristan, Isolde; Isolde, Tristan! Queen,
I know more about you than your cousin, more
Than a thousand roles of actors, more than yourself!
You can't remember how or why you loved
Him who has caused this final shame and exile,
Beautiful Isolde. I found this work,
Knowing how close to your lord was the eager duke,
Certain to follow him would be to find you.
And the night we sailed from Cornwall,
As the troubadours came aboard and the providential
Innocent Ormonds tried to steal their passage –
I watched the Breton rowing his hooded women
Over the bay towards me, into my arms.
Remember, a single gust
But strong blew your dark hood from your blonde hair
A moment only – but there was Isolde there.
And here was Isolde here.
And here is Isolde here.

The CAPTAIN *leans and kisses* ISOLDE *on the mouth; she
neither parts her lips nor pulls away. This lasts five seconds*

When the moon begins to move between
The North Star and the tip of the Swan's wing,
Open the door and leave it open. It's soon.
Send your cousin away if she wakes up.
After, after,
All pain is over: we land and you heal the sick.
You cure your lover of all in a single drop.
I start to sail west and I do not stop.

Exit CAPTAIN

ISOLDE (*disorientated*)
Tristan? That was a sweet, sickly wine.
Where have his actors gone away to? Tristan?
I'm sick. I'm on a sea. I'm on this sea.
I'll drown in this sea. Try to drown in this sea
Too, Tristan, amour. Then,
A great fish as large as a shire will come
And swallow us two together. That'll make it
Love us, dear. It's dark and it moves here.
God does not desire that I see you, Tristan.
It is not a hope of His, it has not
Entered into His mind,
But He
Has manned this ship with a devil who has your eyes.
Your eyes. And I am afraid of the Lady Isolde
Of White Hands, Tristan, if I should drown
In this sea, of all seas the last sea.

Enter ORMOND

ORMOND
Excuse me, noble lady.
Only a glass of water.
ISOLDE   Yes. Are you English?
ORMOND
Of Wessex, England.
ISOLDE   Is that a peaceful place?
ORMOND
Yes, mostly it is.
ISOLDE   But so is this.
ORMOND
– I think we'll be landed soon.
My Margaret always feels it in her bones.

It's been a pleasure to travel with you. I hope
You're able to work your marvels!
ISOLDE   Thank you, sir.
ORMOND
  So. Good night.
ISOLDE   There you go with your drink.

Exit ORMOND

  Your eyes. The moon, the moon –
  What did I just drink? Tristan? Tristan?

*She ascends and enters her cabin, shutting the door. After a
while, it slowly opens. Enter the* CAPTAIN, *below*

ACT IV

The "Esperance", below deck, dawn on the fifth day of the return crossing.

Deserted and dark. CARDIN *and* VALENTIN *are heard off-stage*

CARDIN
  Not that – beyond the cliff!
VALENTIN   The red cliff?
CARDIN
  It isn't a cliff, it's a rampart – Land! Land!
VALENTIN
  It's your land, sir!
CARDIN   Karke! The voyage is over!

Enter from the direction of the cabin used by RAVAL'S
TROUPE, *surreptitiously,* KARA. *She scurries across and exits*

  And the sun's catching it, making it scarlet – look!
VALENTIN
  I see it, sir, I see it!
CARDIN   I see the lawns!
  Hoist the white flag at last!

Enter from ISOLDE's *cabin the* CAPTAIN; *he descends and
exits.* YVETTE *enters from the direction of the troubadours'
cabin, looks around with suspicion, and catches sight of the*
CAPTAIN *leaving. She exits. Enter* CARDIN: *he goes up to
the* WOMEN'S *cabin, and knocks.* BRANWEN *appears*

  We've seen the Castle of Karke in all its glory
  Right at the sunrise, Branwen!
BRANWEN   "Mademoiselle".
CARDIN
  Yes, yes, but it's over, we're there, the nightmare,
  I'm home on the fortieth day and it turns the others
  To days that never were! The boy – above –
  We're flying the white flag in the sight of Tristan!
BRANWEN
  Of whom?

CARDIN   I'm sorry – I know. Tell your lady
  To prepare herself, come upon deck, – and bring
  Her comb, the green comb she wears sometimes
  And soon, now, come – I can see the Castle!

Enter RAVAL, GUIDO *and* CLUBS, *somewhat hungover*

RAVAL
  A very theatrical cry is going up.
  I wonder if Ormond scripted our lives this morning.
GUIDO
  We have to speak in his couples, and move like – so.
CARDIN
  We're home, Raval, go up and see for yourself!
CLUBS
  The act in the rain upstairs we can do remember.
CARDIN
  Rain, old fellow? The sun is pouring down
  And every minute laughs at the one that's ended!

Exeunt RAVAL, GUIDO *and* CLUBS

  (*shouts up*) Ladies, slow to rise to see my homeland?

Enter YVETTE *and* FOL

FOL
  This is the man who's always shutting *us* up.
  What a percussion, considering my headache.
CARDIN
  It's Karke, Brittany: we can see its banners!
FOL
  You mean it's time for a drink. There, we differ.
  Be nice to meet some air though, eh Yvette?

Exeunt YVETTE *and* FOL

CARDIN (*shouts up*) Ladies, are you marooned in time?

BRANWEN *appears*

BRANWEN   Sir.
  Your idea it was to locate a certain
  Object we have seen but cannot find.

[281]

CARDIN
  It's green, mademoiselle!
BRANWEN   Green, is it.
  When you said green of course I thought I heard red
  And started hunting a comb the colour of sky.
CARDIN
  Let me find it –

CARDIN *starts to go up. Enter* VALENTIN

VALENTIN   Monsieur.
CARDIN (*stops*)
  Valentin, mon ami, why aren't you up there
  Catching the wind in the sails?
VALENTIN   There's no room.
  The troubadours are generally seeing double,
  And the English family I always mistake for
  Several English families at one go.
CARDIN
  Yes – did you hoist the white flag? Is it flying?
VALENTIN
  Yes, monsieur, and I'm afraid, suddenly, no.
CARDIN
  What does that mean – afraid, suddenly, what?
VALENTIN
  Yes, it's hoisted. No, it is not flying.
  The wind we had has died.
CARDIN
  Died, what do you mean?
VALENTIN   Died, like a person.
  The breathing it was doing it has ceased,
  All of a sudden, to do.
CARDIN   But we are in sight
  Of Karke, Valentin!
VALENTIN   Very striking it is,
  Its redstone walls but sir:
  If the wind has died we cannot move, and it has,
  And we cannot.
BRANWEN   So, a little less hurry
  In your dawn manner, would I be right in saying?
CARDIN
  My God, a thickening prison.
  Somebody drag this moment back to its cell.
  Bran – Mademoiselle, still bring the lady –
  We can be seen from the land, and our still flag

Is nevertheless a pure, pure white –
And find – forget the comb, bring the lady now.
BRANWEN
By all means, C-Ca-Car-Monsieur.

Exit BRANWEN

CARDIN
Valentin, what can we do?
VALENTIN   Hope for a breath.
The Captain knows how to work the sail so the slightest
Whisper from a petrel, even a dolphin's
Gossiping can edge us on our way.
CARDIN
Can only the Captain do that?
VALENTIN   He's a sailor,
A born sailor. Of course.
CARDIN   Could anyone swim?
– I could swim there, raise the villages, bring
Fishing boats out here.
VALENTIN   Well, if you made
The coast by way of zigzag between serpents
And turned to wave you'd find us all in a line,
On our knees to Triton.
CARDIN   I know,
I know this stretch of coast. – Valentin,
Find the Captain and bring him here.
VALENTIN   Sir,
I saw him enter his cabin. This is his hour
Always to sleep.
CARDIN   If he's asleep, wake him.
If he is dead, wake him and cook him breakfast.
If he never existed, wake him, cook him breakfast
And shave his damnable head.
VALENTIN   Very good, monsieur.

Exit VALENTIN. BRANWEN *and* ISOLDE *appear above*

CARDIN
Ladies, at last, and by this – ghastly time
The news has turned its back and is bad news.
ISOLDE
She told me. Not a breath and we can't move.
CARDIN
Inches forward and inches backward.

But we can be seen, my lady, from the Castle,
And our white flag clearly flying.
BRANWEN   Hanging.
CARDIN
But white where nothing else is white, woman.
ISOLDE
I'd like to go up and see the Castle, Cardin.
CARDIN
Yes – I'm afraid the deck is littered with all
The other people.
BRANWEN   We like other people.
ISOLDE
Cousin, let's go up. The entire world
Has ended but let's have a view of it.
BRANWEN
Fine, but we both know
If this boy doesn't, a castle is what but a great
Sarcophagus of gulls, flies and adders.
It may be fun to see a new design
But it'll smell the same. I was rather banking
On sea-entombment finally: no questions,
No ceremony, evidence, or visitors.
ISOLDE
All is ended, cousin. You rage and sputter
Like you were alone on the low
Jetty into Hell: we are all there.
CARDIN
Or none of us – this is the last day
Of the allotted time but the time is not
Over! He will live until it is!
While he has hope I swear he is alive
And breathing.
BRANWEN   Fine. So he can suck us home.
ISOLDE
Thank you, Cardin. Come on, cousin: above.

As ISOLDE *and* BRANWEN *make to leave they encounter the*
CAPTAIN *coming in*

CAPTAIN
Pardon me, ladies, this schoolboy
Has woken me with his wailing of kings and castles.
You catch me not at my best.
BRANWEN   Didn't I catch you

[284]

Once, in a garden, hanging upside-down
Being spoonfed boiling oil by dwarfs
With hooves cloven and tails forked? Pardon:
I took that for your best.
CAPTAIN   That's what it was.
What an abrasive relative you have,
Clinging to you cursing, healing lady.
BRANWEN
A day will come when mouths like yours'll be healed.
CAPTAIN
The day they catch the god who gashed them open.
ISOLDE
Follow me to Heaven, cousin, the Heaven
There is where he is not.
CAPTAIN   Or not today.
Noble ladies . . .

Exeunt ISOLDE *and* BRANWEN

SCENE II
The same, continuous.

CARDIN
I sent for you to experience the joy
Of sending you away. Go up on deck,
And wait for the slightest breath – Valentin says
You work the sail so well –
CAPTAIN   Valentin says?
Hmm, I wonder, is this one of those
Lengthy and sleepy dreams that come as you lie
Intending to rise: or are you growing insane,
Captain Cardin? You appear
To have sprouted an admiral hat, and the boy become
A master mariner non-pareil. The minor
Point you have omitted from the agenda
Is that I know your name. Ah no – another:
That I know their names. Oh, wait, another:
That I am the Captain of the "Esperance",
(Which of itself should puff your orders back):
That Valentin's a boy – how many is that? –
A clueless apprentice only – and, in fact,

Last-remembered, most-pertaining point,
I do not wish to go on deck, monsieur.
I wish to yawn: there. It's very early.
CARDIN
Do you fear nothing?
CAPTAIN   Stowaways and Germans.
You're Breton and invited, so all's well.
CARDIN
All's well where you are.
CAPTAIN   Also, you also.
For as I say: it's early, admiral.
Very early upon the fortieth day.
Id est: You have come home and you are in time.
Id est: The sun is up and strumming his lute.
Id est: how about a shade of danke schoen?
CARDIN
We can't move. Don't you know the wind has dropped?
CAPTAIN
Look at you: you're about to say I dropped it,
Aren't you, boy? But another reason I won't
Go on deck, is I've been on deck already,
While you were doing the Dance of the Fresh Daisies.
CARDIN
You've seen the Castle?
CAPTAIN   Yes, and I've seen the Ormonds,
Ranged about the deck, each with a finger
Sucked and held to the air, wet: for example,
Daddy to the west, the girl to the east, the doctor
Doing it wrong, the mother somewhere between.
I hope no ship comes by: to see this English
Candelabra of amateur sailors, a poor
Fisherman might take it for the fabled
Dawn nightmare boat. Then there's the gang,
Stale and sweating, slumped on the deck in a ring,
Each head on the neighbourly belly, so that one
Giggle convulses the next, the next the next,
And so on like one single
Newly created pentagrammatic fool.
The girl says an English word – that does the trick.
Raval snorts and that's the joke of the age.
I hope I can use these fools inland.
CARDIN   Inland
Expect nothing but trial.
CAPTAIN   I expect little

Enough as it is, but a trial would be a bonus.
If I'd not had my bonus already.
I'm glad I'm not a Breton, though. The tradition
By which a captain, hired to sail to Cornwall
With hired dissemblers, hired to take a secret
Duke along so he could pluck two women,
One the Queen of the country visited,
(A fine memento that for a trip, I think)
Safely out of that country, hooded, in no more
Than forty days, and who then does this exactly
And to the letter, the tradition by which that captain
Is in sincere gratitude court-martialled –
This tradition I can live without, admiral.

CARDIN

That history was not so much one-sided
As one-worded and that word was a lie.
Somehow, I don't know how,
You have extorted acts of obedience.
That I could believe it plausible the wind
Has died at your command, ought to expose
The nub of what I think of you.

CAPTAIN   It is
A hot, dusty shame, that lack of a breeze.
That's ocean life all over. But we had luck
With your storm after all, blowing us on.

CARDIN

Luck for us. You would prefer this ship
To creak to the last months of the millennium,
Crewed by skeleton personnel.

CAPTAIN   Why not?
Skulls are dramatic; two can bang on a ribcage.
So the actors wouldn't mind, so long as they found
A recipe for cheap wine from seaweed.

CARDIN

What's that in your hand?

CAPTAIN   It is a comb.

CARDIN

It's a green comb.

CAPTAIN   It is, for when at last
Our galleon goes down, and the crabs applaud.

CARDIN

It is my lady's.

CAPTAIN   Is it. Have it. Return it.
If you would be so kind.

CARDIN Where did you find it?

CAPTAIN

I found it on her floor, and I absently
Put it into my pocket.

CARDIN

What were you doing – what were you doing in there?

CAPTAIN

Are you old enough to learn, I wonder? . . . no.
If you were old enough you wouldn't ask.

CARDIN

This nightmare doesn't work.
I know it for a nightmare.

CAPTAIN Then, of course,

By all means execute your fondest wish
As one would in a discovered dream and kill me.
Then wait for another storm to blow a heavenly
Mariner aboard.

CARDIN

We're visible from the shore: they might send boats.

CAPTAIN

Why would they believe we needed their boats?
We're only a speck in the distance. If you saw us
Would you cry: "Look! They have no landing-boat!
And a poor, homesick Breton is surely among them,
For whom today is the final and fortieth day!"
No, you would say: "What a still and peaceful morning
They chose to sail beside the Breton coast!
How amiable's the world . . ."

CARDIN Whose ghost or demon

Are you? One my master destroyed – which one?

CAPTAIN

How boastful on another's behalf you are!
And superstitious as a born shipman. No,
I am a real, urgently busy human,
Bereft of the pleasure of a head-to-head with your
Superhuman lord.
You'll have to wait for the wind now and trust me.

CARDIN

Trust? What were you doing in the ladies' cabin?

CAPTAIN

The Royal Quarters? Let's not have a secret,
Cardin: but this was unfinished business
And not especially yours.

CARDIN Don't speak my name.

CAPTAIN
  Now why, of many reasons?
  Unintroduced as an Englishman? Or shy?
  Or isn't it your name? Are you an actor?
  Well if you are you're quite the pick of the cargo.
  I took you for an over-excited noble.
  Everybody else believes you're a Breton.
CARDIN
  I'll be myself to the end. Don't speak my name
  Because your breath infects it, and I need it.
  What was your business?
CAPTAIN   Love.
CARDIN
  – That wriggles out at the far end of a lie.
CAPTAIN
  Believe it then. I do. We had a – tryst.
CARDIN
  The air is turning colour as you bruise it.
CAPTAIN
  Look at the comb. You say it's hers. It is.
  How else would I get it? Why else show it you?
  I feel an innardly gust of honesty.
  I did want you to know.
CARDIN   A gift of hatred?
CAPTAIN
  A gift, at all accounts. But I love Isolde.
CARDIN
  Half the world does too, but she loves only
  Tristan, and your words are below shame.
CAPTAIN
  For once I hear no denial of the name.
  – When you were kind enough to let us alone
  And be my lookout above,
  I told her how and from where I knew her, how
  I've followed her for love,
  And then we drank, and reminisced, and played
  Our duet of the way it was. After,
  She took to her bed and, after, so did I.
CARDIN
  She would have locked the door.
CAPTAIN   She opened it.
CARDIN
  She would have screamed.
CAPTAIN   She did it soundlessly.

CARDIN
She would have killed you.
CAPTAIN   "Would" as in "wanted to",
But then again, this ship would have no captain,
And be dragged westward, fortieth night, forty-
First night, fiftieth, hundredth, thousandth, on
And on to the Great Whoops.
CARDIN
The boy can steer the ship.
CAPTAIN   No, he cannot.
Not into a harbour: that's a skill.
The boy knows only words and those the wrong ones.
CARDIN
Taught him by you.
CAPTAIN   Most diligently learned.
CARDIN
She – can't love you.
CAPTAIN   Doubtless she abhors me.
CARDIN
She – would have told me.
CAPTAIN   I have saved her trouble.
CARDIN
You did – your worst.
CAPTAIN   I did my best. I thought so.
CARDIN
– Death you merited, sir, so long ago,
I cannot – add to death. You have to die.
CAPTAIN
That I understand. You love her, clearly,
But how will you get home?
CARDIN   It's not for me
To do the act, it's for a Court Assizes
To listen and determine.
CAPTAIN   Merciful,
I'm sure, monsieur. But I won't have you charge me
With loving the wrong lady. Loving a Queen
Is oh, a public quartering at the least,
And forty Bretons banqueting on the quarters;
Having her cousin should mean a commutation
Perhaps to a hanging or burning.
CARDIN   Her . . . cousin?
CAPTAIN
Yes, it's hardly the regicidal
Crime against humanity you seem

[290]

To think I spent the thirty-ninth night
Tangled up in.
CARDIN   Horrid: the Irish cousin?
CAPTAIN
Branwen, yes, a vigorous staring woman
When vertical – when up against it, heavens,
All stars mixed in the dark with sudden fumes
Of wine and embittered life: now I know first hand
How trusting, dull, was that Cornwall King Mark,
Stroking the glossy brass he mistook for gold
When, with the candles blown on the honeymoon,
Cousin gave up her innocence for Queen.
How blind are the lovingly open-eyed, Cardin.
How sighted are the ones as – gone as I am.
CARDIN
The cousin, you and the cousin.
CAPTAIN
And what appals me now,
Beyond that to repeat the treacherous plot
They spun some twenty years ago to gull
A panting King – was so predictable,
So easy to imagine, to perform –
Is that they must believe they were successful,
That I am fooled, thinking I had the Queen,
And not the gasping, wine-polluted –

CARDIN *draws a dagger, pushes the* CAPTAIN *against a wall
and holds it to his throat*

CARDIN   Captain!
CAPTAIN
Oh-ho, a Bretonic tantrum.
CARDIN   Do not move!
CAPTAIN
I'll act the role of my ship. There, there.
Now what.
CARDIN   I do not know.
Is it, anywhere – known that the Queen and Branwen
Gulled the King like this?
CAPTAIN   Look about you.
Ask the Ormonds, tell the troubadours.
It's the secret of the age.
CARDIN   So how do you know it?

[291]

CAPTAIN
  I sailed on the ship that brought Isolde to Mark.
  Saw her and Tristan engage on their Great Rumour.
  More than a rumour then, whatever came later.
  I had an interest – I heard them lay this plot
  To forge her bygone chastity with this
  Young dissembling cousin.
  I know all the secrets of the age . . .
  I'm still here, Cardin. Being my ship.
  Shame if the wind gets up
  And here I am, nailed to the ocean floor.
  The girls might get quite cross at that.
CARDIN   Be quiet.
CAPTAIN
  Still, at peace, sailing.
CARDIN   Yes, yes.
CAPTAIN
  Pity about not having a landing-boat.
CARDIN
  The boy told me he knew it was sabotage.
  You don't, therefore, need to tell me whose.
CAPTAIN
  Fine, I shan't.
CARDIN   Nor that your sea-instinct
  To sail east was not sea-instinct
  But trying to slow us down. My land-instinct
  I should have trusted: a spasm of foreboding
  The hour I set my eyes on you.
CAPTAIN   Indeed.
  No breeze as yet.
CARDIN   An angel's holding his breath,
  Astounded by a sight of the depths at which
  Evil swims in you.
CAPTAIN   Evil. Oh,
  Love and a plan, Love and a plan, Cardin.
  How else have your beloved Queen and her cousin,
  Your Tristan and his enemies in England,
  His friends in Karke, giants and men he slaughtered
  Chivalrously – how else have these lived?
  Tristan loves Isolde, so he plans.
  The Captain loves Isolde, so he plans.
  Because he loves Isolde, she plans
  And uses yet again her agreeable cousin.
  You and she should get along, you are both

Useful to lovers' plans: you move your square
With dignity on the chessboard, while the game
Soars and whistles above and around your heads.
Evil, Cardin? Love and the next plan.
Now, move wherever you can.
Everybody is quiet. Listen.
CARDIN   Look.

CARDIN *stabs the* CAPTAIN *in the ribs. They stare at each other. The* CAPTAIN *smiles and looks down at the dagger*

CAPTAIN
How is that done?

He puts his fingers to the point of entry: they come away bloody and he looks up at CARDIN

                        How is this done?
CARDIN (*driving in the blade*)   Thus,
Diagonally!
CAPTAIN   Euch. – Truer – .

CARDIN *pulls out the blade, and the* CAPTAIN *falls to the ground*

CARDIN
Remember, remember:
I am the one on this ship who is playing himself.
And this is what I have done. (*hisses*) Valentin!

Exit CARDIN

(*off, urgently*) Valentin!

Enter CARDIN *and* VALENTIN

                        Look.

VALENTIN *goes to the body*

VALENTIN
Well, there's his blood on the floor already.
Was it a duel?
CARDIN   No. It was a murder.
I'll answer it ashore. Before it happened

He told me your marine education
Was worthless. That he had taught you falsely.
VALENTIN
So blooms a growing feeling. The English actor
Kept saying so.
CARDIN   So you can't work the sails?
VALENTIN
Only with a strong wind, and then –
Maybe. Not like he could. But – Ormond.
He seems to know some principles I couldn't
Understand.
CARDIN   That would be Providence.
VALENTIN
With the wind dead, monsieur, we cannot move,
Captain alive or no. Either we swim
Or hope another passes.
CARDIN   Go on deck.
Say nothing about anything, but let
Nobody come down. I'll find a sheet
To curl this shipman in.
VALENTIN   Was it one wound?
CARDIN
Yes.
VALENTIN   A deep one?
CARDIN   Deep enough, yes.
Go up and pray.
VALENTIN   I will, monsieur, thank you.

Exit VALENTIN. *Exit* CARDIN. *After a moment, the* CAP-
TAIN *stirs, tries to rise, can't, but drags his body off, like a
snake*

SCENE III
The same, continuous.

Enter CARDIN, *and sees the body is gone*

CARDIN
Valentin, I said, I'd do this.

*Noticing a trail of blood leading off, he starts to follow it, but
enter* VALENTIN, *trying to keep out* ORMOND *and* ELINOR

What did you do?

VALENTIN   I can't stop him, sir.

ORMOND
  We have an end to stopping, good monsieur!
  We waited, as a family, for that breath
  To help us in, we waited in a ring,
  As I instructed, I myself taught
  When a mere boy, –

VALENTIN   He says he felt a breath.

ORMOND
  Do we have time to jump ahead like that?

CARDIN
  It's all we have, Mr Ormond: say what you felt.

ORMOND
  I: nothing. Elinor . . .
  Say what you felt, Elinor.

ELINOR   Nothing, but look!

ORMOND
  See? Her hair! Always so bunched and tidy,
  Now – see? This: wild and indicative!
  Does it not stand out, sir?

CARDIN   It does. Where
  Exactly were you standing?

ORMOND   I thought of that!
  It means it came from the north! Am I not wrong
  In stating that is precisely what we require?

CARDIN
  Yes, you're right. Was –

ORMOND   Thanks be to the saints,
  Elinor I had posted there! The doctor's
  Hair is either flyaway or gone,
  And Kara's like she permanently walks
  In beauty through a whirlwind. Elinor,
  Excellent weathervane!

CARDIN   Go up on deck,
  Mr Ormond, and feel what you can feel.
  If the wind rises, as this suggests it might,
  We certainly need your help in recollecting
  Knowledge of the sails.

ORMOND   You need my help?
  I had of the Captain inferred otherwise.

CARDIN
  We cannot find the Captain. We believe
  He may be lost.

[295]

ELINOR   Heavens!
CARDIN   This is, please,
  Not to be mentioned above. Mr Ormond, please,
  Go up and be prepared.
ORMOND   Be prepared?
  I always tell my young ones "Be prepared".

Exeunt ORMOND *and* ELINOR

VALENTIN
  They didn't see his blood.
CARDIN   It's just as well.
  His body's gone. He couldn't have been dead!
VALENTIN
  You said the cut was deep.
CARDIN   It was, it was.
  – I don't see what to do but find him and kill him.
VALENTIN
  A second heat of the moment?
CARDIN   I never said
  It was the heat. I said it was a murder.
VALENTIN
  And now it isn't one.
CARDIN   Go up again,
  And wait with Ormond. Send the ladies down.

Exit VALENTIN

  Only a devil crawls away with that.
  Tristan would have cut him into forty.
  But a devil would crawl away with that too.
  God send a breeze, for Isolde, for my lord.
  Is this them?

Enter RAVAL, YVETTE, FOL, CLUBS *and* GUIDO, *with a
piece of paper they are fighting over and laughing about*

FOL   I saved it in time, just
  A breath from gliding overboard! here,
  Read –
YVETTE
  And so it was King Mark espied a naked
  Sword between the two, and wanted to take it
  And cut his nephew down, but then he knew
  The sword was but a symbol of the true

Friendly love, not more, between the friends
Whom he had banished. He would make amends,
Apologise that ever he could think
His comely Queen Isolde would ever sink
To an adulterous passion, or that his favourite
Tristan would (though if he did he'd pay for it).

FOL
Vas-y, Raval.

RAVAL (*improvising*)
. . . For it is widely known that the best of fellows
Always employ enormous swords for pillows,
And show their loyalty to God and King
By sleeping with the nearest Queen, a thing
Mark had often noticed. It's a tradition!
He cried, I'd do it myself in his position!

FOL (*improvising*)
If you like the Queen, don't take her to a tavern,
Strip her naked and lay her in a cavern!
What better way to prove you love the King
And everything he stands for? Everything!

RAVAL
Space for a song, I think.

YVETTE   Not in this throat.

Enter ISOLDE *and* BRANWEN *from the deck*

CARDIN
Ladies, to the cabin – we must speak!

Enter KARA *in distress: she falls into the arms of* RAVAL

KARA
Haiee, the swimmer, the swimmer!

YVETTE   Raval, a duet?

RAVAL
What's the matter, my dear?

YVETTE   Oh a dear duet.

KARA
I fell asleep in the hold, I woke and looked
Out at the underwater where a pale man
Was swimming at the window – the porthole!

CARDIN
A dream, a dream – ladies, follow!

[297]

Enter VALENTIN

VALENTIN   A mercy!
A wind is up from the north and Ormond stands
Whistling at the helm – we are heading in!
CARDIN
Heavenly mercy! Ladies, come!
VALENTIN   And the coast
Is lined with little boats that increase in size!
CARDIN
We're seen and recognised!
VALENTIN   The sails are full,
And the white flag is billowing in the breeze!
CARDIN
All of you, go up and help Ormond!
Ladies, into your cabin, for we must speak
Before we pray!

RAVAL, KARA, FOL, YVETTE, GUIDO, CLUBS *and* VALEN-
TIN *move towards the deck exit, as* BRANWEN *reaches her
cabin door and opens it. The* CAPTAIN's *body rolls out and
down the steps to the bottom.* KARA *screams*

CARDIN (*to* VALENTIN)
Get that doctor.

Exit VALENTIN

YVETTE   Finally, Captain Blood.
KARA
Don't touch him, he's the swimmer!
RAVAL   Be calm, be calm.
I think he's dead.
KARA   Haiee!
BRANWEN
One less act to perform in a new life.

She pushes ISOLDE *into their cabin and shuts the door. Enter*
VOGEL *and* VALENTIN. VOGEL *goes to the body*

FOL (*to* CARDIN)
He isn't a medical doctor, m'sieur.
CARDIN   I know.
Whatever he is he can make the sign of the Cross.

[298]

FOL
So can we all.
CARDIN   Some can mean it too.
VOGEL
Dead, stabbed, lately, loss of blood.
Difficult to pinpoint, but yes.
CARDIN
Raval and your fellows, help
The doctor with the body. Dr Vogel,
Make the sign of the Cross and throw him over.
VOGEL
I shall indeed.

VOGEL, RAVAL, CLUBS *and* GUIDO *carry the* CAPTAIN *off;*
KARA *clings to* RAVAL

CARDIN
What kind of a man was this?
VALENTIN   He had no home.
CARDIN
He has one now. Go up and help Ormond.

Exit VALENTIN

All of you, to your quarters, gather your things.
This voyage is in the past.

CARDIN *exits to the ladies' cabin*

FOL
Damnable thing is, whom can we say has won?
Our Judge has no opinion now.
YVETTE   Our team captain
Seems preoccupied with something.
FOL   The maid?
Yvette, ta bouche. It's hardly the first time.
YVETTE
So that makes it right?
FOL   Ask me one Sunday
We wake up in the morning and I've never
Had a drink in my life. Then I'll be honest.
YVETTE
We shan't always live this kind of a life.
Sometimes I'm somebody's wife.

FOL
   Come on, Queen of the Circuit.

Exeunt FOL *and* YVETTE

ACT V

The Castle of Karke, Brittany, at dawn on the fortieth day; and a hill overlooking the bay, that morning.

Lights up on TRISTAN *where he lies, his skin white, his eyes sunken. On the other side of the stage, the* LOOKOUT *sits on a small hillock, looking out over the audience*

TRISTAN
    What is your name. Tristan. So is mine.
    But they call me Dwarf Tristan, because a giant,
    Estult li Orgillus, ran away with the bride
    I was to marry. Now, he has six brothers,
    Each the boldest alive except for the others,
    And guards her in his fortress. Tristan, you,
    I plead you help me, and I claim the right
    Of namesake that you do, against Estult,
    In rescuing my Lady . . . Then Cardin said:
    "There is no time to help this Dwarf Tristan."
    But Tristan said: "Are we not both Tristan?
    Then there is time to help this Dwarf Tristan,
    And all the time there is." Had he not,
    No Tristan would have killed two brothers, Cardin
    Killed two others, no Dwarf Tristan the rest,
    And no Dwarf Tristan killed by Giant Estult,
    No Tristan killed the Giant to avenge the name,
    And no Tristan split in two by a spear
    Dipped in a spreading death. – What is my name?
    Tristan. So is mine.
    Why are you named for sorrow? To suffer sorrow.
    What is your sorrow? A lady and nothing at all.
    Why do you love a lady who is not there?
    Because I am named for sorrow. What is your name?

he rouses from the delirium

    Day has come? Day. Exacting day,
    Exposing, scorching, shining, exhorting day:
    I could have been this Tristan, and still lived

A happy life, had it not been for the daytimes,
The gentlemen that come. There's one here.

Enter ISOLDE OF THE WHITE HANDS, *with a white sheet*

WHITE HANDS
How do you do, my Lord? It's the fortieth day.
TRISTAN
Duchess, how many nights?
WHITE HANDS
Thirty-nine. Yesterday, thirty-eight,
Last night a superadded one and it reaches
Thirty-nine now. Let me add this sheet.

WHITE HANDS *removes* TRISTAN'*s fur covering. The sheet
beneath is stained, damp and solidly red near his wound,
brown and black around it, white only at the edges. It is a
dreadful sight. The new sheet which* WHITE HANDS *lays
upon it instantly absorbs fluid from the mess beneath. She
replaces the covering*

So your wood-spirit is almost late, my darling.
Not unlike a doctor – unlike a spirit.
TRISTAN
There is no pain.
WHITE HANDS   Maybe she'll come tomorrow.
TRISTAN
If that's the fortieth day as well.
WHITE HANDS   Oh then
She'll come soon, on a horse-drawn boat.
TRISTAN   Isolde.
WHITE HANDS
Yes?
TRISTAN   What did he say, the boy on the hill?
WHITE HANDS
Oed und leer das Meer.
TRISTAN   Sprichts du Deutsch?
WHITE HANDS
No. The sea is empty and deserted.

Exit WHITE HANDS

TRISTAN
Empty – in another man's language.

And in another world – deserted.
Let me create a sight as simple as this.
One ship, a silver sea, and the crow-black rocks
Of Brittany, sunshine, a masthead
Flying a white flag, a golden masthead
Flying a golden flag below it. Cardin:
Young and proud; beautiful Irish Branwen,
Eyes to the cheering shore. Deep inland,
Infections and contaminations turn
Tired as death and flee the rejoicing body,
Blurting out their sins to the priestly blood
As a white forgiveness spreads from brain to toenail
And washes the days away. Enter, Isolde!
. . . Imagined in the clarity that kills.
No man can prophesy what he merely wishes.
I must begin at once on a new world.
A one where what I see is, and is.

The LOOKOUT *stands*

LOOKOUT
 Yes! or a leaf fell out of Heaven, a ship!
 Lady Duchess Blanchemains, our Lord's
 Flagship in the sunlight!

Enter WHITE HANDS

WHITE HANDS   I can't see it.
LOOKOUT
 Can I now? – yes, yes, I can see it barely,
 It's barely daylight enough but there – no,
 There – yes!
WHITE HANDS I see it now, it's unmoving.
LOOKOUT
 Last night the wind dropped, Lady Duchess: perhaps
 They're waiting?
WHITE HANDS Damn the world for waiting. Boy,
 Run to the fishermen's wharf and give them these
 Crowns to take their boats out to meet it.

The LOOKOUT *runs off*

 Now the sun is letting me look at his picture
 Over his shoulder. Now I can see the sail.

– Now I can see the flag.
It is a surprising colour on such a morning.
Whatever life it saves, the lives it means
To kill outnumber it. If she is here
There is a green green nation across that water
Whose brows are blackening to such a black
It blanches the poor word. And I have sat
Forty days beside and hundreds more
A caring wife unkissed and I see unloved,
To have this billowing sight. Oh Blanchemains,
Spit your Christian name into the air
To merge with all the insects flying towards me
Over the waves and humming, humming, "Isolde,
Isolde the Fair Maid of Ireland!" – clad
In lies, cloaks, disguises, a wood-spirit
Inflammably so, Isolde! Oh Blanchemains . . .
Do as your own name, you must. You are not
A palace-intriguer, are you? No, no.
So he will survive, and live, and she depart?
No, to return home then would be her death.
So he will survive, and she remain? And I?
No, that's war on us. My father would send
Them both away in his fury at these abuses.
There is no end to this I can envisage.
Not with the colour it is.
Oh, wander a slow way back to where he lies.
Take your entire name and entire heart:
Suffer its white half, bear its black part.

WHITE HANDS *moves slowly to where* TRISTAN *lies*

Lord, Duke, Tristan, husband . . .
TRISTAN   Lady?
WHITE HANDS
  A ship is on the sea.
TRISTAN   – In this world?
WHITE HANDS
  It is the very ship.
TRISTAN   – On this day?
WHITE HANDS
  I saw it plainly, sir, with these eyes.
TRISTAN
  And I, with these. I saw it when it sailed,
  Saw who was aboard, it was

[304]

Hard to see, so bright, so bright it was
But I could see your brother at the prow,
Lady, and an Irish confidante . . .
It flew across the sea.
And now it sails into our harbour, silent,
Her spirit is aboard, it is so bright
The Bretons fall and pray, dazzled and still:
The healing spirit strides into the light –
The flag moves in the breeze!
WHITE HANDS   – It doesn't at all.
There is no breeze. The flag I saw was black.

Exit WHITE HANDS. *A long pause, during which the*
LOOKOUT *returns to his little hill, and sits there, head bowed*

TRISTAN
Black. Isolde. Black. Isolde.
Another world has settled on this world.
It is a lookalike world but a different world.
In it, all the things there are are not.
The lovers don't. The ladies aren't. The sailors
Can't – seem – to – sail.
Three words drop into it from the Heaven
It was when it was this. The words are
"Tristan" – and – "And" – and – "Isolde".
The gentlemen who aren't – have come for them . . .
Tristan, we have taken back our golden
"And", and we have taken back our silver
"Isolde". Now we think we will take "Tristan".

– What did he use to say in the world there was?
He did talk of a God.
What did he use to do in the world there was?
Love, battle and sing.
Where is he now? He lives in the world there was.
He slows down into it and will always be there.
There he goes now, beginning to slow –
He has two words with him, to slow with him –
Dearest Isolde. Dearest Isolde. Dearest . . .
Isolde – Dearest – Isolde –

He dies

[305]

Lights up on the LOOKOUT, *who is crying. Enter* WHITE
HANDS, *who finds that* TRISTAN *is dead, and falls to her
knees by the bedside*

Enter ISOLDE, CARDIN *and* BRANWEN *to where the*
LOOKOUT *sits*

LOOKOUT
  You came from the shore, lady.
ISOLDE   And over the sea.
  You have a beautiful country, and it's a fine -
  Looking day, I'd be happy if I were you.
  Why were you crying?
LOOKOUT   My favourite lord is dead.
ISOLDE
  – I imagine Tristan was your favourite lord.
LOOKOUT
  That's kind, lady, he was.
ISOLDE
  Gone, no call to worry.
LOOKOUT   Yes, lady.

ISOLDE, CARDIN *and* BRANWEN *proceed slowly on to
where* TRISTAN *lies, and* WHITE HANDS *is kneeling*

CARDIN
  Sister.
WHITE HANDS   Brother, I have too much to say!

They embrace

  I must – I must – oh lady, do look away!
CARDIN
  Sister, come, I'll hear you. Branwen,
  If there's a lost trail of goodwill in you
  Towards me, stay with your lady, protect her.
  I must attend to my sister.
WHITE HANDS   Oh, Cardin,
  I never thought he'd die for the name of a colour!

Exeunt CARDIN *and* WHITE HANDS

BRANWEN
  What was that, a wife?

ISOLDE His duchess,
White Hands. Cousin, here's a whiteness
Beyond healing, beyond my mother's hands.
Promise now you will let me heal my life
Without a breath of sorrow or prolonging.
BRANWEN
My last act as Branwen is to hug you.
My first as a byway traveller is to depart
And free you. Now, now.

ISOLDE *and* BRANWEN *embrace.* BRANWEN *exits.* ISOLDE
*goes to the bed, lifts the covers and sheets and embraces the
body of* TRISTAN, *as* CARDIN *runs in too late, followed by*
WHITE HANDS

CARDIN
More harm to all!
ISOLDE Hold, I am infected
Happily already. Forgive my cousin,
Friend, she is gone now.
CARDIN
My sister –
ISOLDE Is mine in name and spirit.
CARDIN Oh Queen Isolde –
ISOLDE
We are too late, good friend, we were in time
But for the sun, the wind and the devil there was,
We were in time, good friend, but we are too late.
There is no cure for that but to lie here
Until I rise, and now I do, and this
That speaks to you is Tristan. He says: Friend,
Isolde is gone now: we are together.
I am learning of her voyage, she of my fading
Light in Brittany. To you she wanted
Dearly to say she loves you in spirit forever
And thanks you for your courage and your time.
You are a faultless, noble man. There was one
Last word she had for you, and it was –
"Now I have kissed my death – will the Mariner
Kiss me now?" but then she felt such peace,
Such quiet, nothing needed saying
And she let those words fall and vanish, fall
And vanish.

[307]

She dies. CARDIN *and* WHITE HANDS *cover the bodies with the fur. Both kneel. Lights down on this*

SCENE II
Continuous: the hill overlooking the bay.

Enter ORMOND, MRS ORMOND, ELINOR, KARA, VOGEL, RAVAL, YVETTE, FOL, GUIDO *and* CLUBS *to where the* LOOKOUT *sits*

ORMOND
  Hoy there, little boy!
MRS ORMOND   It's a little boy.
  Look, Elinor, Kara.
KARA   What are we doing,
  Buying him?
MRS ORMOND He seems like a sad fellow.
ORMOND
  Hoy there, can you tell us the way to the church
  And a crossroads where four roads meet?
RAVAL
  Henry, maybe in Brittany crossroads don't have
  Four roads, maybe seven, or one, or none.
MRS ORMOND
  He's shaking his head, Henry.
FOL   Don't we all,
  When Henry takes command.
CLUBS   In these countries,
  That may mean "yes", remember, or "now it's raining".
FOL
  If it means "it's raining", Count, we've found a fool,
  Or should I say a foil? a perfect foil
  For you, and we will have to outbid the Ormonds.
LOOKOUT
  Where are you going, sir?
ORMOND   We are headed south,
  Towards the hills.
LOOKOUT   So look to the horizon.
RAVAL
  Ah-ha, some native wisdom!
ORMOND   There they are!

MRS ORMOND
Such a way away, Henry.
ORMOND   Indeed,
But Margaret, so is England now.
MRS ORMOND   Alas.
ELINOR
There's plenty we can do while we're walking.
VOGEL
That's the spirit, Elinor. The spirit of –
The spirit of that grand battle we won.
MRS ORMOND
What's the matter, little friend?
LOOKOUT   It's nothing.
I promised the last lady not to worry,
And it's not a thing that touches –
MRS ORMOND   Perhaps,
But would it help you out to tell us?
LOOKOUT   Only –
A nobleman who passed away this morning.
ORMOND
Ah, always a cause for proper grief.
LOOKOUT
Yes, sir. But down in the fishermen's village
There are strange fears. In the middle of the morning
A body was washed ashore, a bad omen.
ORMOND
Was it – a known body?
LOOKOUT   No, a stranger.
VOGEL
Yes, well I think we know him better than that.
A bloodless body?
LOOKOUT   No, he died of drowning.
The villagers are worried. Just now
They are burning him to save the year's catch.
MRS ORMOND
I'm sure it shall be saved.
LOOKOUT
– It was so much to happen in a morning.
You see, I know you came up from the shore.
I was the one who saw your ship first,
Spotted the white flag when the sun came up;
I watched you get in the boats.
But all the time I watched, these clear eyes
Hurt and filled with water, somehow, the nearer

[309]

You came in the small boats the fishermen rowed.
My eyes sparkled the sea already sparkling.
I mean, my eyes were full before I heard
The bells at Saint-Antoine and guessed their cause.
I seemed to have seen that sadness
Early and then cried to have had that sight.
Is all I can say of it.

VOGEL
Poor boy, you're sitting too high.
Look at the sea forever all sorts of things
Bound to blossom inside.

MRS ORMOND   You should come with us!
Keep your mind on the road.

KARA   See? we are.

ELINOR
We are what?

KARA   Buying him. Or is he free?

RAVAL
Henry, before you Ormondise this poor
Defenceless local, let me ask him too –
Which is the best road east, little hawkeye?

KARA
East?

RAVAL   Yes, to Germany.

ORMOND   Ah, Germany.

LOOKOUT
This road but that way, sir.

RAVAL
Well, Mr Ormond, the oracle has spoken.
Looks like each has a road to disappear on.

ORMOND
It does, I grant you, yes.

RAVAL   And as for our contest?

ORMOND
An honourable stand-off!

FOL   It can't be a stand-off.
Standoffishness, the English win hands down.

RAVAL
Peace, wolf. Raval accepts a draw.
May we all live to clash another day.

MRS ORMOND
I very much enjoyed your acting style,
But it was very fast, and I didn't always
Understand.

[310]

YVETTE   A compliment indeed,
  Mrs Almond. I'll not forget your Norwegian.
FOL
  What about the prize?
VOGEL   It's on the ship.
  We'll share it half and half.
LOOKOUT   If it's on the ship,
  Sir, the fishermen will by now have shared it
  Half and half and half and half and half.
RAVAL
  Then we will share no points, England and France.
GUIDO
  España also, no point, no point!
FOL
  Marvellous, an all-round pointless draw.
YVETTE
  Goodbye, doctor, Elinor, Kara.
  I do hope you meet a young man soon.
KARA
  That would be super, wouldn't it, Yvette?
YVETTE
  Suitable.
MRS ORMOND Not suitable at all,
  Kara.
RAVAL   Kara, au revoir.
KARA   Another
  Breton word? Uh-huh. So long, mister.
VOGEL
  Best of luck, old fellow.
CLUBS   In all cases.
  Wrap up well and in the mean time.
MRS ORMOND
  Have you a home to go to, little lookout?
LOOKOUT
  Yes, the cottage over by that bridge.
  But I'll walk a mile with you, or more. It must be
  A day for only unexpected things.
MRS ORMOND
  We'll eat some cake on the way, and look about.
  It's very new to us.
LOOKOUT   It's dangerous.
  I'll show you a busy road where carts go by.
RAVAL
  Enough, enough, enough, or I will start

[311]

Rhyming like an Ormond. Allons-y. Sir,
May every village have its Henry Ormond
One day, and its Mrs Ormond too;
Its daughter who stays, its daughter who goes, its doctor
Of something more than medicine.
ORMOND   Henri,
May you perform your wild quickfire turn
Upon a hill so high a thousand thousand
Watch it at a time, a thousand thousand
Laugh at everything there is to see,
Good or bad, half-true or patently false.
You are a villain.
RAVAL   Lord Pomposity,
Farewell, farewell.

RAVAL *and* ORMOND *shake hands. The two parties exit on
opposite sides.* KARA *lingers at one side;* RAVAL *at the other.*
YVETTE *comes back, and playfully pulls* RAVAL *off: both he
and she blow kisses to* KARA *as they go.* KARA *hesitates,
throws a V-sign in their direction, and follows her family off.
Enter* VALENTIN, *with a thick sheaf of paper*

VALENTIN
Off they go, to countries foreign to them,
Our precious cargo. The field is left to me,
Who knew one thing and one thing only
About the "Esperance".
Where to hide and listen. Now,
I have a dozen stories of the age.
I held them up in the air as I was wading
On to the shore but some I can see are damp,
The ink faded and faint. I need to eat.
I'll take these to some grand royal court
And write them up for somebody.
I'll never go to sea again, I reckon.
All my words were wrong, but I did know them.
And I never stopped a deed from being done.
I'll travel south and dry this in the sun.
Now for a cart to take me.

VALENTIN *stretches his right thumb out towards the audience and faces off, in the original hitch-hiking stance, the
sheaf of papers tucked under his left arm. Lights down on
this*

CURTAIN

[312]